THE CIO EXPEDITION: MASTERING THE DIGITAL LEADERSHIP IN IT

A Comprehensive Guide for IT Leaders

DR. JIPSON THOOMKUZHY

COPYRIGHT PAGE

This is a work of non-fiction. All of the characters, organizations, and events portrayed in this book are either product of the author's experience.

THE CIO EXPEDITION: MASTERING THE DIGITAL LEADERSHIP IN IT

Copyright © 2024 by **DR. JIPSON THOOMKUZHY**

ISBN: 978-93-6128-799-2

DEDICATION

This book is lovingly dedicated to a select few individuals who have played an immensely significant role in shaping my life. Though two of them have departed continue to guide me. First and foremost, I dedicate this book to my paternal grandfather, who taught me to write my first letter. Your boundless love has left an indelible mark on my heart. To my mother, whose unconditional love nurtured and shaped me into who I am today. May you find eternal tranquility and endless happiness in Paradise. Though your time with us was brief, your memory will forever live in my heart.

To my father, who stood with me, and instilled the principles of hard work and perseverance. Your guidance and strength have been my support pillars, lifting me above life's obstacles. Furthermore, I express my heartfelt gratitude to my beloved spouse, devoted son, cherished daughter, and the Almighty God for their unwavering encouragement and support throughout the challenging journey of completing this book. Your unconditional love has been my constant source of inspiration, propelling me forward at every step of this extraordinary endeavor with love, appreciation, and eternal gratitude.

PREFACE

The Chief Information Officer (CIO) plays a crucial role in today's business climate as the conductor of the complex and dynamic digital symphony that determines the fate of organizations. The book " *The CIO Expedition: Mastering the Digital Leadership in IT*" explores the inner workings of this arrangement, revealing the intricate interplay of duties, developments, and necessary skills that characterize the CIO's position in the digital age. The book delves into the duties and essential skills that distinguish the contemporary CIO in spearheading digital transformation. It explores the history of the CIO position and shows how it developed into a crucial strategic component for businesses. Trends and tactics influence the basis of a harmonious digital environment in IT governance and organizational structure. We encourage readers to investigate how CIOs handle these crucial components, adjusting to the constantly shifting environment to guarantee peak performance and alignment with corporate goals.

We look at the strategic frameworks and designs that drive CIO leadership and point enterprises toward IT excellence. Through the book, readers can discover how CIOs strategically arrange themselves to manage resources, foster innovation, and negotiate the challenges of the digital world. The critical role that CIO leadership plays in promoting smooth business-IT coordination is emphasized, assuring that technology is an essential component of the broader company plan rather than merely a tool. The book also delves into the complex idea of business-IT alignment, examining its definition, associated difficulties, and indisputable benefits. Readers will see how CIOs handle this complex alignment to promote corporate performance and discover the keys to creating synergy while coordinating IT and business goals to provide unmatched values.

Techniques and perspectives are examined to enable CIOs to improve their companies via peaceful cooperation. The unraveling of the intricate threads of IT governance, strategy, and leadership defines the journey of the CIO. The book guides readers on a strategic journey through the IT frontier, guided by the CIO's vision for evolution, synergy, and success, shedding light on the significance of good navigation of the IT landscape for attaining organizational goals. Investigating the worldwide aspects of IT administration occurs when CIOs engage in strategic leadership across international borders. The potential and challenges of managing IT globally are explored, providing readers with a thorough grasp of an ever-changing environment. The book looks ahead, emphasizing innovation and new technologies in the CIO space. It shows how CIOs keep ahead of the curve by adopting cutting-edge technologies to spur innovation and preserve a competitive edge.

Lastly, through incisive case studies highlighting effective CIOs, theoretical notions are finally anchored in actual situations. These case studies present real-world implementations of the tactics and ideas the book covers, providing insightful insights for both seasoned and novice CIOs. As the book delves into the nuances of CIO leadership and composes the digital symphony to create a future where businesses thrive in the constantly changing world of technology and business, readers are cordially invited to embark on a transforming journey.

ABBREVIATIONS

5G: 5th Generation

AI: Artificial Intelligence

AR: Augmented Reality

CapEx: Capital Expenditure

CCPA: California Consumer Privacy Act

CDO: Chief Digital/Data Officer

CEO: Chief Executive Officer

CFO: Chief Financial officer

CIO: Chief Information Officer

CISO: Chief Information Security Officer

CMMI: Capability Maturity Model Integration

CMO: Chief Marketing officer

COBIT: Control Objectives for Information and Related Technologies

COO: Chief Operating Officer

COSO: Committee of Sponsoring Organizations of the Treadway Commission

CRM: Customer Relationship Management

DDDM: Data-Driven Decision Making

E-Commerce: Electronic Commerce

EHRs: Electronic Health Records

ERP: Enterprise Resource Planning

FAIR: Factor Analysis of Information Risk

FCPA: Foreign Corrupt Practices Act

GDPR: General Data Protection Regulation

HIPAA: Health Insurance Portability and Accountability Act

HR: Human Resources

IaaS: Infrastructure-as-a-Service

IoT: Internet of Things

IPR: Intellectual Property Rights

IS: Information Systems

IT: Information Technology

ITGF: Information Technology Governance Framework

ITIL: IT Infrastructure Library

KPIs: Key Performance Indicators

ML: Machine Learning

ODC: Offshore Development Centre

OPEX: Operational Expenses

PaaS: Platform-as-a-Service

PCI: Payment Card Industry

R&D: Research & Development

RMM: Remote Monitoring and Management

ROI: Return on Investment

RPA: Robotic Process Automation

SaaS: Software-as-a-Service

SAF: Service Annual Function

SD-WAN: Software-Defined Wide Area Network

SLAs: Service Level Agreements

SLM: Service Level Management

SWOT: Strengths, Weaknesses, Opportunities, Threats

VR: Virtual Reality

WCAG: Web Material Accessibility Guidelines

CONTENTS

CHAPTER 1

MASTERING THE DIGITAL SYMPHONY: UNRAVELING THE EVOLUTION, RESPONSIBILITIES, AND KEY COMPETENCIES OF THE CIO ROLE

INTRODUCTION:

The CIO plays a vital role in the dynamic world of technology-driven businesses, coordinating strategy, innovation, and business operations. This chapter explores the complex character of a CIO, looking at the historical background and the process of transformation that has formed this significant function over time. Comprehending the CIO requires investigating their many duties, which transcend the conventional boundaries of information management. The CIO's job is dynamic and flexible, involving everything from directing organizational strategy to negotiating the complexities of industry-specific requirements. We will explore the unique roles that characterize a CIO's mandate as we set out on our trip and how these obligations differ throughout industries.

A CIO's effectiveness is based on their key competencies, highlighted in this chapter. A successful CIO possesses specific fundamental abilities and knowledge bases. In addition, we look at the methods and approaches CIOs can use to develop and improve these skills to succeed in the dynamic and ever-evolving field of technology leadership. The position of a CIO is constantly changing in tandem with the business landscape. We explore how this role is changing and consider the benefits and problems that come with industries changing due to technology. This chapter seeks to provide a thorough understanding of the role of a CIO and how they manage the challenges of the contemporary digital world by examining historical turning points, present duties, and future opportunities.

1.1 WHO IS A CIO

A CIO is the highest-ranking IT officer in an organization and is responsible for managing the IT department toward achieving its goals. A CIO oversees and manages the organization's operations and data as part of the strategic leadership function. The CIO's role is critical in turning ideas into actual outcomes working with teams to produce new solutions that promote the effective execution of the organization's IT and digital strategy. The CIO has to have a good understanding of all elements of IT, from cybersecurity and automation to software development and communications.

According to Aarti Shah, CIO & CDO of Eli Lilly organization, "*The role of a CIO has expanded to encompass not only technology but also digital leadership in which collaboration is key. CIOs must partner with other C-suite executives and adapt to change rapidly to keep their organizations competitive.*" The research paper published by Hütter *et al.*, 2017 mentions that the title of CIO is commonly used across industries, government sectors, and non-governmental organizations worldwide. The CIO typically reports to the CEO; there are instances in which a CIO may report to a CFO within specific organizational structures. The reporting structures are subject to change based on the industry and type of organization the CIO works.

Similarly, Barnes *et al.,* 2021 in their research paper, states that the CIO position holds significant leadership prominence within the organization, as the individual oversees and implements IT systems. The CIO's impact extends to every facet of the organization, from operational efficiency to fulfilling technology requirements. The CIO must ensure the IT infrastructure aligns with the CEO's overarching goals, providing relevant and practical support. The article by Nenkov *et al.* (2017) states that developing a relationship between CIOs, CMOs (Chief Marketing officer), and various C-suites has significant implications for organizations. As technology evolves, more and more IT-related tasks get assigned to the CIO. For this reason, every large organization must have a CIO position.

CIOs are now managing electronic information and driving innovation to support corporate objectives. As a result, CIOs have become strong advocates for how development can help companies achieve their goals and handle the most pressing concerns. CIOs must be in charge of technology transformation programs and exercises that result in widespread progressive change. During one of my research interviews with a CIO, when asked about the CIO about his version of who a CIO is, he answered that *"when IT is transforming from a cost center to a profit center in many industries, a CIO should be called as a chief involvement officer when the market calls him a CIO."* He explained that in the past, the CIO's objectives were to keep the light on, but now, the business transformation using it has become a significant task for the CIO. Due to this, the CIO has to get involved with all the business functions, understand the underlying problems, and look at digital and transformation initiatives to bring value through IT, so the CIO role gets involved everywhere in the business, just like the CEO function.

Netflix, a global streaming entertainment firm, demonstrates the emergence of the CIO job. The primary job of the CIO at Netflix was the technology infrastructure that facilitated streaming services. However, the CIO's duties extended to strategic decision-making as the organization grew when data analytics and customization became crucial in the entertainment sector. Netflix's technology team led by the CIO, used data insights to improve user experiences. The strategic involvement of the CIO is evident in Netflix's recommendation engine, which offers personalized content to users. The CIO built and tuned this algorithm with data scientists and engineers, significantly enhancing customer engagement and retention. This shift from monitoring IT operations to driving strategic initiatives exemplifies how CIOs are increasingly critical in determining goals and objectives.

Enhancing the customer experience within an enterprise involves more than just technology; it requires a collaborative effort between CIOs and CMOs. A CIO must recognize the criticality of the partnership; organizations strive to foster effective communication and alignment between these key leaders to harness technology and cultivate innovative strategies that drive overall corporate success and sustained customer satisfaction.

Starbucks, a huge coffee shop chain, offers an interesting case study of how CIO-CMO collaboration may result in strategic innovation. A good example is the organization's mobile ordering and payment app. Starbucks' CIO and CMO collaborated to create and deploy a smartphone app that allows users to pre-order and pay for their beverages, reducing wait times. In addition to increasing customer experience and happiness, this initiative gathered helpful information about client preferences and behaviors. The application succeeded due to the CIO's technological prowess in creating a flawless interface and the CMO's grasp of customer preferences. This collaboration shows CIOs' evolution from mere IT managers to strategic partners driving innovation and customer-centric initiatives.

1.2 HISTORICAL CONTEXT AND EVOLUTION OF THE CIO ROLE

The CIO role started in the 1980s, and during that time, the CIO's primary role was coordinating specialized departments, overseeing the budget, and leveraging technology to increase efficiency and production while reducing costs. The CIO job has seen significant development from its inception in the early days of computing, matching the fast advancements of technology and its integration into organizational strategy. The challenge of managing information systems during the early phases of technology adoption gave rise to the position of CIO.

In the middle of the 20th century, computer systems were innovative tools mainly used for information processing. The CIO function's initial version focused on supervising information centers and assuring the reliability of mainframe systems. At one point during this period, the CIO's responsibilities were primarily operational and focused on maintaining IT infrastructure. As time advanced, the role of the CIO evolved significantly, transforming into a critical facilitator of corporate operations. Technical control gave way to strategic engagement in the late 20th century, and CIOs realized that technology might be used to force aggressive gain. This period saw CIOs emerging as strategic consultants, convincing top-level executives to integrate IT duties with broader business goals. The

CIO's responsibility expanded beyond maintenance to encompass innovation, focusing on harnessing generation to drive growth.

The CIO role had evolved into its current shape by the turn of the century. CIOs played a crucial role in navigating the complexities of the virtual world as digital technology and the internet expanded rapidly. The dot-com boom highlighted the importance of organizations' solid online presence, propelling CIOs into critical roles to drive E-Commerce initiatives and customer-focused digital methods. As the digital transformation period progressed, CIOs evolved from being era-focused to strategic leaders that promoted corporate collaboration and innovation.

Trendy CIOs are critical in creating digital strategies, promoting innovation, and coordinating technology-driven business changes. Various reasons have contributed to the growth of the CIO's position from technical management to strategic leadership at the heart of organizational change. Below are the essential factors which decide the progress of the CIO role.

Rapid Technological Developments: The fast growth of technological innovation has been the primary driver of the evolution of the function of the CIO. The CIO must modify and incorporate the latest tools in business activities as new technologies emerge. The role of the CIO has evolved beyond managing IT infrastructure to investigating opportunities presented by emerging technologies like cloud computing, artificial intelligence, data analytics, and the IoT.

The shift from cost center to value driver: IT departments and their leaders, such as CIOs, have traditionally been perceived as cost centers; nevertheless, they attempt to reverse this perception. A value creation center is replacing the cost center model in information technology. Organizations have begun to demonstrate the ability of technology investments to provide significant returns by improving productivity, consumer experiences, and corporate profits. CIOs have become value drivers throughout this transformation, contributing to revenue growth and strategic initiatives.

Digitization and Advanced Change: The increasing importance of computerized innovation in numerous corporate sectors led to the development of enhanced change engines. CIOs found themselves at the forefront of these activities, pushing growth and supporting organizations in adapting to rapidly changing business sector settings. The need to rethink organization procedures, implement light-footed technologies, and create uniform digital interactions for clients and employees propelled the CIO role to the forefront of the audience's attention.

Information as an Essential Resource: Amidst the rapid expansion of knowledge, organizations recognized the transformative potential of information in guiding decision-making, enabling personalization, and revealing profound insights. In response, CIOs transitioned from overseeing data storage to actively overseeing data administration, analysis, and developing strategies for converting data into a valuable resource. This shift underscored the pivotal role of CIOs in shaping business processes in the era of data-driven insights.

Developing Cybersecurity: Because of internet security's growth, cybersecurity and data breach prevention have become a mandate for all organizations. CIOs and IT departments must protect sensitive data, implement adequate cybersecurity measures, and closely adhere to legal standards. As the scope of cybersecurity threats broadens, CIOs have assumed a critical role in managing risks and building solid digital defenses to protect their enterprises from emerging attacks.

Changing Expectations and Demands: In response to the growing importance of technology for corporate success, partner expectations have changed significantly. Expectations for CIOs included collaborating with other C-suite executives and playing an active role in strategic decision-making rather than merely providing support for IT. This move demanded a shift in skill sets, with a greater focus on leadership, effective communication, and the capacity to bridge the gap between technology and long-term organizational goals.

Globalization and Complex Business Operations: The globalization of operations and the connectivity of supply chains increased the complexity of corporate processes. CIOs enabled seamless technology integration across several geographical locations, languages, and regulatory contexts. Their responsibilities included the harmonization of disparate systems as well as the encouragement of cross-functional collaboration.

Client Centricity and Client Experience: CIOs should realize the necessity of creating excellent customer experiences as technology's role when consumer interactions grow. This requirement requires CIOs to modify technical solutions to align with consumer demands, tastes, and habits, emphasizing the CIO's duty to improve customer-centric activities. In doing so, CIOs play a pivotal role in meeting current customer expectations and anticipating and adapting to evolving consumer preferences to ensure sustained satisfaction and business success.

Social and Organizational Change: A change in organizational culture is frequently necessary for successful digital transformation. CIOs were critical in driving cultural change, supporting innovation, and promoting a technologically aware attitude across several departments. These forces have impacted the CIO function's growth and positioned CIOs as critical catalysts for innovation, strategic vision, and organizational agility in the ever-changing digital ecosystem.

1.3 RESPONSIBILITIES OF A CIO

CIOs are seasoned industry experts entrusted with managing vital data that holds immense significance for organizations. Over the past few decades, their expertise has led to a transformative evolution of the IT team's role. A CIO has to play a critical role in transforming IT from a cost center to a profit center rather than being restricted to administrative duties. CEOs rely on CIOs to help them develop their businesses and find new income sources.

CIOs are also responsible for ensuring the security and integrity of the organization's information systems, managing IT infrastructure, and mitigating cybersecurity risks. "*With great power comes great responsibility*," Voltaire accurately observed, a notion that applies to all leaders, including CIOs. The CIOs are responsible for overseeing an organization's entire information technology landscape. Their multifaceted role encompasses managing IT strategies, ensuring data security and integrity, implementing technology solutions, and optimizing IT operations. CIOs are instrumental in aligning technology with business objectives, driving innovation, and fostering digital transformation. They must navigate the evolving technological landscape, stay abreast of emerging trends, and make informed decisions on technology investments.

The research paper authored by Bongiorno *et al.* (2018) outlines the key responsibilities of a CIO as follows:

Innovation Leadership: The CIO plays a crucial role in fostering and actively seeking creative ideas within their organizations. CIOs need to be very good with innovation because they have to be able to handle innovation difficulties to make sure their companies succeed.

Value Creation: CIOs play a critical role in creating value for the company through technology development projects. Any financially oriented business is built on return on investment (ROI), and to add value, CIOs must skillfully manage organizational resources to create value.

Strategic Alignment: One of the primary responsibilities of the CIO is to guarantee that the organization's goals are fulfilled through its objectives. The organization's executive viewpoints provide the knowledge required to modify the organization's activities to meet specific needs.

Leading the Workforce: The CIOs oversee the strategic management of their workforce, ensuring that IT specialists can access the resources and tools necessary to meet organizational objectives. Additionally, CIOs are crucial in fostering a collaborative and innovative work environment and liaising between the IT department and overarching corporate goals and technological advancements.

Quality Control: CIOs are responsible for creating IT policies and processes to develop robust quality control techniques, utilizing improvements to optimize operations.

Financial Management: CIOs are responsible for financial resources and allocations, ensuring they allocate funds to projects that benefit the organization.

Cross-Departmental Liaison: CIOs maintain open contact channels with all organizational divisions to ensure seamless operations. This constant communication acts as a foundation for accountability and feedback as needed.

In the rapidly evolving corporate landscape, CIOs must adopt a holistic perspective, recognizing that technology's exponential advancement is more crucial than ever in driving corporate innovation and success. Consequently, CIOs forge deeper connections with their organizations to meet evolving expectations and requirements effectively. Banker *et al.* (2019) highlight emerging innovations such as cloud computing, data transformation, DevOps, the Internet of Things (IoT), augmented reality (AR), virtual reality (VR), artificial intelligence (AI), and robotic process automation (RPA) empower CIOs to fulfill their role of future-proofing their organizations. As the technological landscape transforms, CIOs are assuming more prominent executive positions and expanding their responsibilities to lead their enterprises into the future.

Frequent introductions of groundbreaking technologies fuel the rapid pace of technical advancement, leading executives to rely on CIOs for their expertise increasingly. It is commonly known that keeping up with technology advancements is highly beneficial for CEOs. Urbach et al. (2019) underscore in their research article that CIOs must critically assess how their technical proficiency, adaptability, and customer-focused approach can confer a competitive edge in today's market. As companies adopt a more collaborative stance, CIOs are at the forefront of leading cross-functional initiatives that require diverse skill sets. In contrast to the past, where CIOs often followed a traditional career path, today's CEOs recognize the value of having individuals in high-level roles that can enhance organizational structure and champion disruptive change.

1.4 CIO RESPONSIBILITIES BASED ON INDUSTRY

The CIO's responsibilities depend on their industry and are closely linked to the quickly changing market dynamics. The type of work the CIO does varies according to the particulars and requirements of the sector in which they work. The unique possibilities and constraints in their particular industry setting influence the CIO's job.

As a result, the market's dynamic character demands that the CIO's duties be explicitly approached.

The responsibilities of the CIO in the retail industry are mainly in terms of E-Commerce and customer experience; retail CIOs work on improving the online shopping experience, optimizing E-Commerce platforms, and employing data analytics for tailored marketing and suggestions. Furthermore, supply chain management has also emerged as a critical position where CIOs may increase supply chain efficiency using technologies like RFID and IoT to ensure product availability.

In the software and technology sectors, innovation and product development are the purview of CIOs. Technology companies' CIOs are at the forefront of innovation, spearheading R&D initiatives and creating state-of-the-art goods and services. Another crucial duty for CIOs is to ensure that IT infrastructure can grow swiftly to accommodate expansion. This is especially important for startups and rapidly growing IT companies.

CIOs in healthcare play a pivotal role in leveraging technology to enhance patient care, optimize operational efficiency, ensure regulatory compliance, and drive digital transformation within the complex and dynamic landscape of the healthcare industry. Healthcare CIOs are primarily responsible for ensuring the security and privacy of patient data and compliance with strict healthcare regulations (e.g., HIPAA in the United States). Similarly, health CIOs are liable for Electronic Health Records (EHRs), which are significant in adopting and improving EHR systems to improve patient care and streamline procedures.

Financial sector CIOs seek comprehensive cybersecurity solutions to safeguard sensitive financial data from cyber-attacks and breaches. These CIOs are also in charge of Fintech Integration, which entails overseeing the integration of cutting-edge FinTech technologies, including mobile banking applications and digital payment systems, to fulfill client needs for ease and security. Regarding the energy and utilities industries, CIOs are implementing innovative grid technology to improve energy distribution and increase sustainability activities. CIOs are also in charge of energy data analytics, which involves using data analytics to monitor energy use, eliminate waste, and increase resource efficiency.

CIOs in the manufacturing industry are held accountable for Industry 4.0 and IoT, and CIOs embrace Industry 4.0 principles and use the IoT to improve automation, optimize production processes, and monitor equipment health. Furthermore, predictive maintenance becomes essential, and they use data analytics to create predictive maintenance techniques, minimizing downtime and enhancing overall operational efficiency.

CIO responsibilities in government and the public sector are mainly related to digital transformation, with CIOs focusing on digital transformation efforts to improve citizen services and government efficiency. Another significant area on which the CIO focuses is data accessibility, and they try to make government data more available to the public while protecting data security and privacy. Finally, while CIOs have similar tasks, each industry's unique problems and possibilities determine their objectives and areas of expertise. CIOs must adapt to industry-specific needs to foster innovation, competitiveness, and success in their particular industries.

The responsibilities of a CIO can vary significantly among sectors and companies. These distinctions originate from elements such as the nature of the firm, its scale, its dependence on technology, and its principal goals. This range demonstrates the versatility and complex nature of the CIO function.

1.5 CIO RESPONSIBILITIES BASED ON SITUATIONS

CIOs' roles change dynamically in response to various business environment circumstances. CIOs are entrusted with evaluating and implementing cutting-edge technology to boost corporate efficiency during times of technological progress. Their attention turns to guaranteeing the resilience and security of digital infrastructures during times of crisis, such as cybersecurity threats or worldwide outages. CIOs must emphasize their strategic leadership by coordinating IT projects with changing corporate objectives in response to shifts in the scope and direction of their businesses. Their roles are further impacted by regulatory changes and compliance requirements, which calls for a thorough awareness of legal frameworks. One of the most notable aspects of CIO roles is their flexibility, which demonstrates their capacity to handle various situations and make a strategic contribution to the company's success.

Let us take a closer look at how the CIO's responsibilities might vary depending on the situation:

Industry-Specific Technology Demands: Different industries have different technology requirements based on their primary functions. For example, a CIO may be particularly concerned with deploying electronic health records (EHR) systems and the most excellent protection of patient data in the healthcare industry. The emphasis in financial services may be on maintaining robust cybersecurity safeguards and adhering to high regulatory regulations. The focus in manufacturing may be on integrating the IoT and leveraging data-driven advancements for supply chain optimization.

Business Size and Scope: The business size can significantly influence the scope of the CIO's responsibilities. The CIO may be responsible for various technological initiatives within more prominent organizations, including enterprise resource planning (ERP) systems, customer relationship management (CRM) platforms, and complex data analytics projects. In smaller firms, on the other hand, the CIO may be more hands-on, overseeing day-to-day IT operations while still contributing to high-level strategic planning.

Strategic Orientation: CIO duties differ substantially depending on whether the firm perceives technology as a constant capacity or a critical facilitator. In technology-driven industries such as E-Commerce or software development, the CIO may significantly impact the fundamental goods or services. In conventional sectors, the CIO may emphasize streamlining internal processes and guaranteeing technological dependability.

Innovation & disruption: Rapid technology disruptions and advances characterize specific sectors. In industries such as retail or media, the CIO may play an essential role in recognizing emerging trends, directing new digital efforts, and staying ahead of industry trends to maintain competitiveness.

Regulatory & Compliance: CIOs must manage complex regulatory frameworks in highly regulated industries such as healthcare, banking, and pharmaceuticals. The CIO's duties may include creating technological solutions to maintain compliance, protect sensitive data, and support audits.

Global Operations: In multinational enterprises, the CIO's responsibility may include integrating technological systems, communication platforms, and security measures across several areas. In such situations, ensuring smooth technical integration and resolving local regulatory intricacies becomes critical.

Customer-Centric Focus: In consumer-driven businesses like hotels and retail, the CIO's responsibilities may include improving customer experiences via digital channels. This category falls under implementing omnichannel strategies, tailored efforts, and leveraging technology for improved consumer interaction.

Digital Transformation Stage: The level of digital transformation at which a business is also impacting the CIO's responsibilities. In firms just beginning their digital journey, the CIO may prioritize infrastructure modernization. The function in mature digital organizations may change toward fostering innovation, data monetization, and sophisticated analytics.

In Summary, the CIO's obligations are not one-size-fits-all but tailored to each sector and organization's needs, goals, and challenges. The ability of the CIO to adapt their talents, approaches, and demands to different settings demonstrates their dynamic,

influential position in the ever-changing landscape of innovation and business.

1.6 KEY COMPETENCIES OF A CIO

To create world-class IT, the CIO must first set the mentality and conviction that the organization is a world-class IT organization. A CIO should be able to make a vision for IT, and the CIO should be able to amplify the team's ideas, validate them with others, and develop them. Because the CIO knows that technology is underpinning and digital is generating value, the CIO should grasp the business values expected from the transformation strategy. A CIO's duty is analogous to a pendulum spanning the total distance, with one side being technology and the other being business, and the swinging pendulum should touch both sides, technology, and business. The CIO should have the skills necessary to develop rules and regulations inside the firm. These regulations should be process-centric, favoring organized processes over personality-driven methods, which may frequently lead to prejudice and failure. Furthermore, IT, like HR, is a cross-functional business unit that requires approaches that integrate smoothly with other business units.

A forward-thinking CIO should possess strong research-oriented skills, including keen observation and analysis. Such a CIO, driven by a research-oriented mindset, envisions the future and diligently strives to transform that vision into concrete reality. As a CIO, one must develop the capacity to identify business difficulties and build IT solutions correctly. Quick decision-making based on calculated risk assessments becomes critical, especially considering the possible implications of ignoring risk concerns while making rash decisions. They should be able to see things from two perspectives: neutral spectator and active participant. Because of this dual approach, the organization can comprehensively study challenges and design complete solutions. The CIO should retain neutrality as an observer, allowing participants to produce ideas and conclusions freely. Having observer and participant skills is critical to the success of any invention. Furthermore, the CIO should have a *"third eye,"* which they should use to make judgments by combining ideas gathered from observation and engagement. This third eye acts as a link between disparate thoughts, allowing for more informed decisions.

Competency is not synonymous with succeeding in every element; it is about recognizing one's talents and successfully using them. A CIO and their organization must embrace the customer service philosophy that transcends transactional interactions. This approach is particularly suitable for a business in constant evolution. In manufacturing, CIOs need to shift their leadership focus from being plant-centric to adopting a customer-centric mindset. The CIO should be able to take decisive action by using a holistic approach, stepping back from the current situation, and examining the larger context. The temptation to play the blame game during serious emergencies could seem more productive, but a crisis needs a collaborative approach and a mentality shift.

It is vital to emphasize that the attitude necessary on the production floor is fundamentally different from that required for research. Before making judgments in analysis, considerable evidence is gathered and intensively considered to ensure the study's thoroughness. On the other hand, it is critical to respond quickly and make quick judgments on the production floor. A CIO's research-oriented mindset finds its place in strategic aspects, where thoughtful analysis is crucial while making prompt decisions is paramount when managing production. These represent two distinct facets of the CIO's role spectrum.

Another ability I have investigated is that a CIO should have one attitude and one language while speaking with colleagues but a different language and viewpoint when speaking with customers. The CIO should be able to generate a value addition to the business and sell the value proposition to management. As a C-level executive, the CIO must be able to give a holistic picture of the interaction between IT and the larger business landscape. This approach helps the capacity to identify numerous variables that contribute to growing workloads, the environment in which work is expanding, the excellent impact of these efforts on the business, their relevance to the CIO's role, and the expected acknowledgment from others.

The CIO should take a strategic approach to building a presence in various parts of the business ecosystem regarding technology and human skills. As a leader, the CIO should always approach problem-solving systematically and analytically. Furthermore, they should deliberately orient themselves and their organizations toward customer-centric, prioritizing their clients' requirements and preferences. The more we understand a customer's DNA, the better we can serve them. With this approach, the CIO or IT team can program the dopamine levels required to understand and manage customer requirements.

Another critical attribute of a CIO is the ability to bring out the best in everyone, whether a partner employee or an internal employee. The CIO, as a leader, must understand his partners and customers. Determining visitors' intent to an organization's website or dealership is the most excellent method to understand customer behaviors and transform the user experience. The CIOs can overcome specific fear issues by utilizing comedy to overcome their worries. Employing wit to counter emotions like jealousy and envy represents a clever strategy. Through humor, a leader can jest with the team, ultimately aiding to overcome the fears of self or team. CIOs should be competent to recognize that everything is constructed twice: first in the mind and then in physical reality. Therefore, it is essential to program one's mind and adapt to the practical aspects to ensure the success of their decisions.

CIOs can enhance their learning experiences through micro-learning and conversations with influential figures, vendors, partners, and more. CIOs should be able to grasp that everything is built twice: once in the imagination and again in physical reality. As a result, it is critical to train one's mind and adjust to practical issues to ensure the success of their judgments. CIOs may improve their learning experiences by engaging in dialogues with notable personalities, suppliers, partners, and others. Partners and participation in workshops contribute significantly to their learning. CIOs also rely on respected sources like IDC, Forrester, and Gartner to broaden their knowledge. Accepting humility is essential for learning and progress. One's capacity to learn new skills and information also depends on humility. Those who are humble succeed as problem solvers and learners. In reality, people who are humble and open to critical comments often outperform their highly gifted friends who are too proud to receive input. A CIO must learn the foundations and engage in his growth to strengthen his capabilities.

In summary, the CIOs can develop the competencies like technology proficiency, strategic vision, leadership, communication, business acumen, change management, financial management, vendor and supplier management, cybersecurity expertise, innovation, project management, data management, regulatory compliance, strategic sourcing, adaptability Etc to drive an organization effectively.

1.7 KEY COMPETENCIES FOR MODERN CIOS

CIOs must constantly improve and enhance their skill sets to flourish in this dynamic industry. Insights from many sectors provide vital views and assistance to CIOs on their journey of competency development. Here are the primary abilities that CIOs may develop to navigate varied industries effectively:

Pioneering Cutting-Edge Technology: CIOs must support a forward-thinking attitude and control IT operations. CIOs act as catalysts for change within their organizations, fostering a culture of adaptability and continuous learning. They inspire teams to embrace new technologies, providing the necessary training and support to ensure a smooth transition. By championing a tech-savvy culture, they position their organizations to be agile in responding to market dynamics and staying ahead of the competition. For example, a CIO in the manufacturing industry converts the IT division into a strategic ally by deploying modern technology such as IoT sensors. This change resulted in considerable cost savings and increased efficiency due to real-time production line monitoring.

Technology and Business Demands Must Be Balanced: CIOs are crucial in managing the delicate balance between innovation and stability. While the infusion of cutting-edge technologies can drive progress, it must be done judiciously to avoid disruptions to existing operations. CIOs must assess the potential impact of technological changes on the organization's infrastructure, security, and overall business continuity. By maintaining a delicate equilibrium, CIOs can position their organizations for sustained growth, resilience in the face of change, and a competitive advantage in the dynamic and technology-driven business landscape. A CIO in the healthcare business is an outstanding example. He promotes technical advances like telemedicine platforms while working with medical specialists to ensure solutions align with patient care goals.

Informed Decision-Making and Research Attitude: Successful CIOs develop a research attitude. A banking sector CIO believes a comprehensive study is essential before introducing new technologies. The CIO diligently investigated customer demands and market developments to ensure that the CIO's recommendation was made based on a thorough understanding of the environment. CIOs are the linchpin between technological advancements and organizational objectives; their ability to make well-informed decisions is crucial for the enterprise's success. By leveraging a research-oriented mindset, CIOs contribute to the efficient and effective use of technology and their enterprises' overall resilience and competitiveness in an increasingly digital world.

Customer-Centric Leadership: Customer-centric leadership signifies a strategic orientation where technological decisions and innovations are deeply rooted in understanding and meeting the needs of the end-users. A CIO with a customer-centric leadership approach places the customer experience at the forefront of technological strategies and initiatives. It is critical to lead with a customer-centric mindset. During the research, one retail CIO informed us that he uses data analytics to gain in-depth knowledge of client preferences. He increases customer satisfaction and loyalty by customizing online shopping experiences and improving inventory management. A CIO practicing customer-centric leadership becomes a catalyst for positive technological change, where every innovation is viewed through its impact on the end-user. By intertwining technology decisions with a deep understanding of customer needs, CIOs play a pivotal role in creating a technology landscape that meets operational requirements and contributes significantly to the organization's customer-centric ethos.

Continuous Learning and Adaptation: In today's fast-paced technological world, CIOs must demonstrate a commitment to lifetime learning. CIOs champion a culture of learning within their teams. They encourage professional development, provide opportunities for skill enhancement, and foster an environment where team members feel empowered to explore new technologies and methodologies. This collective commitment to continuous learning ensures that the IT department remains at the forefront of innovation. CIOs prioritizing continuous learning and adaptation position themselves and their organizations for sustained success in a dynamic digital landscape. By embracing a mindset of perpetual learning, staying adaptable, and fostering a culture of innovation, these CIOs lead their teams effectively and contribute to their organizations' overall resilience and competitiveness in an ever-changing technological landscape. Illustrating this concept is a scenario where a CIO promotes reverse mentorship, wherein younger IT staff provides insights into emerging technology. This approach ensures that the organization stays at the forefront of technological advancements.

Creating Value and Building Relationships: A CIO's success is measured by technological prowess and the strategic impact they bring. Delivering demonstrable value by connecting IT projects with larger business objectives is a fundamental capability of CIOs. Modern CIOs go beyond the traditional role of technology overseers; they are value creators and relationship builders. Their ability to align technology with business goals, cultivate strong internal and external relationships, form strategic partnerships, and effectively manage risks positions them as integral contributors to the success and competitiveness of their organizations in the digital age. During the research, a CIO from the hotel industry illustrated that improving the visitor experience with self-check-in kiosks and mobile app connections has resulted in customer satisfaction and has encouraged loyalty and repeated business.

Embracing Humor and Overcoming Fear: CIOs who incorporate humor into their leadership approach understand the power of levity in creating a more engaging and enjoyable workplace. They utilize humor not only as a stress reliever but also as a tool to break down communication barriers, enhance team collaboration, and stimulate creative thinking. By embracing comedy, CIOs create a workplace atmosphere that encourages open communication and promotes a sense of camaraderie among team members. CIOs may use humor as a great tool to overcome fear. During one of my research interviews, one of the CIOs from the entertainment industry told me once that he uses humor during team meetings to build a healthy work environment. He promotes teamwork and innovation by reducing conflicts and encouraging open communication.

Strategic Planning and Execution: CIOs play a pivotal role in the strategic planning and execution processes within organizations. In the rapidly evolving technological landscape, aligning IT strategies with overall business objectives is critical for ensuring long-term success. CIOs engage in strategic planning and execution to harness the potential of technology and drive innovation, enhance efficiency, and contribute to the organization's overall competitiveness. In the strategic planning phase, CIOs assess the current technological infrastructure, identify gaps, and anticipate future needs. They prioritize initiatives based on potential business impact, cost-effectiveness, and alignment with the organization's vision. CIOs play a dual role as architects of strategic IT plans and orchestrators of their successful execution. Their ability to envision the future technology landscape, align strategies with business goals, and lead effective execution is essential for organizations aiming to thrive in an increasingly digital and competitive world. Strategic planning needs emotional involvement and an understanding of guiding concepts.

Fostering Innovation and Digitalization: By fostering an environment where team members feel empowered to contribute ideas and take calculated risks, CIOs ensure that innovation becomes an integral part of the organization's DNA. CIOs often champion hackathons, brainstorming sessions, and collaborative projects that spark fresh ideas and perspectives, driving the organization forward in a rapidly changing digital landscape. CIOs lead initiatives to digitize workflows, automate repetitive tasks, and enhance operational efficiency. This streamlines internal processes and positions the organization more responsive to market changes. Digitalization efforts extend to customer experiences, where CIOs leverage technology to create seamless, personalized interactions that meet the expectations of modern consumers. CIOs must promote business innovation and digitalization projects. An example is a logistics CIO, who uses robotic process automation to improve supply chain operations. This approach has helped the CIO to increase efficiency, reduce mistakes, and improve client happiness by minimizing manual activities.

Holistic Leadership: Holistic CIOs are strategic thinkers who seamlessly align technology initiatives with broader business objectives. By actively participating in strategic planning, holistic CIOs ensure that technology investments contribute to the organization's growth, innovation, and competitive positioning. Holistic leadership by CIOs combines technological expertise with a deep understanding of business strategy, human dynamics, and ethical considerations. By adopting a holistic approach, CIOs position themselves as integral leaders who drive organizational success by effectively integrating technology into all facets of the business. CIOs must be knowledgeable in all aspects of leadership, including business and technology. A telecom CIO who works with marketing teams to provide new services that match client expectations. His ability to balance technological and economic goals leads to his firm's success. His efforts also demonstrate the importance of understanding the needs of both internal teams and external customers. By implementing a holistic approach, he is able to create successful solutions that benefit all parties involved.

By cultivating a strategic vision that prioritizes agility and innovation, CIOs with holistic leadership skills empower their teams to adapt to evolving technological landscapes, ensuring long-term resilience and competitiveness for their enterprise. Incorporating these abilities positions CIOs as dynamic leaders capable of negotiating the complicated convergence of technology and business and creating digital success in their enterprises.

1.8 EVOLVING ROLE OF A CIO

Traditionally, the CIO has been in charge of managing technology and technology-related risks. However, thought leadership and strategic vision are becoming more critical components of the profession. In this new era, CIOs must collaborate to ensure that technology solutions align with business goals for success. They must also be able to translate complicated technical concepts. Aligning a technological vision with the business strategy is crucial for a CIO seeking thought leadership. The gap between IT and the rest of the company is often painfully evident when choosing which technologies to invest in. Even when there are specific safe solutions, like fixing outdated infrastructure, the discussion frequently ends there. By aligning the technology vision with the business, the CIO can open up new opportunities for innovation and help position the organization for success.

A CIO is responsible for comprehending the intricacies of the business, actively engaging within the organization, and taking a reflective stance to understand the factors influencing the organization's present condition. In reaction to the altering technology landscape, the function of the CIO is experiencing rapid and sophisticated development. CIOs must use technology to alter their processes, staff, and operations to manage this ever-expanding and complex market. First and foremost, CIOs must use technology to automate and standardize procedures wherever possible. Automating the tasks will allow the organization to deal with the increasing complexity of the technological world and free up critical time for more important strategic undertakings. Second, CIOs must identify and create the proper teams to help their workforce and organization evolve.

Mark Zuckerberg quote states, "*In a world that's changing quickly, the only strategy that is guaranteed to fail is not taking risks.*" A forward-thinking CIO in the current corporate environment works closely with business divisions, customers, and stakeholders to get insights into their difficulties and barriers within the existing technical framework. Following that, the CIO works with key business stakeholders to develop a clear and straightforward problem description for the firm. This strategy makes it easier to grasp the firm's goals and build a good relationship with the organization. It also urges the CIO to enquire about the industry's business problem statement. A modern CIO acts as a business partner, collaborating with business divisions, customers, and various stakeholders to identify the organization's challenges, concerns, and opportunities. The most successful method is to encourage people to express their issue statement.

According to Earley's research report published in 2017, CIOs have been crucial in pushing digital transformation projects, introducing cutting-edge technology, and optimizing internal procedures. A poll of over 500 CIOs by professional services firm Genpact and the MIT Sloan CIO Symposium emphasized the shifting nature of the CIO function. CIOs must champion innovation and renewal inside their enterprises to promote change in today's digital world. Failure to innovate may easily lead to an organization slipping behind its competition. The CIO can initiate change and influence the organization's overall strategy by working closely with the CEO and other top-level executives. They are well-positioned to understand the changing expectations of the CIO's role in aiding their organization's growth and success.

According to a recent PwC survey, 84% of CEOs agree that CIOs should be at the forefront of driving innovation and change inside their firms. This proportion has climbed dramatically from the previous years, highlighting the rising importance of CIOs in pioneering innovation. As a result, CIOs must be well-prepared to take on this new position.

CHAPTER 2
OPTIMIZING ORGANIZATIONAL STRUCTURE AND IT GOVERNANCE: TRENDS AND STRATEGIES

INTRODUCTION

This chapter explores the essential elements of setting up an IT organization with the proper framework, which is a fundamental component of any progressive company. In this chapter, we analyze growth methods that place companies at the forefront of market evolution while keeping up with technical advancements. To achieve such heights, we navigate the landscape of high-performance teams, providing insights and guidance on cultivating and guiding teams that consistently deliver exceptional results in the dynamic world of IT.

The chapter also explores organizational design optimization, an essential component of successful IT administration. Organizations may improve their agility and responsiveness and guarantee smooth technology integration into all operations by coordinating their structures with their strategic objectives. We go into the details of this optimization process and clarify recommended methods that support an all-encompassing strategy for IT management; as we acknowledge the critical role that talent plays in the IT world, human resource and skills considerations take center stage. Success depends primarily on developing the proper abilities. Thus, we explore tactics for luring, training, and keeping elite IT specialists.

In this chapter, we also investigate the constantly changing trends in CIO reporting frameworks. The reporting structure that backs the efforts of CIOs is subject to constant change in tandem with the officer's job. We explore new developments and how they affect organizational dynamics, offering insightful guidance on negotiating the challenging landscape of IT leadership. In this chapter's thorough examination of IT management, we go into the complexities of organizational structure, development strategies, team leadership, design optimization, human resource considerations, and the ever-changing landscape of CIO reporting structures.

2.1 ORGANIZING IT WITH PROPER STRUCTURE

Many CIOs still run their organization using outdated, inefficient methods that do not take advantage of contemporary technologies in an attempt to optimize commercial results. CIOs must reevaluate their IT organizational structures and replace them with more modern ones that better meet the needs of modern companies. A well-defined organizational structure can aid in an IT department's problem-solving process, contractor selection, and authority hierarchy. Based on this, we can say that "*A well-organized system is the backbone of efficiency, so structure your work and watch productivity thrive.*"

By organizational requirements, the CIO can embrace either a unified IT department system or a variety of organizational frameworks, as outlined in the IET (2021) article. For CIOs operating within IT, familiarizing themselves with diverse IT organizational structures could prove beneficial in formulating effective processes to align with corporate objectives. Below are the critical organizational structures that a CIO would use for designing his organization.

2.1.1 CENTRALIZED IT

In the past, the primary focus of the CIO was on developing and maintaining the organization's IT infrastructure. However, the CIO's attention has moved to creating commercial value as digital transformation has become a strategic priority for many organizations. The organizational strategy of grouping information technology resources and services under a single team or location inside a business or organization is known as centralized IT. According to this paradigm, a single department or organization manages and provides all IT services. This method contrasts decentralized IT systems, in which separate business units or departments oversee their IT operations autonomously.

"*Efficiency thrives in the heart of centralization, where coordinated efforts lead to unparalleled success.*" Efficiency is one of the main benefits of a centralized IT model. Organizations can cut costs, eliminate redundancy, and streamline operations by pooling their IT resources. Centralization makes better coordination and standardization of IT systems and processes possible, which boosts overall performance. Additionally, it makes managing IT assets easier, guaranteeing that hardware, software, and other resources are used to their fullest potential. Increased security and control are two other significant advantages of centralized IT. Because a single body oversees, controls, and enforces security procedures throughout the company, centralization enables the implementation of more effective security measures. This is especially important since organizations face severe cyber threats and data breaches.

"Strategic resource allocation is the bridge between vision and reality, transforming aspirations into tangible achievements". Centralized IT encourages improved resource allocation and strategic planning. Organizations may more strategically manage resources, efficiently prioritize projects, and guarantee that IT activities align with the overarching business goals when a centralized team monitors IT functions. This centralized method frequently yields a more unified IT strategy that advances the organization's overarching goals. According to its detractors, the drawbacks of centralized IT include the possibility of higher bureaucracy and slower reaction times. Since centralized authorities must review and approve all requests and modifications, centralization can occasionally result in bottlenecks in the decision-

making process. This can provide a problem in dynamic settings where quick decisions are crucial.

Under centralized organizational structures, a single IT team manages the organization's technical assistance, resources, and equipment. Centralized teams perform better because they are more coordinated, have greater oversight, and are more organized. They might be appropriate for small and medium-sized enterprises with minimal IT requirements. A single server should be used by businesses to track the movement of all network data, requiring greater visibility and control over their networks. A centralized IT network can help reduce hardware costs, provide efficiency gains for IT staff, increase purchasing power, and improve industry-standard compliance.

Strategic planning, good communication, and a thorough grasp of the organization's overarching objectives and the particular requirements of its many divisions are necessary for setting up an appropriate structure in centralized IT. A CIO can be assisted in adequately structuring a centralized IT structure that efficiently manages technology resources and effectively supports the organization's broader goals. Some of the strategies that can be used to achieve this include aligning IT with business goals, establishing transparent governance, defining service catalog and SLAs, centralized IT leadership, standardizing processes, implementing a unified technology stack, communication and collaboration, user-centric approach, training and skill development, cybersecurity measures, performance metrics and monitoring, flexibility and adaptability, feedback mechanisms, etc. This strategy ensures that IT provides more than support—it becomes a strategic enabler.

To sum up, centralized IT has several benefits, such as improved security, greater productivity, and improved alignment with strategy. Organizations must carefully consider these advantages against potential disadvantages, such as decreased responsiveness and agility, to choose the best IT structure for their unique requirements and operational environment.

2.1.2 DECENTRALIZED IT

The term "*Decentralized IT*" describes an organizational structure in which the duties and functions related to information technology are dispersed among several departments or business units. Under this paradigm, the choices, systems, and resources related to IT may be independently made by teams or specific units. Decentralized IT systems are frequently distinguished by autonomy and adaptability, allowing any department to oversee its technological requirements. Autonomy and flexibility, customization for business units, quick decision-making, responsiveness to local needs, expertise in business domains, decreased reliance on centralized resources, local innovation, increased user satisfaction, risk mitigation, challenges with standardization, resource redundancy, security, and compliance concerns, communication and coordination are important aspects and considerations of decentralized IT. "*In the world of decentralized IT, collaboration becomes the currency, and collective intelligence propels the organization forward.*"

According to CIOs, decentralized IT seeks to improve its responsiveness, agility, and flexibility to evolving business needs. To do this, IT professionals must be encouraged to work more closely with the companies they support and to make decisions at the edge. IT professionals must be well-versed in the technology supporting organizational goals and objectives. They also need to be able to work with business divisions to determine the best way to leverage these technologies. IT specialists must also have the speed to design and implement solutions that must be modified in response to user input. IT must be knowledgeable about DevOps and the software development life cycle to accomplish this.

IT duties are divided among multiple groups in decentralized organizations, with each group responsible for overseeing IT support for a specific team or business unit. Sub-department supervisors usually oversee their teams, while higher management only intervenes when necessary. Large organizations employ this structure, with teams spread over several sites. Organizations that support groups with varying IT needs might also consider decentralized networks. For instance, it could be better to provide full-time IT support to a team that employs specialist software that requires frequent updates.

It is simpler for upper-level managers to give lower-level managers additional authority because of the decentralized structure. If stated differently, lower-level managers have greater decision-making authority and responsibility. Lower-level managers prioritize less critical tasks above making strategic choices. Executives, for example, make decisions on the organization's mission, vision, and strategic plans. Lower-level managers are entrusted with the remaining findings, giving them authority and accountability for daily operations.

Top-level managers perceive decentralization as a means of motivating employees to do more. They, therefore, grant authority to those who report to them. Consequently, it facilitates decision-making for upper management and increases enthusiasm among those reporting to them. They can, therefore, freely control and make decisions regarding their workspace. They also have the opportunity to develop and improve, increasing their skill. Decentralized IT should be considered by a CIO who wishes to increase the IT organization's agility and responsiveness.

To correctly structure an organization in a decentralized IT environment, a strategic plan must balance the benefits of autonomy and flexibility and the demands of coordination, standardization, and centralized control. A CIO establishes clear governance frameworks, standardizes core technologies, creates communication channels, defines SLAs, implements centralized security measures, and promotes best practices to organize structure in a decentralized organization. Investing in training and development, fostering a collaborative culture, implementing enterprise architecture, establishing change management procedures, centralizing procurement, centralizing vendor management, sharing, providing centralized support services, centralizing procurement, evaluating, and adjusting the delivery can also help the CIO to organize a proper structure in the organization.

A CIO can minimize coordination, security, and standardization issues while leveraging the benefits of flexibility and responsiveness by adopting a deliberate and strategic approach to decentralize IT. The aim is to establish a framework for each unit's best possible IT performance while maintaining a unified and harmonious IT environment.

In conclusion, decentralized IT structures benefit departmental flexibility, reactivity, and creativity. However, they also provide difficulties for resource redundancy, standardization, and centralized security and compliance management. It is essential to strike the correct balance between autonomy and central monitoring to optimize the advantages of a decentralized IT approach while minimizing potential negatives. In a nutshell *"Decentralized IT"* transforms challenges into opportunities, as diverse perspectives converge to solve complex problems.

2.1.3 HYBRID IT

A Hybrid IT Organization is a structure that combines elements of both centralized and decentralized models, allowing for a flexible and balanced approach to managing IT resources. In a hybrid IT organization, different business units or departments may have varying degrees of autonomy in managing their IT functions, while certain core IT functions and services are centrally controlled. The goal is to leverage the benefits of both centralized and decentralized approaches to meet the organization's overall objectives.

CIOs recognize the critical importance of organizational structures and cultures within enterprises, knowing that their decisions significantly impact overall performance. The objective is to strike the right balance between IT and business capabilities, fostering agility, responsiveness, and innovation within the organization. The hybrid IT model is prevalent among the CIO's preferred organizational structures. This hybrid structure pursues a harmonious integration of external resources into IT service lines. IT managers may outsource specific aspects of their services to contractors and specialized professionals. The organization can engage a contractor working across multiple service lines, adapting to changing needs. Typically, IT department management selects contractors from their network, considering reputation and expertise.

Hybrid IT embraces both on-site data centers and cloud technologies. It goes beyond merely connecting disparate IT infrastructure environments that were traditionally kept separate. Instead, this model empowers organizations to manage and govern IT services uniformly, emphasizing adopting cloud computing. Integrating cloud resources into the infrastructure is not just about connecting different environments; it is a deliberate choice to standardize IT services. Business agility takes precedence when selecting infrastructure resources to support mission-critical data workloads and applications. This strategic decision extends beyond cost and security considerations, highlighting a purposeful approach to enhancing the organization's overall efficiency and adaptability.

Key characteristics of a hybrid IT organization are centralized core functions, decentralized business units, flexibility and adaptability, optimized resource allocation, scalability, integration of cloud services, risk management, innovation, and collaboration. Implementing a hybrid IT organization requires careful planning and effective communication to realize the benefits of both centralization and decentralization. It is a strategy that acknowledges the diverse needs of different parts of the organization while maintaining control and standardization where necessary for overall efficiency and security. Organizing a proper structure in a hybrid IT organization involves careful planning, strategic decision-making, and practical implementation.

Below are key steps and considerations that a CIO might take in managing a Hybrid IT:

Assessing Business Needs: Understand the organization's goals, objectives, and challenges. Identify the specific IT requirements of different business units or departments.

Defining the Hybrid IT Strategy: A CIO should define the hybrid IT strategy that complements the overarching business plan of the organization. The CIOs should establish which IT tasks will be autonomous or centralized and the cloud services integration strategy.

Creating a Governance Framework: A CIO should establish a governance framework that outlines roles, responsibilities, decision-making processes, and compliance standards. A governance framework will ensure consistency and accountability across the organization.

Building a Skilled Team: A CIO should recruit and develop a skilled IT team that manages both on-premises and cloud-based IT. This includes expertise in cloud services, security, compliance, and integration.

Implementing Centralized Core Functions: A CIO should identify core IT functions that must be centralized for standardization, security, and compliance. This may include governance, cybersecurity, and specific infrastructure components.

Facilitating Decentralized Business Units: A CIO should empower business units with the autonomy to manage their IT needs. Define the boundaries of decentralization, considering factors like budget allocation, decision-making authority, and technology adoption.

Integrating Cloud Services: A CIO should develop a strategy for integrating cloud services into the IT infrastructure. This may involve choosing the right cloud providers, establishing connectivity, and implementing cloud-native solutions.

Implementing Hybrid Infrastructure: A CIO should deploy a hybrid infrastructure that integrates on-premises data centers with cloud services. This may involve using technologies like containers and microservices for better compatibility.

Ensuring Security and Compliance: A CIO should implement robust security measures and compliance protocols across both on-premises and cloud environments. Address any regulatory requirements relevant to the industry.

Monitoring and Optimization: A CIO should implement monitoring tools to track the performance of both on-premises and cloud-based systems. A CIO should regularly assess the efficiency of the hybrid IT model and make adjustments as needed.

Training and Communication: A CIO should provide IT staff and end-users training to adapt to the hybrid environment. Communicate the benefits and changes effectively to ensure a smooth transition and user adoption.

Continuous Improvement: A CIO should foster a culture of continuous improvement. A CIO should regularly review the hybrid IT structure, assess its effectiveness, and adjust based on evolving business needs and technological advancements.

Following these steps, a CIO can establish a well-organized and effective structure in a Hybrid IT organization. The key is to strike a balance between centralization and decentralization, leveraging the strengths of each approach to meet the organization's specific goals and requirements. In a nutshell *"Hybrid IT is the bridge connecting the best of both worlds — the reliability of the past and the limitless possibilities of the future".*

2.1.4 VIRTUAL IT

An IT department or team that works remotely, with its workers dispersed across different locations instead of operating from a single physical office, is commonly called a *"Virtual IT"*. Another name for this strategy is distributed or virtual IT. Within a virtual IT business, team members utilize technology to cooperate and communicate efficiently, even when physically separated. A new IT era has emerged due to the rise of digital transformation, where the conventional IT structure is no longer sufficient. The CIO must establish a virtual IT organization emphasizing innovation and value generation.

A virtual IT organization is a system of individuals, procedures, and tools arranged according to the company's requirements. Under this new organizational structure, the organization's success is shared by all organization members. A virtual IT organization that can meet the business expectations for speed, agility, and flexibility must be established by the CIO. To achieve this, the CIO must concentrate on three crucial areas: personnel management, organizational design, and operational efficiency.

With the primary goal of achieving predetermined objectives, the virtual IT structure is a modern approach to structuring roles, teams, or other units within various IT organizations or entire companies. A Virtual IT normally has no unique legal name, physical assets, or workers connected only to one company. The network and the virtual enterprise are the essential elements of a virtual IT organization structure. Partners' rapid communication abilities are critical to maintaining healthy partnerships in this approach. The foundation of a virtual IT organization is network computing and communication technology.

Because the IT world is changing, businesses must face new challenges and adapt to incorporating new IT solutions. All members of this virtual IT company are treated equally, regardless of where they are in the organizational hierarchy. When the company enters into contracts with particular customers, tasks are broken down, and procedures are strictly watched. A virtual IT organization's lifespan can change depending on how long it takes to finish a specific project or execute an order. A virtual IT organization must be set up correctly for successful project execution, efficient operations, and effective communication.

Below are some tactics a CIO can use to set up a suitable framework in a remote IT-based company:

Remote Work Policies: A CIO should establish clear remote work policies that outline expectations for working hours, communication channels, and deliverables. A CIO should communicate guidelines for handling work-related issues, such as troubleshooting, support, and collaboration.

Clear Organizational Goals and Objectives: A CIO should clearly define and communicate the organization's goals and objectives to all team members. A CIO should ensure alignment between individual and team goals with the organization's overall strategic objectives.

Virtual Team Building: A CIO should organize virtual team-building activities to foster a sense of camaraderie among team members. A CIO should encourage regular informal interactions to build relationships and strengthen team cohesion.

Training and Development: A CIO should provide ongoing training and professional development opportunities to keep team members updated on relevant technologies and best practices. A CIO should foster a culture of continuous learning to enhance the skills of the virtual team.

Team Collaboration Tools: A CIO should implement and leverage tools that facilitate communication and project collaboration, such as video conferencing, messaging platforms, project management software, and shared document repositories.

Performance Measurement: A CIO should establish key performance indicators (KPIs) to measure the performance of individuals and team performance. A CIO should regularly review and assess performance, providing constructive feedback and recognition for achievements.

Communication Strategies: A CIO should consider developing effective communication strategies, considering time zone differences and cultural diversity. A CIO should ensure regular team meetings, one-on-one check-ins, and open lines of communication to address concerns and share updates.

Security Measures: A CIO should consider implementing robust cybersecurity measures to protect sensitive data and ensure the security of remote work environments. A CIO should educate team members on cybersecurity best practices, including using secure communication channels and adherence to security policies.

Agile Methodologies: A CIO should consider adopting agile methodologies to enhance adaptability and responsiveness to changing project requirements. A CIO should implement agile practices such as regular sprint planning, daily stand-ups, and retrospectives.

Leadership and Empowerment: A CIO should consider empowering team leaders and managers with the skills to lead remote teams effectively. A CIO should foster a culture of trust and autonomy, allowing team members to own their work.

Regular Performance Reviews: A CIO should conduct regular performance reviews and provide constructive feedback to help team members improve and grow in their roles. A CIO should recognize and reward outstanding contributions.

Employee Well-being: A CIO should prioritize employee well-being by promoting work-life balance and mental health awareness. A CIO should offer support services and resources to help employees cope with the challenges of remote work.

By implementing these strategies, a CIO can help create a structured and supportive environment for a virtual IT organization, fostering collaboration, innovation, and success. To conclude "*Virtual IT is the portal to a realm where ideas take flight in the virtual wings of innovation, navigating the vast expanse of the digital sky*"

2.1.5 MULTIMODAL IT

Multimodal IT recognizes that different projects or business functions may require different approaches. It involves employing various IT methodologies or models depending on the specific needs of each initiative. For example, a project may benefit from an agile methodology, while another may follow a more traditional, structured approach. The multi-model IT organizational structure for the CIO is a management tool designed to enhance the efficiency and optimization of IT service delivery within an enterprise. It operates on the principle that the CIO holds responsibility for the strategic planning, execution, and day-to-day management of all IT resources and functions. The CIO also ensures that all IT-related initiatives are aligned with the overall organizational strategy. The CIO is also responsible for the budgeting, cost control, and risk management of IT operations. Finally, the CIO must ensure that the IT security systems and protocols are up to date.

Adopting multi-modal IT is like having a versatile toolkit – combining the strength of proven methodologies with the flexibility needed to navigate the complexities of the modern IT landscape. The multi-model IT organizational structure for the CIO provides a framework for the CIO to align IT with business goals and objectives and to create a system that supports the efficient and effective delivery of IT services. The multi-model IT organizational structure for the CIO can be adapted to any organization of any size and can be used in conjunction with other management tools, such as the IT balanced scorecard, to create a comprehensive approach to IT management.

IT transformation is a widespread process undertaken by many organizations. Organizations undergoing transition shifts relied on traditional IT infrastructure consisting of physical or virtualized servers running N-tier or monolithic apps and using waterfall development processes. As part of the transition, organizations are moving their workloads and servers from on-premise to the cloud. Legacy applications undergo rapid conversion into containers or micro-services. Consequently, these organizations operate within a multimodal IT environment, seamlessly coexisting with traditional and software-defined infrastructures.

Multimodal IT is a strategic approach whereby firms recognize the various requirements of various projects and applications and use a variety of approaches to fulfill those needs suitably. Multimodal IT enables CIOs to modify their strategy to the particular needs of various applications, projects, or business operations. Depending on variables, including project scale, complexity, and deadline, CIOs can use a variety of approaches, including agile, traditional waterfall, or a hybrid of the two.

In a multimodal IT environment, CIOs combine more contemporary, agile techniques and technologies (Mode 2) with more traditional IT practices (Mode 1). Cloud-based platforms, containerized development, micro-services architecture, and other modern technologies are frequently used with the existing infrastructure for this integration. For more dynamic projects, CIOs can encourage innovation and adaptation through agile approaches (Mode 2), but for stable, well-understood projects, they can employ established methodologies to improve IT operations for efficiency (Mode 1). By striking a balance between these modes, the organization may maintain a solid, organized base while being able to react swiftly to shifting business needs.

CIOs are essential in making strategic decisions because they select the best approach for any project or use case. The degree of unpredictability, project complexity, time-to-market demands, and the necessity of quick iterations and collaboration are a few factors to consider. Managing a hybrid infrastructure that combines conventional on-premise solutions with cloud-based services is a common task for multimodal IT. CIOs should invest in building an adaptable IT staff with a wide range of competencies that can work with various approaches and technology. Team members can adjust to the constantly changing IT world with training programs and continuous learning initiatives. A CIO should foster a culture of continuous improvement by encouraging feedback and lessons learned from traditional and agile projects.

A CIO should evaluate each mode's efficacy regularly and modify tactics in response to changing organizational requirements and market trends. Every mode has risks that CIOs must carefully manage, considering security, compliance, and possible interruptions. A CIO should establish robust risk management procedures to reduce difficulties from multimodal IT's heterogeneous nature. Organizing a proper structure in a multimodal IT organization, where different projects or functions may require varied approaches, requires a thoughtful and flexible approach.

Here are some strategies that a CIO can employ in managing a multimodal IT:

Define Project Criteria: A CIO should clearly define the criteria for determining which projects or functions fall under each mode (e.g., agile, traditional, hybrid). A CIO should establish guidelines for project teams to assess and select the most appropriate methodology based on project characteristics.

Resource Allocation: A CIO should assess the skills and expertise within the IT team and allocate resources accordingly. A CIO should ensure that team members are well-versed in the methodologies they will be working with. Consider training programs to enhance the team's proficiency in various methodologies.

Communication and Collaboration: A CIO should foster a culture of open communication and collaboration among team members and across modes. A CIO should implement tools and platforms that facilitate communication and collaboration, particularly in a virtual or distributed work environment.

Project Portfolio Management: A CIO should implement robust portfolio management practices to oversee and prioritize projects across different modes. A CIO should regularly review and reassess the portfolio to ensure alignment with business goals and adapt to changing circumstances.

Flexible Governance Framework: A CIO should consider establishing a framework for flexibility and adaptability across different modes. A CIO should define each mode's clear governance structures, decision-making processes, and escalation procedures.

Knowledge Sharing and Learning: A CIO should encourage knowledge sharing among team members across different modes. CIO should also Facilitate forums, workshops, or knowledge-sharing sessions to discuss experiences and lessons learned and establish a culture of continuous learning to adapt to evolving methodologies and best practices.

Performance Measurement: A CIO should develop key performance indicators (KPIs) tailored to each mode. Measure and assess performance against these indicators to identify areas for improvement. A CIO should use performance data to make informed decisions about the effectiveness of different modes in specific contexts.

Change Management: A CIO should consider implementing effective strategies to help team members transition smoothly between different modes. The CIO has to communicate the benefits of Multimodal IT and provide the necessary support and resources for a successful transition.

Customer-Centric Approach: A CIO is expected to ensure that the selection of IT modes aligns with the needs and expectations of internal and external customers. The CIO should continuously gather feedback from stakeholders to improve and refine the Multimodal IT approach.

Risk Management: A CIO should implement a robust risk management framework that considers the unique risks associated with each mode. CIO should regularly assess and mitigate risks to minimize potential project timelines and deliverables disruptions.

2.2 TRENDS IN CIO REPORTING STRUCTURE

The CIO plays a flexible role in company strategy. CIOs can maximize IT by demonstrating their business acumen, developing relationships with the C-suite, and balancing design with mission and identity, regardless of who they report to. According to a study by Kark et al. (2018), CIOs are becoming more concerned with integrating cutting-edge infrastructure and apps with crucial business and IT operational activities and setting clear guidelines for remote workforce that include deadlines, contact information, and expected results—providing guidelines for resolving issues at work, including cooperation, assistance, and troubleshooting. This integration aims to support creative business models, generate top-line value, and give the company a competitive edge. CIOs now operate at the nexus of strategic technology adoption and business growth as the role of IT shifts from protecting value to actively creating income.

Because of the speed at which technology is developing, CIOs must be quick thinkers and decision-makers. This highlights the collaborative nature of navigating the changing technological world and calls for solid assistance from all organizational levels. In this context, the CIO's responsibilities go beyond typical IT management, including actively promoting the company's success by utilizing technology to boost competitiveness and profitability.

CIOs have long needed help with where they should best report. Over the years, there have been several trends in CIO reporting structure, with no clear consensus on which is best. The CIO's position is becoming more and more aligned with other organizational departments as it becomes more strategic and business value-oriented. In the past, the CIO reported directly to the CEO, but now we see a trend where the CIO reports to the Chief Operating Officer

(COO) or the Chief Financial Officer (CFO). Several factors have contributed to this trend. First, the CIO role has become more strategic and focused on business growth rather than operational efficiency. Second, with data and analytics playing a more significant role in business decision-making, the CFO is now viewed as the CIO's natural business partner.

2.2.1 CEO-CIO REPORTING LINE

In today's corporate environment, a CEO and a CIO's relationship is crucial when technology is essential to an organization's performance. The CIO is in charge of the information systems and technology infrastructure that support the business goals, whereas the CEO is generally in charge of the company's overall performance and strategic direction. The nature of this reporting relationship is synergistic; the CEO looks to the CIO to help align technology projects with the company's objectives and improve operational efficiency.

As IT has evolved within firms, there is a growing tendency for CEOs to supervise CIOs directly. This change is evident in the CEO-CIO reporting line, which highlights the increasing importance of IT in corporate planning. This tendency is anticipated to continue as companies rely increasingly on technology to drive expansion and preserve their competitiveness.

Kark *et al.* (2018) assert that the growing number of CIOs who answer directly to CEOs highlights how vital technology is in determining corporate strategy.

An examination of the reporting structures of over 500 CIOs unveiled that 46 percent of global enterprise CIOs are accountable to the C suites of their organizations. Notably, 51% of CIOs in the United States maintain a direct reporting relationship with the CEO, surpassing the global average. This inclination towards reporting directly to the CEO is more conspicuous in the U.S. The noteworthy observation is the heightened prevalence of a direct reporting link to the CEO, especially among CIOs guiding their organizations through digital transformation. The research also states that 55 percent of the CIOs creating their company's digital strategy report directly to the CEO. In contrast, most CIOs (51%) who support the creation of digital strategies report to the CFO, with only approximately a quarter (27%) reporting to the CEO.

This change in reporting structures highlights the strategic role of technology leadership and its direct impact on organizational success. Since CIOs are increasingly involved in developing digital strategies and corporate growth, the trend of them reporting directly to the CEO indicates their crucial position in defining the future trajectory of their organizations. According to the study, 77% of CIOs who report to the CEO say that their companies have some digital strategy.Also, 38 percent of CIOs report to the CEO in companies with enterprise-wide digital strategy, while only 8 percent report to the CFO. However, when CIOs say digital is not a priority for their organization, far fewer (25%) report to the CEO, and many more (27%) report to the CFO. Even when an organization has a Chief Digital Officer (CDO) in charge of leading and implementing the digital strategy, 74 percent of CIOs say that both the CDO and the CIO report to the CEO.

It is common for CIOs to report directly to the CEO in areas where technology is causing major disruptions or changes. The dynamic between the CEO and CIO regarding reporting is changing with the rapid evolution of technology. CIOs are becoming increasingly viewed as strategic partners that help with operational efficiency, new revenue stream creation, and market differentiation. To stay flexible and adaptable to new technology, an organization's ability to navigate the dynamic environment of digital disruption depends on the cooperation of its CEO and CIO. Retaining a competitive advantage in today's fast-paced business world depends on a robust and cooperative CEO-CIO reporting relationship that fosters innovation and growth.

2.2.2 CIO-CFO REPORTING LINE

The CFO and the CIO are essential to an organization's strategic management and decision-making processes, and they each contribute to various aspects of its success. The CIO manages the IT infrastructure, ensures that technology supports organizational objectives, and optimizes effectiveness. When reporting to the CFO, the CIO's primary responsibility is to convey the value of IT investments, their effect on operational procedures, and how technological efforts support the company's financial stability. To make well-informed financial decisions, the CFO needs this reporting relationship to provide insights into the organization's technology capabilities, threats, and possibilities.

CEOs and CFOs are two of a corporation's most essential and influential executives. CIOs and CFOs have diverse areas of expertise, yet they both oversee crucial tasks that directly impact the bottom line. Their shared objective is to add value to the company. This objective can be accomplished through collaboration and using one another's advantages. Instead of being rivals, CIOs and CFOs should be allies. Through collaboration, they may give their companies a competitive edge.

Deloitte's research highlights the frequent and productive collaboration between CIOs and CFOs, driven by their shared objective of enhancing organizational performance through a strategic balance between top-line contributions and bottom-line efficiencies. CIOs, especially when reporting to finance, delve more extensively into technology budgets, business cases, and return on investment—especially for sizable projects with extended timelines and significant assets. When the reporting relationship is to the CFO instead of the CEO, daily operations claim a more significant portion, constituting 60% of the IT budget compared to 53% under CEO reporting. Moreover, companies following this reporting structure tend to allocate less budget to small-scale business transformation and innovation initiatives. Collaborative efforts between the CIO and the finance leader can be advantageous, allowing them to showcase technology's importance and value collectively. In such cases, having the CIO report to the CFO ensures a technology advocate within the finance leadership, supporting the strategic role of technology in the organization.

In today's business environment, where technology is vital in accomplishing organizational goals, the collaboration between CIOs and CFOs is critical. These two executives' cooperation guarantees that IT expenditures meet budgetary goals and advance company success. Organizations differ in how CIOs and CFOs are expected to report. The fact that both executives in some businesses answer directly to the CEO emphasizes the strategic significance of the finance and IT departments. In other situations, there may be a closer synergy between financial goals and technological initiatives as the CIO reports to the CFO.

Effective communication and coordination between the CIO and CFO are critical, regardless of the reporting structure. CIOs and CFOs must work together to make sure that technology spending is in line with the organization's financial priorities and strategic goals. The CIO's job is to comprehend how technology may spur innovation, increase productivity, and provide a competitive edge. The CFO's priorities in the interim include cost control, financial performance optimization, and a strong return on investment. The convergence of these perspectives is crucial for making informed decisions about IT investments.

Typically, the CFO holds responsibility for expenditures and plays a pivotal role in budgeting. Achieving IT budgets that are rational and aligned with the organization's strategic objectives necessitates close collaboration between the CIO and CFO. This entails assessing cost-benefit evaluations, discussing the possible financial effects of technological initiatives, and ranking projects according to how well they connect with overarching corporate objectives. While CFOs focus on financial risk and compliance, CIOs address technological risks, including cybersecurity attacks and system breakdowns. To ensure that the company has a comprehensive approach to risk management that considers both technological and financial issues, the two executives must work together on risk assessment and mitigation measures.

Setting up KPIs is essential for assessing budgetary plans and IT project success. The CFO and CIO should establish measurements supporting the business's goals. This could involve calculating how technology expenditures affect financial performance, cost savings, and revenue growth. Effective and transparent communication is essential to the CIO-CFO partnership's success. Collaboration can be facilitated by setting up cross-functional teams, holding regular meetings, and participating in collaborative planning sessions. Both executives should know each other's goals, difficulties, and communication styles to build a solid collaboration.

Reaching company objectives requires the CIO and CFO to collaborate and communicate effectively. Modern corporate success is primarily influenced by the dynamic interaction between technology and finance, and a strong working relationship between these two executives guarantees that the company can successfully traverse the challenges of the digital world without jeopardizing its financial stability. Regular reporting and open communication between the CIO and CFO foster a comprehensive awareness of the organization's operations. This understanding enables well-informed decisions to be made that support both financial sustainability and technical growth.

In conclusion, the interaction between CIOs and CFOs is critical in the current corporate landscape. Together, senior leaders can ensure that financial objectives and technological investments are correctly matched, boosting company performance and providing them with a competitive advantage in the marketplace.

2.2.3 CIO-COO REPORTING LINE

The reporting lines of the CIO and Chief Operating Officer (COO) within an organization play pivotal roles in shaping the strategic direction and operational efficiency of the company. The CIO typically reports directly to the CEO or sometimes to the CFO depending on the organizational structure. This reporting arrangement reflects the critical role technology plays in modern businesses, as the CIO is responsible for overseeing the company's information technology strategy, infrastructure, and digital initiatives. The direct reporting line to the CEO emphasizes the importance of aligning technology with overall business objectives and ensuring that IT investments contribute to the organization's success.

The CIO and COO's relationship has been changing over time. Traditionally, the COO has concentrated on business procedures, whereas the CIO has concentrated on technology. Nevertheless, the functions and responsibilities of the CIO and COO are beginning to overlap due to the growing significance of technology in business. Under these circumstances, IT would be seen as a shared service, and CIOs might need help to break the myth that IT is only an execution-driven function. However, CIOs may find it helpful to report to a COO to get business leaders to agree on standard technology, structures, and procedures—especially when bringing about changes that affect the entire organization. This framework supports a coherent strategy for accomplishing corporate objectives by facilitating collaboration and alignment between technological initiatives and operational needs.

An organization's ability to operate effectively depends on the interaction between the COO and CIO. They may have different duties and responsibilities based on the industry and organizational structure, but cooperation amongst them is crucial to coordinating technological initiatives with overarching business goals. The CIO and COO must collaborate closely to ensure that technological efforts align with the organization's operational objectives. Technology can better support overall company strategy, increase efficiency, and streamline procedures through this partnership. Organizational structures for reporting can differ. The strategic significance of operations and technology is highlighted by the CEO receiving direct reports from the CIO and COO in certain businesses. Alternatively, the CIO might report to the COO, emphasizing the close relationship between technology and day-to-day operations.

The CIO and COO should hold strategic planning meetings to find areas where technology might improve operational efficacy. This entails evaluating the processes in place, projecting future requirements, and matching business priorities with technological investments. Risk management is a shared duty of the CIO and COO. Whereas the COO oversees operational risks, the CIO concentrates on cybersecurity, data protection, and technology-related hazards. Working together to develop risk reduction techniques guarantees an all-encompassing strategy for protecting the company.

An effective CIO-COO collaboration requires open communication. Frequent updates and meetings allow information sharing about technology projects, operational difficulties, and new opportunities. Transparency guarantees that both leaders are aware and contribute to developing trust. The CIO is crucial when assessing, choosing, and implementing IT solutions. The COO, on the other hand, ensures that these solutions are seamlessly integrated into daily operations. Continuous collaboration is necessary to address any operational challenges during the implementation phase.

A shared set of performance indicators must be established to assess collaborative projects. Metrics include cost reductions, successful technological project execution, and increases in operational efficiency. The alignment of operations and technology goals is strengthened via shared KPIs. The COO and CIO must both be flexible and receptive to new ideas. Since technology is constantly changing, so too must an organization's methods of operation. The collaboration's success mainly depends on an innovative culture and an openness to new technology.

Cooperation between the CIO and COO reporting lines fosters synergy between operations and technology inside a business. The alignment of these responsibilities becomes essential to accomplishing organizational goals as companies depend increasingly on technology to improve operations and obtain a competitive edge. The CIO and COO work together to create a harmonious and productive ecosystem that supports the company's overall success by ensuring that technical investments complement operational goals.

In summary, a strong collaboration between the CIO and COO is essential for organizations to thrive in today's rapidly changing business environment. The alignment of technology and operations, coupled with effective communication and a shared strategic vision, ensures that the organization can leverage technology to achieve its operational and business objectives.

2.2.4 CIO AND BOARD RELATIONS

In today's technology-driven business environment, the CIO's connection with the board of directors is crucial. The company's success depends on the CIO's critical role in coordinating IT strategy with overarching business goals. To guarantee that technological projects serve the company's long-term goals and enhance its competitiveness in the market, there must be effective communication between the CIO and the board.

For the board and the CIO to work together, complicated technical information must be translated into business language that the board members can comprehend and utilize to make decisions. The value of technology investments, cybersecurity precautions, and digital transformation initiatives in terms of risk reduction, operational effectiveness, and revenue growth must be communicated by the CIO. Frequent reporting on cybersecurity resilience and return on investment are two crucial performance metrics linked to IT projects that assist the board in evaluating the efficacy of the technology strategy and making decisions.

The needs of the company, the board, and the shareholders will eventually trickle down to the CIO if directed toward a well-known business leader who recognizes, advocates for, and pushes technology as a critical element of corporate strategy. Ultimately, it matters that the CIO and IT are represented at the strategic decision-making table. Consistency will be facilitated by matching an organization's strategy to its mission and brand. The CIO's goal and brand must reflect business requirements before the IT staff and design can align with the corporate strategy. For example, does the CIO have to manage business change, enforce operational discipline, or spearhead technology-enabled business strategy? The CIO's vision may be strengthened, and the IT staff can benefit from clarity and consistency when purpose and brand align with business needs.

CIOs, especially those who do not go directly to the CEO, can increase their visibility and obtain a place on the executive leadership committee by demonstrating their business acumen. Regardless of the CIO's reporting structure, developing solid organizational relationships with the CEO, CFO, COO, senior C-suite occupants, board members, and other functional leaders can help them be more strategic. A CIO should develop a relationship road map that considers personality, motivation, and expectations and incorporates planned, formal, and informal interactions. Furthermore, CIOs may empower their IT teams to form relationships to drive confidence and develop trust at all levels across the enterprise. CIOs should also ensure their IT teams are regularly encouraged to network with each other and with other departments. This will help to develop a better understanding of the organization's operations and create better working relationships. Finally, CIOs should also provide their team with the opportunity to build relationships with key stakeholders across the enterprise.

Within the boardroom, the CIO assumes a vital role, providing strategic leadership in leveraging technology to achieve organizational goals. They align IT projects with the company's vision, ensuring synergy with overarching strategy development and implementation. Recognizing the increasing reliance on technology, the CIO shoulders the responsibility of identifying and mitigating IT-related risks, including data breaches and cybersecurity threats, while ensuring compliance with relevant laws. The CIO's expertise becomes invaluable in discussions around risk management and the security of sensitive data.

The CIO's proactive role in fostering innovation and leading the organization's digital transformation projects is another aspect that defines the relationship between the CIO and the board. To maintain competitiveness in ever-changing markets, the CIO actively assesses developing technology, considers any potential ramifications, and proposes tactics to take advantage of opportunities. Understanding that technology requires significant financial outlays, the CIO plays a crucial role in effective IT budget management. The CIO ensures that technology expenditures align with business strategies and yield a positive return on investment by balancing innovation and cost considerations. To lead the company toward success in the rapidly changing fields of business and technology, the CIO and the board must work together.

The board receives regular information from the CIO regarding IT initiatives, cybersecurity precautions, and the general condition of the company's IT infrastructure. The board needs effective communication to comprehend how technology affects corporate success. The CIO has to lead the company through changes and disruptions brought about by technology. This includes overseeing the implementation of new systems, resolving issues with outdated infrastructure, and promoting an environment that values flexibility and ongoing development. Stringent laws control how data is used and protected in many different businesses. The CIO ensures the company complies with these rules by addressing any potential legal and regulatory issues related to IT operations.

It is becoming increasingly crucial for the CIO to participate in strategic conversations as companies depend increasingly on technology for innovation and competitive advantage. The CIO is looked to by the board for knowledge about new technologies, possible hazards, and chances for digital disruption. A collaborative environment in which both the CIO and the board have a significant role in determining the organization's digital destiny is fostered by a strong relationship between them. As a strategic partner, the CIO assists the board in navigating the complexity of technology and ensures that IT expenditures align with the overarching business plan.

In summary, the CIO's role in the boardroom is multifaceted, encompassing strategic leadership, risk management, innovation, cost management, collaboration, effective communication, adaptability, and regulatory compliance. As technology continues to evolve, the CIO's contribution becomes increasingly critical in shaping the organization's future success.

2.3 HOW CIO LEADS HIGH-PERFORMANCE TEAMS

The contemporary CIO faces significant challenges because of the intricate relationship between policies, organizational procedures, and human resources. Leaders frequently find themselves torn between answering incessant emails and satisfying demands from stakeholders, which can distract their attention from actively contributing to the development of their teams. CIOs understand this difficulty and agree that bringing in the appropriate personnel, providing them with the necessary resources and tools, and encouraging open communication channels through frequent check-ins and engaging walkabouts can help find a workable solution. Moreover, fostering a culture of innovation and adaptability within the organization is paramount, ensuring that the team is well-equipped to navigate the ever-evolving technological landscape and meet the dynamic needs of the business environment.

"The strength of a team lies not just in its ability to do great things, but in its unwavering belief that together, they can achieve the impossible." Demonstrating genuine interest in coworkers by physically immersing oneself within a team is a highly effective strategy. In addition to being a helpful activity, this intentional

interaction conveys a deep awareness of each team member as a person. Building a trustworthy and committed team is greatly aided by creating an environment where the CIO actively values and interacts with every team member. The focus on personal interests acts as a spark to create an environment at work where team members are inspired to perform well and feel valued. The CIO strategies for creating a high-performance team are mentioned below.

2.3.1 CIO STRATEGIES FOR CREATING HIGH-PERFORMANCE TEAMS

CIOs are essential in helping organizations create high-performing teams by implementing a strategic plan that combines human potential with technology skills. CIOs must, above all, promote an innovative and collaborative culture where team members are encouraged to exchange ideas and try out novel solutions. Having efficient official and informal communication channels is crucial to ensuring everyone is on the same page regarding the organization's objectives. CIOs should place a high priority on hiring new employees, looking for people who have a desire for lifelong learning as well as a variety of skill sets. Furthermore, giving teams continual opportunities for training and growth keeps them abreast of technical developments. CIOs use agile approaches and give the team's decision-making authority to increase productivity while encouraging a sense of accountability and ownership. Lastly, recognizing and rewarding team achievement cultivates a positive work environment, motivating individuals to contribute their best to the team's success.

In addition to this below is how a CIO can create high-performance teams:

Vision and Strategy: "*The journey to success is paved with a well-crafted strategy, but a clear vision illuminates the path ahead.*" A visionary CIO's primary responsibility is to provide the IT department with a clear strategic direction and vision to encourage the development of high-performing teams. This entails having the CIO coordinate aligning specific IT goals with the company's overall objectives. The CIO ensures that everyone understands their part in accomplishing the organization's strategic goals by giving the team a clear road map. The view goes beyond satisfying the market needs of a CIO leading a technology company. Instead, it involves imagining and shaping the course of the next big technological breakthrough wave. This forward-thinking vision motivates the team to push the boundaries of innovation continuously.

An example is a financial institution's CIO taking a strategic stance around digital transformation. This strategy plan can include strengthening cybersecurity defenses, implementing artificial intelligence to generate individualized client experiences, and streamlining internal operations for more agility in the quickly changing financial technology sector. Essentially, the team is guided towards excellence by the organization's broader strategic goals by the CIO's vision, which functions as a roadmap.

Get to Know the People: "*Understanding is the foundation of leadership; by getting to know your team members, you can help them reach their full potential.*" Creating and leading a high-performing team starts with connecting and conversing. A CIO should talk to and get to know your teammates as much as possible. Everyone possesses abilities, life experiences, information, and skills that a CIO can utilize. As the CIO cultivates the CIO's leadership skills and interacts with them, the CIO will often see potential in team members before they do. The CIO can help them see new opportunities. A CIO should find out their objectives and whether the CIO can assist them in achieving them. Once the CIO knows this, he or she can allocate project duties by determining what motivates each individual. The CIO may suggest that they benefit from books, webinars, seminars, and courses, among other educational resources.

Effective Communication & Collaboration: "*Effective communication and teamwork create a symphony of success, with each note resonating with clarity and purpose. This is the symphony on which leadership thrives*". It is imperative for CIOs to proficiently convey their vision, goals, and modifications to their teams. This calls for explicit goal-setting and attentive listening to fully grasp other team members' concerns and opinions. Creating a teamwork and interdisciplinary collaboration culture is essential for solving complex problems and delivering integrated solutions. Cross-functional collaboration enhances innovation and agility. A CIO should actively listen to the team's problems to facilitate successful communication. The CIO can foster cooperation and trust among the team members by attending to these issues and incorporating insightful input into the decision-making process. To create a shared understanding of the ultimate objective, the CIO should make clear to all team members the expectation that they will all participate in the new endeavors. A CIO may rapidly address the entire team in an emergency using a video conference or real-time messaging system. The CIO might also choose in-person encounters for deeper conversations to guarantee a thorough sharing of views.

Empowerment and Delegation: *Empowerment is the fuel for individual growth; delegation is the roadmap to collective success.* Empowerment and delegation are crucial elements in developing individuals into high performers who, when assembled, become high-performing teams under solid leadership. An organization should examine the characteristics and duties of the CIO, considering factors like education, experience, and resources. The aim is strategically leveraging the CIO team's experience while supporting their development through growth, learning, and effective communication. Leaders frequently hesitate to spend money on team development because they are worried about possible employee attrition. Retaining employees boosts satisfaction and performance, the CIO should work towards improving the performance and increases satisfaction. Environments characterised by comfort or stagnation should be avoided by the CIOs. Developing a high-performing team requires competent personnel. In addition to attracting and keeping top talent, the CIO is essential in establishing a culture that encourages continuous learning and skill development. The CIO ensures the team stays on the cutting edge of technology innovations by investing in team members' professional development.

"In a high-performing team, collaboration is not a task, but a culture. Success is not a goal; it's a journey where every member contributes their best, making the team unstoppable." The CIO deliberately delegates authority to team members by empowerment. This entails giving them authority over tasks and discretion in their areas of specialization. This approach promotes a sense of ownership and enhances teamwork. Assigning tasks to team members boosts job satisfaction and contributes to better results. The focus on delegating and empowerment highlights the CIO's commitment to developing a dynamic, competent, and self-directed workforce that helps to strive for excellence.

Give precise, timely, and valuable feedback: *"The ability to provide feedback that is timely, meaningful, and enlightening enough to spur change and drive ongoing progress is a critical component of leadership competence."* Even though the CIO may only have 15 to 20 minutes each day to speak with the team members one-on-one, checking in with them routinely is imperative. The CIO can receive updates on assignments and tasks, understand what has to be done, and, if needed, offer support and encouragement. Take swift action when the CIO observes someone continuing a pattern of errors or not altering their behavior in response to a previous reprimand. The faster feedback and correction are provided, the more likely a behavior change will occur. We naturally look for feedback since it enables us to assess our performance and decide whether to put in more effort. CIOs set KPIs to gauge the IT department's performance. Team members can better understand their performance, pinpoint growth areas, and be acknowledged for their accomplishments by participating in regular feedback sessions. Constructive feedback is essential for ongoing development.

Lead with a Weakness: *"True leadership lies in the courage to lead with vulnerability, turning weaknesses into beacons of strength."* Leading with weakness is a leadership style in which CIOs publicly own their flaws and shortcomings. CIOs who embrace weakness foster an honest and trustworthy culture within their teams instead of presenting an appearance of infallibility. When a CIO exhibits vulnerability as a leader, the team members feel free to express their doubts and difficulties. This collaborative environment is fostered by an open culture, which promotes open communication and the sharing of different viewpoints. Recognizing their shortcomings as a leader creates the foundation for an environment of ongoing learning. CIOs showcasing a commitment to advancement inspire their staff to create a growth mindset and promote empathetic leadership. When CIOs openly share their challenges, it gives a perception of the human aspects of work. This empathy creates a supportive work environment where team members feel valued not just for their skills but as individuals with unique experiences and challenges.

Adaptability and Change Management: *"Those who skillfully modify their sails in response to changing winds will ride the growth currents to new heights."* Organizations continually change in the dynamic world of high-performing teams to meet changing expectations, promote growth, and advance. Given the speed at which activities, conventions, and technology are evolving, giving the human side of this transition top priority is critical. The CIO is essential in promptly explaining the changes taking place, their reasoning, and their effects on the team. Success in navigating change requires the team to understand its needs. Just as successes and failures mold an organization, feelings of pride and emotion are infused into the important job that people accomplish. The world of high-performing teams moves quickly, and technology is developing even faster there. CIOs must be skilled at managing change and guiding their teams through transformations. This competence includes embracing new technologies, keeping up with industry trends, and deftly leading the team through the necessary modifications.

Risk Management: "*High-performing teams use risk management as a catalyst to drive their creativity, resiliency, and continuous excellence rather than as a restraint.*" One of the most important aspects of a CIO's job is managing risks effectively, particularly when leading high-performing teams in the constantly changing technology field. CIOs are essential in ensuring that their teams develop creative ideas and reduce risks that could affect the company. Teams with high-performance levels frequently take on projects that have inherent risks. The CIO needs to be a substantial risk assessor and manager to ensure the team is ready to face obstacles and unknowns. This entails creating backup plans and cultivating a culture that values flexibility in the face of unanticipated circumstances. In addition to other crucial factors, cybersecurity management, strategic technology adoption, effective talent, and team management, adherence to regulatory and compliance standards, project oversight, business continuity and disaster recovery planning, and financial risk management are all important factors for CIOs to take into account when managing risks while leading high-performing teams.

In conclusion, a CIO must have a combination of strategic vision, effective communication, talent development, collaboration, empowerment, adaptability, and a results-driven mindset to lead high-performance teams. By exhibiting these attributes, a CIO may foster an atmosphere where IT teams flourish, innovate, and contribute substantially to the organization's overall success.

2.4 HOW CIO LEADS ORGANIZATION WITH GROWTH STRATEGIES

As the twenty-first century unfolds, CIOs ought to advocate for a new model of leadership that prioritizes the common good over personal gain. "*Great leaders inspire greatness in others. Leading with growth strategies is cultivating a team that continually strives for progress and embraces change.*" Organizations must adopt this paradigm to succeed despite hitherto unseen opportunities and challenges. Moreover, this leadership style needs to support the psychological development of staff members, understanding the significance of their welfare for attaining organizational success. The last few years have been turbulent and unsettled, posing severe difficulties for leaders. In a hybrid workplace, leaders—including CIOs—must prioritize their and their team's well-being, embrace mass reinvention, and maintain motivation. With the epidemic's end comes a timely chance to reassess leadership values and readjust expectations. "*True leadership is not about having all the answers but about fostering a culture where everyone is encouraged to ask questions and seek innovative solutions for continuous growth."*

From the context of CIOs leading teams implementing growth initiatives, studies such as Stiglitz's (2002) explore the changing standards that companies set for their executives and provide insights into the consequences of leadership development. Organizations today face great uncertainty due to the epidemic, navigating a business environment marked by ongoing disruption and rising economic and geopolitical unpredictability. With the public, media, and investors paying more attention, leaders—especially CIOs—struggle with the complexities of the environmental, social, and governance agendas. The workforce landscape is characterized by risks and rewards associated with simultaneous technology developments and problems posed by an aging and declining labor supply.

Although the epidemic may not have wholly altered the core principles of good leadership, leaders must encourage new attitudes, actions, and approaches to performance. The rise in remote work has necessitated the development of creative approaches to building rapport, establishing clear expectations, inspiring staff, and effectively tracking performance. CIOs need to adapt quickly to these changes and actively participate in developing innovative leadership techniques that align with the opportunities and challenges of the digital age to lead enterprises toward new paradigms or growth plans.

2.4.1 CIO STRATEGIES FOR LEADING ORGANIZATION WITH GROWTH STRATEGIES

As technology increasingly intertwines every aspect of operations, CIOs are pivotal in driving innovation and leading their organizations into new growth paradigms. Below are the key strategies and considerations CIOs employ to spearhead transformation and propel their organizations forward.

Visionary Leadership: CIOs must function as visionary leaders, not just technology managers. By understanding the broader business landscape, market trends, and emerging technologies, CIOs can articulate a compelling vision for how technology can catalyze growth. This vision serves as a guiding force for the entire organization, aligning teams and strategies toward common goals.

Strategic Alignment: Successful CIOs work closely with other C-suite executives to ensure that IT strategies align seamlessly with overall business objectives. By fostering collaboration and breaking down silos, CIOs create an integrated approach that maximizes the impact of technology on all facets of the organization. This alignment is critical for driving efficiency, reducing costs, and identifying new avenues for revenue.

Innovation Advocacy: CIOs need to champion a culture of innovation within their organizations. This involves encouraging experimentation, embracing calculated risks, and creating an environment where creative solutions are valued. By fostering a culture of continuous improvement, CIOs can position their organizations to adapt quickly to changes in the market and proactively identify growth opportunities.

Data-Driven Decision-Making: Leveraging the power of data is a core competency for CIOs. They should implement robust data analytics tools and strategies to extract meaningful insights. This enables organizations to make informed decisions, optimize processes, and identify areas for improvement. CIOs guide their teams in turning data into a strategic asset that informs and drives growth strategies. Embracing innovation, they navigate dynamic landscapes, fostering adaptability and resilience for sustained success.

Agile Methodologies: CIOs understand the importance of agility in a fast-paced business environment. Organizations can respond more rapidly to changing market conditions and customer expectations by adopting agile methodologies. CIOs play a crucial role in instilling agile principles in their teams, fostering adaptability, and ensuring technology initiatives are delivered efficiently and effectively.

Customer-Centric Focus: CIOS must implement customer-centric growth strategies. CIOs use technology to improve the consumer experience, whether it is via customized digital products, improved web interfaces, or cutting-edge services. The CIO creates customer value by leveraging technology, resulting in growth and loyalty.

Outside-in reasoning: Developing the potential for foresight requires leaders to scan their external environment for market signals, spot patterns, and generate insights.

Creation of purpose-anchored adaptive strategies: The development of purpose-driven adaptive strategies is crucial for CIOs. Leaders in information technology must structure their organizations to remain agile and responsive while staying focused on a consistent goal and purpose.

Understanding complexity: Leaders must be able to navigate highly ambiguous circumstances, find connections between parts of the system that appear to be unrelated, and make judgments based on conflicting or inadequate information.

Leading in the era of digital activism: The social contract between businesses and key stakeholders, including employees, governments, media, investors, and local communities, is evolving. CIOs must be prepared to embrace greater transparency and visibility in their leadership approach.

Increasing execution agility capacity: By incorporating agility into their decision-making and execution processes, CIOs must be able to react quickly to growing competition threats and altering customer expectations.

Create a culture that values research and experimentation: A CIO should embrace an experimental mindset in the organization, enabling the prototyping of diverse options before widespread implementation. This approach might present challenges for CIOs and IT leaders who do not recognize the importance of learning from instances that may be perceived as *"failures."*

Managing hybrid and remote teams: Due to developments in the market and technology, the hybrid workplace will persist. CIOs should use virtual technologies to ensure equity between in-person and remote groups, sustain performance and motivation while working remotely, and promote real employee engagement and team cohesion.

Leaders as people-enablers: Expectations in the realm of CIO leadership are shifting from dictating tasks to adopting a coaching style that empowers team members to define their success and reach their goals. CIOs must exhibit compassionate, curious, and modest leadership and understand that they might not have all the answers.

Promoting well-being and inclusion: In the realm of CIOs, it is imperative to cultivate an inclusive culture that empowers all team members to unleash their maximum potential, irrespective of their backgrounds. Simultaneously, CIOS needs to prioritize its staff's well-being, particularly in remote work.

CHAPTER 3
NAVIGATING IT EXCELLENCE: UNVEILING THE STRATEGIC FRAMEWORKS AND DESIGNS OF CIO LEADERSHIP

INTRODUCTION

Starting the path to mastering IT success necessitates delving deeply into organizational structure and metrics' critical role in promoting excellence. As we peel back the layers of this extensive manual, CIOs and IT executives will gain critical perspectives on the essential elements that characterize success in the always-changing field of IT. This chapter also covers a thorough understanding of key KPIs, which serve as the compass for IT initiatives. These indicators capture performance, efficiency, and innovation in their purest form, pointing businesses toward a future in which technical advancements are perfectly integrated with business goals.

The chapter breaks down an IT organization's numerous units and explores the art and science of developing and structuring an IT organization. This chapter offers practical ideas to build an IT ecosystem that thrives on innovation and operational excellence, from reporting formats that support transparent communication to strategic service orchestration that embodies a CIO's vision for service excellence. As we manage the symbiotic relationship between technology and organizational design, we realize how vital digital maturity is. Determining how to account for digital maturity becomes essential in creating an IT environment that is flexible, adaptable, and prepared for the future.

Frameworks and techniques for business and IT strategy take center stage and serve as the cornerstone of efficient IT governance. This chapter examines frameworks that ensure a strategic synergy that drives enterprises forward by coordinating technological initiatives with broader business goals. Unified dashboards are revolutionary instruments that help to propel integrated KPI reporting. The CIO should be able to use these dashboards effectively to create a broad perspective of an organization's performance landscape and become the cornerstone for strategic decision-making.

This chapter delves into the idea of metric mélange, which is the smooth convergence of business and technological KPIs. This chapter is a compass for IT executives, giving them the information and resources they need to successfully negotiate the complex terrain of organizational architecture, strategic decision-making, and IT governance. Equipped with this manual, IT executives can confidently lead their companies to unparalleled success in the digital age.

3.1 HOW TO MEASURE THE SUCCESS OF IT

In the world of technology, metrics are the compass that guides us toward IT success, ensuring we navigate the digital landscape with precision. CIOs are crucial players in information technology, and their performance depends on essential criteria that determine how healthy investments in technology are working. Innovative technologies are becoming increasingly important in the changing business landscape. Therefore, CIOs must carefully consider their options and make investments that maximize their company's competitive edge. While costs are significant, the business will determine how much technology is invested.

CIOs must weigh the 30% cost vs the 70% effect quandary when assessing their technology solutions. This ratio becomes the pivot for well-informed decision-making, allowing CIOs to identify innovations that will impact their company. Careful thought must be given to the difficult choice of weighing impact for organizational growth versus cost for operational stability.

A vital component of a CIO's accomplishments is their capacity to express and measure the business benefits of IT initiatives. The CFO's decision to allocate higher IT budgets favorably correlates with this proficiency. To do this, CIOs need to become proficient in business language and convert IT objectives into results that the company can embrace. After these results are achieved, quantifying the return on investment becomes possible. Delivering quantifiable business value is the new operational mandate of CIOs as the business landscape changes. The quantifiable impact of IT efforts should ideally be ten times the CIO's budget, as required by the developing function. Cooperation with the CFO becomes essential to achieve this kind of impact, highlighting the requirement for alignment between IT and overall.

A few IT-related KPIs are particularly illuminating for CIOs in this context. Nine essential internal and external IT indicators are listed by Edwards (2019) and can be used as valuable benchmarks to gauge how well IT plans are working. With the help of these indicators, CIOs can confidently navigate the complexity of technology management, knowing that their choices support the organization's continuous development and happiness in addition to operational stability.

3.1.1 ESSENTIAL METRICS USED FOR IT MEASUREMENT

The success assessment of IT efforts depends on IT metrics, which offer measurable perspectives on effectiveness and performance. System uptime, reaction time, and resolution speed are examples of KPIs used to measure IT services' responsiveness and dependability. Furthermore, project delivery metrics like budget adherence and on-time completion add to a thorough evaluation of the overall impact and performance of IT in a company. Here, we explore some of the essential metrics that CIOs prioritize to ensure their IT endeavors' effectiveness, efficiency, and strategic alignment.

Business Alignment Metrics: CIOs constantly assess how well IT efforts fit the company's larger goals. This entails monitoring KPIs that show how IT contributes to revenue growth, cost savings, and other critical business outcomes. Aligning business metrics is essential to IT performance because they objectively assess how successfully IT activities complement and advance the organization's objectives. CIOs can use these KPIs to ensure that IT delivers value, innovation, and alignment with the overarching business plan, acting as a strategic facilitator. IT must align with business goals for the firm to succeed and remain competitive. Assessment of business alignment metrics helps the CIOs in measuring alignment with business strategy, demonstrating value to the business, ensuring compliance with governance frameworks, measuring project alignment with business outcomes, assessing stakeholder feedback, integrating it with business processes, speed of technology deployment, measuring user engagement, assessing innovation's contribution, evaluating portfolio alignment, staying aligned with market dynamics, measuring communication impact.

Cost-revenue ratio Metrics: When CIOs evaluate the accomplishment of IT projects, the cost-revenue ratio is one of the most important metrics, especially regarding digital transformation. The shift brought about by digital transformation not only creates new sources of income but also improves cost-effectiveness by removing costs associated with marketing, sales, and human resources. CIOs are essential in tracking necessary expenses and revenue data to traverse this disruptive journey successfully. The cost-revenue ratio is the strategic focus of the CIOs' attention. This measure gauges how well a company uses its resources in the context of the digital revolution. Monitoring the relationship between financial markets and operations performance is necessary to make informed decisions. The CIOs should calculate the components of the cost-revenue ratio, including administrative, operational, and client acquisition costs, to better understand the nuances. Comparing the performance of new and established digital revenue streams is a crucial component of this assessment, as it offers important insights into the overall viability and financial sustainability of the company's digital endeavors.

Technology ROI Metrics: Technology ROI metrics are crucial indicators that give CIOs the power to decide wisely, match IT projects to organizational goals, and show technology's tangible benefits. It acts as a guide to help navigate the tricky terrain of IT management and ensure that financial investments in technology improve organizational performance. CIOs keep a tight eye on the ROI of their technology spending. This indicator includes the broader effects of technology on productivity, innovation, business operations, and financial gains. Technology ROI helps CIOs in cost justification, resource allocation, the effectiveness of IT solutions, linking IT to business goals, identifying high-impact technologies, iterative assessment, communicating value to stakeholders, agility in technology adoption, ensuring long-term value, etc.

IT Operational Efficiency Metrics: Efficiency, which measures how well IT systems and processes function, is a crucial indicator for CIOs. This entails evaluating IT services' efficiency, dependability, and general efficacy to guarantee top performance throughout the enterprise. IT operational efficiency is crucial to IT success because it enables CIOs to manage risks, optimize resources, provide dependable services, and Integrate IT with the broader organizational plan. CIOs enhance their firms' effectiveness and competitiveness in a fast-changing digital landscape by concentrating on operational efficiency. IT operational efficiency helps the CIO in cost management, timely and reliable services, adaptability to change, user experience, security and compliance, optimized data handling, seamless integration of technologies, monitoring and analysis, value for investments, and aligning IT with business objectives.

System Downtime and Availability Metrics: System availability and downtime directly impact corporate operations, user productivity, customer satisfaction, and financial results, making them essential indicators for IT success. Implementing plans and tactics to reduce downtime, guarantee high system availability, and enhance the general robustness and success of the company's IT infrastructure is primarily the responsibility of CIOs. A CIO ensuring business continuity and user experience necessitates minimizing downtime and optimizing availability. The availability metrics help the CIO minimize disruptions, maximize user access, enhance customer satisfaction, reduce downtime, meet SLA commitments, address vulnerabilities, proactive monitoring, effective recovery processes, infrastructure scaling, continuous improvement, etc.

Cybersecurity Metrics: Due to the growing threat landscape, CIOs are concentrating on cybersecurity metrics, such as the number of security incidents, response times, and the efficacy of security solutions. Priorities include safeguarding confidential information and maintaining a strong cybersecurity posture. Cybersecurity metrics are essential for IT success because they help CIOs manage risks, respond to incidents efficiently, maintain compliance, and continuously strengthen their cybersecurity posture. In an increasingly digital and linked world, these measurements help the company fend off cyberattacks and enhance overall business resilience and success. The assessment of cybersecurity metrics helps the CIOs in identifying and assessing risks, measuring incident response effectiveness, ensuring compliance, utilizing threat intelligence metrics, tracking vulnerabilities, assessing security awareness, monitoring patching and updates, identifying insider threats, evaluating SOC efficiency, demonstrating ROI on cybersecurity investments, cultivating a security culture.

Innovation Metrics: CIOs evaluate the effectiveness of innovation projects by gauging the rate at which new technologies are incorporated into the organization and how innovation affects overall competitiveness. This includes metrics about the practical application of cutting-edge technologies and initiatives towards digital transformation. Creativity Metrics are essential to the success of IT because they offer an organized method for gauging and encouraging innovation inside the company. CIOs use these KPIs to promote resource optimization, boost customer happiness, foster strategy alignment, and establish a dynamic and competitive IT environment. Innovation becomes a critical component of company success in a technical environment that is changing quickly. Assessment of innovation metrics helps the CIOs in measuring the impact on business objectives, speed of innovation implementation, measuring idea generation, assessing employee involvement, optimizing resource allocation, impact on customer experience, promoting collaboration metrics, quantifying innovation value, learning from pilots, benchmarking against competitors, measuring technology adoption, failure as a learning metric.

User Satisfaction and Experience Metrics: CIOs know how critical end-user experience and satisfaction are. Metrics that reveal how successfully IT services satisfy the demands of stakeholders and employees include response times, issue resolution rates, and user feedback. User satisfaction and experience metrics are critical for IT success because they show how successfully IT services meet user demands and expectations. CIOs use these indicators to align IT with business goals, increase efficiency, and foster a pleasant, user-focused IT environment. Good user experiences are essential for the success of IT efforts and the company's general well-being and productivity. These metrics help the CIOs measure impact on business goals, enhance user productivity, optimize customer experience, gather user feedback, monitor service desk metrics, ensure inclusive user experiences, assess training impact, optimize system responsiveness, adapt to mobile and remote work, balance security , user experience, iterative enhancements, and measuring technology adoption success.

Project Delivery Metrics: The success of IT depends on timely and effective project delivery. The CIOs oversee project objectives, budgetary compliance, and schedules to ensure IT endeavors support corporate goals. Project metrics are essential for IT success because they offer a methodical approach to managing, measuring, and optimizing project outcomes. CIOs use these data to ensure that initiatives meet deadlines, stick to budgets, and produce high-caliber outcomes. Efficient project management, directed by pertinent metrics, substantially contributes to the overall prosperity and competitiveness of an organization's IT department. The assessment of project delivery metrics will help the CIO in aligning projects with business goals, defining and measuring success, monitoring budget performance, meeting project timelines, optimizing resource allocation, identifying and mitigating risks, ensuring high-quality outputs, gathering stakeholder feedback, evaluating agile development, measuring communication impact, learning from project experiences and technology adoption rates.

Digital Maturity Metrics: CIOs utilize digital maturity indicators to gauge an organization's digital sophistication during its transformation. Assessing the uptake of cutting-edge technologies, data analytics prowess, and general digital preparedness are all included in this. Because they offer a complete picture of an organization's capacity to use digital technology strategically, digital maturity metrics are essential for IT success. CIOs use these indicators to promote innovation, propel digital transformation, and ensure the company stays resilient and competitive in the ever-changing digital market. The assessment of digital maturity metrics will help the CIOs in aligning digital initiatives with business strategy, measuring innovation capabilities, tracking technology adoption rates, assessing data utilization, measuring customer experience initiatives, evaluating organizational agility, assessing workforce digital competency, ensuring digital security, measuring ecosystem connectivity, quantifying returns on digital initiatives, iterative enhancements, comparing with industry peers.

Talent and Skills Development Metrics: CIOs understand the value of having a highly qualified IT staff. Metrics about hiring, retaining, and continuous skill development aid in making sure the IT staff is prepared to handle new and developing technical issues. The development of talent and skill set metrics is essential to the success of IT because it allows CIOs to develop a staff knowledgeable about current and emerging technology. CIOs enhance the overall competitiveness, innovation, and resilience of the IT department inside the company by emphasizing ongoing skill development. The assessment of talent and skill development metrics helps the CIOs in skill alignment with technology trends, measuring the impact of training programs, identifying and addressing skill gaps, tracking certification achievements, identifying potential leaders, promoting diversity and inclusion metrics, encouraging cross-functional training, quantifying returns on learning investments, linking skills development to engagement, assessing adaptability metrics, leveraging feedback metrics, comparing skills with industry benchmarks.

By actively monitoring and optimizing these critical metrics, CIOs not only measure the success of their IT initiatives but also contribute to the overall success and competitiveness of the organization in an increasingly technology-driven business landscape.

3.2 HOW CIO DESIGNS STRUCTURE OF AN ORGANIZATION

One of the most important tasks assigned to CIOs is designing and arranging an IT organization. The organization's overarching strategy should align with the structure, supporting business goals and encouraging creativity and agility. The CIO is pivotal in designing the organizational structure and defining how technology is integrated across the enterprise. The effectiveness of a deployment configuration in aligning with the company's objectives is a critical consideration in the CIO's strategy for IT structure. There are various approaches that a CIO would use for designing an IT organization. The needs and goals of an organization shape the proper design and use of people.

IT departments range significantly in terms of their size and specific objectives. Below are the factors that a CIO considers for designing the structure of an IT organization:

Structure Based on Size of Business: For instance, the IT director of a small business can be in charge of many different IT responsibilities, including planning, budgeting, and IT operations. Some tasks, such as cyber security, could be contracted out. The company's size frequently influences whether to centralize or decentralize IT services. While larger firms may choose more decentralized approaches for agility, smaller businesses may gravitate toward centralized structures for cost-effectiveness. In light of the organization's magnitude, the CIO maximizes the distribution of resources, encompassing funds, staff, and technology. Larger organizations will hire excellent resources for specialized jobs and technologies, while smaller organizations may prioritize cost-effectiveness. While smaller firms prioritize cost-effective solutions, larger businesses may allocate resources toward more robust and scalable systems. In addition, the size of the organization matters to the CIO in terms of right-sizing teams, agility and flexibility, vendor and outsourcing strategy, communication channels, scaling cybersecurity measures, training and development, innovation capacity, compliance, governance, user support, service delivery, collaboration, and integration, etc.

Structure Based on Type of Business: CIOs take great care to specify and organize an IT organization according to the specific business model they are operating in. IT requirements and challenges vary throughout business models and industries. Different industries could have different legal systems, standards for compliance, and technology needs. CIOs consider how their industry's particular regulations and compliance standards impact IT. They ensure that the IT infrastructure conforms with regulations, such as PCI, HIPAA,

GDPR, etc. CIOs sometimes assess the sensitivity of data and implement security measures based on the nature of the firm. Robust security protocols are essential in several industries, such as healthcare and banking, where sensitive data is handled. CIOs modify IT solutions to meet the unique needs of various types of organizations. For example, manufacturing, retail, healthcare, and finance may require industry-specific software and technology. E-Commerce platforms, user-friendly interfaces, and CRM systems are a few examples of technology that CIOs in customer-focused companies prioritize. Depending on the industry, the CIO must also look into innovation, research, health IT systems, online presence and E-Commerce, supply chain integration, telecommunications infrastructure, and more.

Structuring by bridging past and future: The building of the structure has to happen fast—between now and tomorrow. Since the organizational structure is based on changing circumstances, it must adjust to the times. The system ought to be adaptable enough to accommodate modifications as needed. A strategic approach that enables the CIO to strike a balance between future technologies and innovations and legacy systems and processes is to design an organizational structure that spans the past and the future. The strengths, limitations, and dependencies of the current configuration should be thoroughly examined by the CIOs, together with the legacy systems, technologies, and organizational procedures that are currently in place. CIOs ought to appreciate the importance of legacy systems and refrain from replacing them immediately. Instead, concentrate on methods to combine these systems with more recent technologies to ensure a seamless transition. The CIO needs to develop a strategy to ensure harmony between modern technology and legacy systems. This might involve implementing middleware solutions, APIs, or other integration technologies to facilitate smooth communication. Additionally, the CIO should recognize the expertise of staff members with legacy systems experience. The CIOs create hybrid teams that blend traditional and contemporary skill sets or design training programs to preserve their knowledge. The CIO should Invest in training programs to upskill staff in both legacy and emerging technology. This guarantees that the labor force will remain flexible and competent to manage the changing IT environment.

Designing by promoting accountability: A culture of accountability within a business is cultivated when workflows are organized systematically. The hierarchical command structure instructs lower-ranking individuals to report to their superiors. Employees are held accountable for the quality of their work when communicating with their managers. Additionally, managers are obligated to report their responsibilities to the central authority.

Designing by aligning succession planning: The IT department's structure is paramount for a business's smooth operation and the security of its assets. A poorly organized IT department can adversely affect the business, while a well-structured IT department can provide a competitive advantage in the industry. Planning and establishing the proper structure for the IT department are crucial steps for ensuring the business's success.

Centralized vs. Decentralized: A CIO should decide on the degree of centralization or decentralization based on the organization's size, industry, and strategic requirements. Some organizations benefit from a centralized IT structure, while others may require a more decentralized approach.

Identify Key Functional Areas and Define Roles and Responsibilities: A CIO should define the core functional areas within the IT organization, such as infrastructure, applications, security, data management, and project management. A CIO should clearly outline the roles and responsibilities within each functional area. This includes positions like system administrators, developers, analysts, project managers, and security specialists. Each role should be assigned specific tasks and goals. Additionally, it is important to document the roles and responsibilities of each role to keep track of performance and progress. Finally, it is important to assess the roles regularly to ensure that the roles remain effective.

Matrix vs. Hierarchical Structure: The CIO should evaluate the benefits of matrix structures, where employees report to functional and project managers, and this approach can enhance flexibility and collaboration in an organization.

Agile and DevOps Integration: A CIO should incorporate agile methodologies and DevOps practices into the organizational structure to enhance agility, collaboration, and continuous delivery.

Cross-Functional Teams: A CIO should form cross-functional teams with members from different IT disciplines to foster collaboration and innovation.

Customer-Centric Approach: A CIO should design the structure to include customer-facing teams directly engaging with internal and external stakeholders. This approach will ensure a customer-centric approach and align IT services with business needs.

Cybersecurity Integration: A CIO should ensure that cybersecurity is a fundamental part of the IT structure. A CIO should establish dedicated teams and roles responsible for cybersecurity and integrating security practices across all IT functions.

Talent Development and Training: A CIO should develop talent development and training strategies. Creating a culture that encourages continuous learning and skill development to keep the IT team up-to-date with evolving technologies will benefit the organization in various aspects.

Risk Management: A CIO should designate roles or teams responsible for risk management within IT. This approach involves identifying, assessing, and mitigating risks associated with technology initiatives.

Diversity and Inclusion: A CIO should create an inclusive environment within the IT organization and foster diversity in skills, backgrounds, and perspectives to drive innovation and adaptability.

3.3 SERVICE DELIVERY DESIGN BY CIO

The CIO's primary duty is to align the organization's technology and support its business strategy and goals. To accomplish this, the CIO needs to have a thorough understanding of the business objectives, as this is the foundation for coordinating service delivery and organizational structure. Ensuring the technology team has the requisite skills and capabilities to support the company efficiently is imperative for the CIO.

The CIO must also encourage cooperation between the organization's IT departments. This partnership is accomplished by establishing open lines of communication, holding frequent progress reports, and encouraging the exchange of best practices between the two departments. The CIO assumes a crucial function in guaranteeing the seamless incorporation of technology into the overarching business plan by aligning the organizational structure and service delivery. This alignment may lower expenses while improving organizational effectiveness.

Effective CIOs emphasize listening to the business more than just pushing technology. They move away from strictly technical decision-making procedures and instead view IT administration as an art. Instead, they concentrate on building rapport with the company and repeatedly identifying ways to solve problems to reach particular objectives. Maintaining a solid process orientation throughout the company is essential to the CIO's job since it guarantees that different teams and departments collaborate well to achieve shared goals. This calls for the CIO to be highly knowledgeable about how the company functions and help departments collaborate, which could be problematic.

CIO to determine the significance of each business function and the main stakeholders: One of the biggest tasks for CIOs and their teams regarding service design is figuring out who the main customers are and how vital each business service is to the organization. Each service holds varying significance levels, and the CIO is responsible for evaluating and establishing its hierarchy. This evaluation could help the organization save costs. The CIO must consider several things when determining the main stakeholders and evaluating the significance of each business service. The first stage assesses the market's demand for different services in the business sector. This evaluation helps identify which services are currently the most important to the company. Proactive planning is the next step, in which the CIO projects future requirements by analyzing trends and projecting the services that will be critical in the changing business environment. With this proactive strategy, the CIO can stay ahead of schedule and be ready to handle the organization's changing needs in terms of services.

CIO to make a list of business services for the enterprise for effective service delivery: To ensure efficient service delivery, the CIO should compile a list of business services for the company. The CIO is accountable for effectively delivering business services in an enterprise. The enterprise's business services should be enumerated, and the CIO is responsible for ensuring these services are provided efficiently. To determine the business services that the enterprise needs, the CIO must collaborate with the enterprise architects. The application development teams and the CIO must collaborate to create these business services. The CIO is responsible for ensuring the business services are deployed on the appropriate platforms and accessible to users when needed. The CIO needs to work with the operations teams to ensure that the business services are running smoothly and are meeting the SLAs. The CIO is responsible for collaborating with the enterprise security team and ensuring the security of business services. Usually, with the assistance of senior managers and directors, CIOs prioritize services based on their importance and the value they contribute to the business. The security posture of the organization is subsequently reviewed with the leadership team.

CIO to socialize the service plan across the enterprise: CIOs must skillfully advocate for the service strategy throughout the organization to flourish as service delivery designers. To do this, it is necessary to convince everyone involved in the project of its benefits and win over people in every company department. CIOs typically call executive team meetings to highlight project goals and findings and share interviewees' thoughts. During these meetings, the CIO ensures that the leadership team gets the IT understanding for fundamental business services that is required to support the organization's primary objectives. The CIO clarifies in these discussions the degree of service required for the company to meet its goals. The CIO must ensure that all executive team members concur on the top priorities of the IT organization. Moreover, the CIO reaffirms that information technology seeks to serve as an essential business team member, focusing on fulfilling the company's unique business needs. This cooperative strategy guarantees the congruence between IT projects and the organization's objectives.

CIO to create and carry out a work plan: Several CIOs often require assistance formulating and implementing a work plan aligned with their organizational goals and objectives. The task of constructing a work plan can be challenging for executives, given constraints such as tight budgets, limited resources, or a lack of clear direction. However, with the appropriate strategy and guidance, creating and maintaining an effective work plan is feasible. Let us delve into the essential steps CIOs should undertake to craft and execute a work plan that effectively addresses the needs of their organization. This exploration spans understanding the goal-setting process to developing the necessary strategies providing insights into how CIOs can maintain organization and direction in their plans.

Evaluating the quality of service: When designing service delivery, the CIO is responsible for guaranteeing the accuracy and timely provision of IT services for the company. Implementing various audits or checks is vital to ascertain the success of these services. These audits play a crucial role in evaluating IT services' functionality, caliber, and security. This will delve into the importance of CIO checks for businesses, their implementation, the elements to incorporate, and their overall value. A CIO must be exceptionally skilled in maintaining the company's service standards. Together with the CEO and other members of the executive team, the CIO actively participates in the creation and execution of policies and processes that ensure all staff members provide high-quality services. In addition, the CIO uses their position to lobby for better chances for staff training and development so that employees are ready to provide exceptional customer service. The CIO is ideally positioned to use data analytics technologies to assess service quality in their capacity as IT leaders. Metrics like customer satisfaction, first-call resolution, and repeat call rates provide the CIO with important information about potential areas of diminishing service quality. Adopting a proactive strategy enables the CIO to promptly detect problems and take remedial measures, upholding a superior level of service delivery inside the firm.

Keep getting better: In service delivery design, astute executives recognize the value of implementing a continuous improvement program. Steve O'Connor underscores the significance of this approach, emphasizing a comprehensive process that assesses service levels from multiple perspectives. This inclusive method allows key stakeholders—IT service owners, business owners, and business users—to engage actively in a program that enhances service delivery. O'Connor successfully implemented such a process elevated service quality and established trust among his business peers. For every CIO, achieving excellence is a primary objective. To foster collaboration with C-suite colleagues and position the CIO as a business partner rather than a mere cost center, building trust is paramount. The CIO can provide outstanding service to the business by leveraging proven processes employed by successful CIOs.

Establishing this foundation enables the CIO to earn trust and serves as a springboard for evolving into a strategic CIO, contributing significantly to the organization's overall success.

3.3.1 CRITICAL ELEMENTS FOR SERVICE DELIVERY DESIGN

Service delivery design by CIOs is a crucial aspect of modern business operations, especially in the rapidly evolving landscape of information technology. As organizations increasingly rely on technology to enhance efficiency and meet customer demands, the role of CIOs in shaping service delivery has become more strategic. Here is an exploration of the critical elements involved in service delivery design by CIOs:

Alignment with Business Objectives: CIOs are responsible for closely coordinating service delivery with the organization's overarching business goals. Designing IT services that directly contribute to the business's success is made possible by their understanding of the fundamental objectives and priorities.

User-Centric Approach: CIOs must approach service delivery from a user's perspective. Understanding the requirements and expectations of both internal and external users is necessary for this. CIOs may improve the caliber of service delivery by taking user experience and feedback into account.

Agile and Flexible Frameworks: The service delivery design for CIOs should prioritize the integration of agile and flexible frameworks. These frameworks should empower prompt adaptation to evolving company needs and technological advancements. CIOs must cultivate a culture that values creativity and the ability to change direction swiftly within the service delivery design.

Integration of Emerging Technologies: For CIOs, staying updated on new technology is crucial. To keep the company innovative and competitive, they should incorporate cutting-edge technology like blockchain, machine learning, and artificial intelligence into their services.

Security and Compliance: CIOs are essential to maintaining the security and legality of IT services. Ensuring compliance with industry rules and safeguarding sensitive data are benefits of designing service delivery with solid security measures. This is especially crucial for industries like government, healthcare, and banking.

Performance Monitoring and Analytics: CIOs should use analytics and performance monitoring tools in the service delivery space to evaluate the services' reliability. CIOs may improve overall service quality by identifying areas for improvement, streamlining processes, and making data-driven decisions using real-time data and insights.

Vendor Management: Many businesses depend on outside providers for service delivery. It is imperative for CIOs to proficiently oversee vendor connections to guarantee that external services conform to the organization's objectives, security processes, and standards.

Scalability and Capacity Planning: Models for delivering services that are scalable and able to meet increasing demand should be created by CIOs. The ability of IT infrastructure to adjust to growing workloads without sacrificing performance is ensured by effective capacity planning.

Continuous Improvement: Providing services is a continual process that needs improvement. CIOs should foster a culture of continuous improvement by motivating groups to evaluate and improve service delivery procedures regularly.

Communication and Collaboration: Collaboration and effective communication are essential for quality services. Encouraging a collaborative culture among IT teams and other departments is crucial for CIOs to guarantee that IT services align with the firm's objectives.

CIOs are essential in creating service delivery strategies that support new technologies, emphasize security and compliance, and support an ongoing improvement culture. CIOs may significantly improve their organization's overall performance and competitiveness in the digital world by concentrating on five essential components.

3.4 FACTORING DIGITAL MATURITY FOR ORGANIZATION STRUCTURING

CIOs are essential in assessing digital readiness for organizational architecture because they manage the complex junction of workforce changes, company evolution, and technology. CIOs must keep up with the most recent technical developments and adjust to how employee workflows and business practices are evolving. They have to take the lead on projects that advance the company, which frequently calls for a willingness to take measured risks.

Within organizational structuring, a CIO's responsibilities extend beyond traditional tasks, including constructing new systems and fostering productive teams. In addition to these roles, CIOs are pivotal in instigating transformational changes. This involves introducing state-of-the-art work processes and adopting emerging technologies. Importantly, CIOs should cultivate a mindset that embraces failure as an integral element of their career journey and recognizes that challenges are often essential in pursuing innovation.

Being a CIO is undeniably one of the most challenging roles. The CIO role demands technical proficiency, creative thinking, and a willingness to explore uncharted territories. CIOs must constantly stay abreast of the latest technological advancements and discern inventive ways to apply these trends within the context of their enterprise. They must maintain their fortitude when confronted with the unavoidable setbacks of trying new things. In IT organizational structures, digital maturity is a benchmark for evaluating preparedness and expertise in the digital sphere. Organizational management is undergoing a paradigm transition as more and more people declare themselves to be involved in the information management sector. Digital maturity progresses from basic functioning to organizational solidity and, finally, to maximum efficiency, operating smoothly and with the least friction.

According to Zhu (2019), a set of characteristics of IT digital maturity include:

Operational Excellence: IT serves as the essential lubricant in the complex architecture of a well-designed business system, guaranteeing stability and operational excellence to brighten the business continuously. To increase digital maturity, IT must proactively carry out modernization, automation, integration, and optimization projects. These actions move the company closer to a higher level of technological development. IT management goes into a never-ending tuning phase in which operations are continuously fine-tuned to maximize efficiency. This calls for an unwavering dedication to improving coordination and cooperation with business partners.

During this process, it is critical to communicate effectively, articulate positive messages, and continuously look for more affordable alternatives to systems that may be unreliable or out-of-date. The CIO's job is critical to starting the IT organization and staying on this innovative path. To achieve operational excellence, the CIO must coordinate efforts to address "*IT effectiveness*" and "*IT efficiency*," seeking a healthy balance. This dual focus ensures that IT runs with a sharp eye on resource optimization and effectiveness and aligns with the overall business objectives.

Tech-savvy People: The three main goals of IT are revenue enhancement, process improvement, and cost reduction. Tech-savvy individuals within IT departments can strategically prioritize the two paramount aspects for businesses: acquiring business knowledge and leveraging technology to their benefit. Businesses will succeed when they realize their digital capabilities may trigger growth and move beyond *"doing digital"* to "*being digital.*" A highly competent digital IT department is essential to the growth of an intelligent, mature, and responsive digital business. This is achieved by adeptly translating business challenges into technology-enabled solutions and efficiently mobilizing resources to address well-defined business problems. In essence, the proficiency of the IT organization in the digital realm becomes a linchpin for steering the business toward a future characterized by adaptability, intelligence, and digital maturity.

People with Innovation Mindset: Businesses look to IT to bring innovative approaches to managing complexity, improving quality, and accelerating digital transformation to increase digital maturity. With the development of digital technologies, innovation is now more affordable and widely available than ever. Innovations include discoveries, efforts toward sustainability, improvements in productivity, and "*soft*" innovations such as those in communication or culture. With its deep integration into all business operations, information technology can spur revenue growth and advance organizational maturity through innovation. To achieve innovative IT, administrative procedures must be reevaluated and reorganized, and strong innovation management capacities must be established.

Simplicity: Simplicity is a new characteristic brought forth by the digital landscape is complexity, which affects people, companies, and society. IT management is critical in reducing needless complexity by managing the complete application life cycle, retiring legacy systems, reevaluating resource-intensive systems, and improving vendor and partner engagement. This strategic approach improves the maturity and reactivity of the organization. A guiding concept that offers qualities like flexibility, balance, and maturity and fits nicely with the new business norm is simplicity. IT management is critical in reducing needless complexity by managing the complete application life cycle, retiring legacy systems, reevaluating resource-intensive systems, and improving vendor and partner engagement. This strategic approach improves the maturity and reactivity of the organization. A guiding concept that offers qualities like flexibility, balance, and maturity and fits nicely with the new business norm is simplicity.

Customer Centricity: The most significant barrier to business success is becoming customer-centric, and the most challenging part of that process is figuring out what the business and the customer anticipate. When it comes to digital operations, individuals are the main focus. An outside-in viewpoint should be adopted to advance digital maturity, and customer-centric operations should be prioritized. Technology is integrated into day-to-day operations, improving customer experiences and frequently going beyond stated IT use cases. It takes more time, money, or influence to navigate the terrain as a corporate partner or consumer advocate to create and carry out these projects. Increasing IT maturity requires giving internal users valuable tools to boost output and satisfaction. Moreover, it increases end-user happiness and engagement by utilizing digital touchpoints and providing tailored experiences.

Adaptability: The ability of people or systems to quickly adjust to changes is referred to as adaptability. Rapid changes, disruptions, a wealth of information, and a shortened knowledge life cycle are characteristics of the digital world. In the digital age, success depends on how quickly and skillfully people and organizations adjust to these changes and overcome obstacles. The dynamic digital landscape necessitates constant perspective changes, openness, and adaptation in the individual and the environment to build flexibility. When people actively engage in organizational transformation, organizational self-adaptation quickens. This starts with building solid interpersonal connections and improving the business's flexibility.

Flexibility: In today's digital landscape, organizational agility is imperative for success. Leaders in the digital realm must adopt a systematic approach to managing their organizations. Maintaining adaptive consistency and fluidity is crucial in the era of rapid digital transformation, ensuring alignment with present needs while preparing for an uncertain future. Businesses that enhance their agility and experience both qualitative and quantitative growth showcase signs of digital maturity. Unlike closed mechanical systems, a digital organization gradually engages in economic activity, pattern generation, structural establishment, self-organization, and innovation. Influential leaders cultivate adaptability by fostering critical thinking and exploring diverse viewpoints, new information, and varied perspectives. This approach establishes a systematic framework for problem-solving and nurtures an environment conducive to continuous improvement and flexibility.

People & Change: People are the driving force behind change and a possible weak point in initiatives to implement digital transformation. Fostering a development mindset, providing value, and abiding by the behavioral norms that characterize organizational alignment are the keys to success. From a people management standpoint, organizational fit depends on balancing "misfit" thinking and a fitting mindset. Reaching a "*fit*" does not mean that beliefs, characters, preferences, or life experiences must all be the same. Instead, it entails balancing "*required misfit*" attributes like creativity and autonomous thought with "*desired fit*" traits like growth mindset, learning agility, positive attitude, and acceptable behavior. By its very nature, the concept of "*fit*" is situational. Organizations must actively seek other viewpoints, promote healthy debate, and cultivate critical thinking in the modern digital environment. IT professionals must have a combination of technical and business abilities to stay digitally resilient, even with the ongoing scarcity of IT talent. In the long run, establishing a people-centered IT-business relationship is necessary for long-term success.

Autonomy: Digital maturity is the same as independence. A company's efficacy, efficiency, responsiveness, and general maturity all increase as it promotes self-sufficiency. The idea of self-organization, which emphasizes empowerment and trust, is fundamental to this strategy. It is centered on fostering workplace mastery, originality, and creativity. Teams with autonomy can better plan and solve issues in their unique ways. The organization's procedures are clear, and managers concentrate on overseeing the team's work rather than micromanaging. "*How*" becomes less critical in digital management and more on "*why*" and "*what.*" The CIO allows the team to experiment with different strategies, find new ideas, and provide the best outcomes. Freedom is a stimulant for increased creativity. This independent culture is fostered by adopting transdisciplinary digital methods, leveraging automation, and encouraging team self-management. The organization functions in a flow state in such an environment, hastening its maturity process.

3.5 BUSINESS & IT STRATEGY FRAMEWORKS AND METHODS

In the domain of CIO business and strategy frameworks, a crucial element emerges in the form of the IT Governance Framework (ITGF). This structured methodology is pivotal in shaping, overseeing, and assessing IT governance within a business organization (Horlach et al., 2018). The ITGF provides guidelines and protocols to optimize the utilization of IT resources and processes, aligning them effectively with the broader business context.

The operational model of the IT governance framework addresses the "*who*" and "*how*," delineating components and providing a structure for decision-making authority, communication methods, and the decision-making process. Flexibility ensures that the IT governance structure can swiftly respond to evolving business requirements. An optimal approach involves a multi-tiered architecture at the executive, commercial, and operational levels (Dempster, 2020). This structure facilitates sound decision-making and provides a clear pathway for resolving disputes.

Performance metrics and reporting specifications are integral components of the IT governance framework. Standardizing management information across stakeholders in the CIO operating model ensures consistency. The IT governance framework serves as a tool for the CIO to evaluate the effectiveness of the CIO operating model. Below are the essential elements that underpin this framework:

Institutional Framework: The Institutional Framework defines decision-making structures, membership, and assigned responsibilities. It answers questions like "*Who decides what?*" and "*What duties will be assigned within this structure?*"

Process: In this stage, the decision-making procedures for IT investments are outlined. This includes the processes for submitting investment proposals, their assessment, approval, and ranking.

Communication: This element focuses on tracking, quantifying, and reporting outcomes, as well as determining the channels for informing various stakeholders—such as the board of directors, executive management, business management, IT management, employees, and shareholders—about IT investment decisions.

CIOs employ various Business/IT strategy frameworks and methods to manage and enhance IT governance within organizations effectively. Some of the commonly utilized frameworks include:

COBIT (Control Objectives for Information and Related Technologies):

- Developed for enterprise IT governance and management.
- Comprehensive framework encompassing globally acknowledged practices, analytical tools, and models.
- Initially rooted in IT auditing, COBIT has fully evolved to support IT governance.
- It is particularly beneficial for organizations focused on risk management and mitigation, with COBIT 5 being the latest version.

ITIL (IT Infrastructure Library):

- Now referred to as IT Service Management.
- Aims to ensure that IT services effectively support essential business operations.
- Comprises five management best practices covering service strategy, design, transition (including change management), operation, and continuous service improvement.

COSO (Committee of Sponsoring Organizations of the Treadway Commission):

- Developed for assessing internal controls.
- Rather than being IT-specific, it focuses more on business elements such as enterprise risk management (ERM) and fraud deterrence.

CMMI (Capability Maturity Model Integration):

- Developed by the Software Engineering Institute for performance enhancement.
- Measures an organization's performance, quality, profitability, and maturity level on a scale of 1 to 5.
- Initially designed for software engineering, CMMI now encompasses purchasing, service delivery, and hardware development procedures.

FAIR (Factor Analysis of Information Risk):

- A relatively new technique for quantifying risk.
- Assists organizations in evaluating operational risk and cybersecurity through periodic reviews.
- Gaining attention from Fortune 500 firms for its effectiveness in making informed judgments.

These frameworks collectively aid CIOs in assessing the overall performance of the IT department, determining key performance indicators (KPIs) required by management, and evaluating the return on investment provided by IT to the business. While ITIL focuses on streamlining service and operations, COBIT and COSO are instrumental in managing risk. Initially designed for software engineering, CMMI has expanded to cover various organizational processes beyond its original scope.

CHAPTER 4

COMBINING SUCCESS: UNCOVERING BUSINESS-IT COORDINATION AND THE CRITICAL FUNCTION OF CIO LEADERSHIP

INTRODUCTION

The CIO becomes a key player in today's changing corporate environment by managing the complex junction of organizational strategy and technology. This chapter dives into the complex position of the CIO, examining how this key executive provides competitive advantage, connects with business needs, and oversees vital duties that are necessary for the organization to succeed. As we progress through the chapters, we will uncover the CIO's primary duties in fostering organizational agility, forming strategic alliances, and leading transformation. We will investigate the crucial role that CIOs play in resilience and crisis management, as well as how they help to navigate the intricate domains of digital transformation, scalability of infrastructure, and strategic leadership.

CIOs play a pivotal role in the dynamic digital era, molding and reshaping companies to prosper in technological innovation and upheaval. In this chapter we will consider how the CIO role will change and examine the issues and developments, determining their strategic importance. The conversation then broadens to include the

CIO's role in promoting sustainability and supporting Green IT projects, considering the necessity of incorporating environmental responsibility into technical solutions. In conclusion, we delve into the ethical aspects of the CIO position, emphasizing their pivotal role in molding and maintaining digital ethics. This chapter explores the many facets of the CIO position, where strategic acumen and technological power collide, and where the CIO's impact goes well beyond IT to shape modern business leadership.

4.1 HOW CIO ALIGNS WITH BUSINESS NEEDS

"When everyone is aligned with the mission, a collective energy takes over." The famous quote of John C Maxwell aligns very well with any leadership role, including the CIO. CIOs must establish relationships with business executives and adequately understand the enterprise results needed to comprehend organizational goals and be effective. Strategic planning and operational strategies are required to meet digital demand, avoid being seduced by the following technology craze, and accomplish the desired results. It is crucial to remember that CIOs are responsible for investments that bolster an organization's operational or growth capabilities. Business leaders establish priorities and objectives and depend on CIOs to assist in transformation projects. It is vital to link the IT organization's aims and objectives to the objectives of the CEO. Monitoring the division's vision, operating model, employees, engagement strategy, and culture is part of IT management.

IT leadership helps business alignment by developing business acumen, reflecting business outcomes, and using metrics to measure key performance indicators. KPIs might help determine the organization's digital transformation plan and support the CIO in achieving business impact through suitable technology investments. CIOs must guarantee that their organizations plans align with their customers' needs. The CIO should prepare their personnel better to meet these demands if they understand the enterprise's customer service and operational requirements. Business executives should also interact with business unit leaders to better understand how IT projects may improve customer service and generate revenue.

The active engagement of the CIO's team with leadership and other groups can enhance efficiency and offer fresh perspectives, thereby ensuring that investment get routed to the right areas. Furthermore, CIOs should work closely with their colleagues in other functions to identify areas of high priority that require greater attention or resources. This strategy helps them sift out potential investments that may not generate the desired returns. CIOs may focus on business success while leading business and technology systems when business and IT objectives are aligned. Many CIOs believe it is vital to align their skills and expertise with business and execution goals and business commitment. Partner influence is critical to success; study findings show that business-oriented CIOs have stronger ties with a more extensive range of stakeholders.

A CIO's skills should have financial knowledge, market expertise, and a comprehensive understanding of intricate dynamics. Many CIOs underlined the crucial role of recruiting, motivating, and developing people for organizational success, recognizing the relevance of attracting and keeping talent. CIOs aggressively foster cooperation among top-performing professionals across the firm as IT leaders, connecting their efforts with career growth and business objectives. They foster an IT culture that provides employees with a thorough understanding of business drivers, consumer expectations, and the ever-changing external market. Astute CIOs appreciate the importance of an adaptive IT strategy capable of meeting current and future business objectives while driving operational efficiency and nurturing an innovation culture.

4.2 HOW CIO DELIVERS COMPETITIVE ADVANTAGE

"*It is not the strongest of the species that survive, nor the most intelligent, but the one most responsive to change*"; Charles Darvin's quote is important in business, too. Taking a competitive advantage is critical for any business. CIO being the technology head, the other members of the C-suite are increasingly pushing CIOs to take the lead on digitizing corporate projects to gain a competitive advantage. As CIOs become full-fledged corporate partners, their increased visibility among other C-suite executives positions them to lead innovation activities. Enhancing reporting skills through technology and exploiting digital data is essential to their function. Additionally, CIOs are essential in helping businesses make sense of vast amounts of data and draw crucial conclusions that affect decisions that are advantageous to the company.

CIOs may help firms obtain a competitive edge by staying on top of technical developments, evolving practices, and creative business initiatives. They may assist in speeding the launch of new enterprises, provide economic value through technologies, and contribute to developing technology-enabled, disruptive solutions. The CIO of today has a unique capacity to identify the sources of competitive advantage accessible to the organization from both a strategic and technological standpoint. Many CIOs foster creative thinking to transform enterprise-grade technology into apps that may give the firm a competitive edge by encouraging business innovation and experimentation.

The most effective CIOs are increasingly pivotal in driving exceptional corporate performance. They achieve this by enhancing competitive advantages through the prioritization of transformational projects. Their role includes educating leaders about the risks associated with innovation and innovative thinking. Furthermore, CIOs are critical in educating CEOs on how technology may generate a competitive edge for the organization. The significance of

CIOs is growing in tandem with technological advancements, shaping how organizations prioritize their technological offerings and influencing overall success. CIOs can push development, solve business objectives, and prioritize efforts that result in products with extensive feature sets. CIOs that remain on top of the newest IT capabilities and emerging technologies can add significant value to their businesses.

As per a 2019 study by Van-Toorn *et al.*, CIOs are urged to prioritize technology-driven growth to shape the course of their enterprises. Forward-thinking CIOs actively pursue groundbreaking and imaginative technologies, often engaging in partnerships or acquisitions to bolster their organizations' innovation capabilities. The study findings indicate that these innovative CIOs critically reassess various operations and procedures, particularly those lacking a competitive edge, to foster a culture of innovation and disruption.

With the customer experience becoming a more critical battlefield in the competition, CIOs are expected to deliver their organizations unmatched insights into customer behaviors and preferences. According to a 2015 research, 45 percent of CIOs cited customers as their primary business concern, which grew by 12 percent the following year. To meet this requirement, CIOs must employ cutting-edge technology to create new, customer-centric business models, products, or markets, all while tightly integrating IT initiatives with overall corporate strategy.

According to Van-Toorn et al. (2019), enterprise digitization is crucial in gaining a competitive advantage. CIOs are pivotal in delivering value to the organization by implementing enterprise-wide systems that leverage digital technology across traditional labor and goods. This involves the application of automation, the IoT, and predictive analytics to streamline industrial operations, establish innovative supply chain models, and enable predictive maintenance for consumer products.

Bongiorno *et al.* (2018) assert that CIOs need a diverse skill set in the ever-evolving business landscape to guide the organization toward a functional and adaptive workplace effectively. Taking on leadership responsibilities within the IT department, they must possess a deep understanding of IT governance and a solid commitment to efficiently managing their teams and achieving objectives. Practical verbal and written communication skills are essential for CIOs to deliver presentations and convey ideas and projects to personnel at all organizational levels.

Moreover, CIOs should demonstrate adaptability and excellent listening abilities, enabling them to navigate diverse personalities and swiftly address varied situations. Maintaining alignment across different teams and departments necessitates exceptional organizational skills and strong communication abilities. In their role as heads of the IT office, CIOs must exhibit substantial expertise in technical fields such as networking and engineering. This comprehensive skill set is crucial for steering the organization through the complexities of technological advancements and digital transformations.

A CIO oversees the division's financial budget and makes strategic investments. To excel in this role, the CIO needs financial acumen, accounting skills, and a firm grasp of utilizing budget resources to optimize outcomes. Furthermore, as a leader, the CIO manages enterprise projects and motivates employees to engage meaningfully. CIOs are responsible for leading a group of experts with different work habits and levels of technical proficiency and assigning them to projects that best showcase their skills. Project management experience and other strategic skills are advantageous but optional. CIOs must actively interact with cybersecurity professionals who excel at spotting possible weaknesses that might lead to security breaches in today's fiercely competitive corporate world. They should also implement robust safeguards to protect their organization's data.

The CIOs must balance corporate objectives with delivering concrete commercial value. For CIOs to thrive in their roles, mastering the art of relationship building is essential. The primary task of a CIO is to build an extraordinary team and optimize resource allocation. The expertise of the CIO should be on integrating the team's efforts with achieving business objectives rather than merely fulfilling deadlines. Furthermore, a CIO's responsibilities go beyond negotiating contracts and SLAs to lower operating expenses. It also means looking for ways to break away from existing suppliers and take advantage of novel services provided by emerging companies. This proactive strategy is critical in keeping the business at the cutting edge of market trends and technology breakthroughs.

4.3 TASK STEWARDSHIP OF A CIO

"Either run the day, or the day runs you." This famous quote by Jim Rohn aligns with the task stewardship of any leaders, including the CIOs. Tasks are the bedrock of any business, but task stewardship goes beyond that. It is about forecasting future corporate needs and deciding whether to build, buy, or rent the necessary skills. CIO task management organizes, coordinates, and directs an organization's operations to achieve its strategic goals. Investment management, resource allocation, schedule development, and priority decisions are all part of it. To maximize operations, they must meet internal customers' IT requirements.

CIOs are crucial in stewarding system automation and information resource management tasks. Their responsibility involves ensuring the successful implementation of plans through IT solutions. This encompasses deploying new software, hardware, and automated procedures to enhance efficiency while maintaining secure access to vital data. Task stewardship for CIOs is indispensable for organizations, enabling them to oversee business initiatives and ensure that computer systems align with operational objectives. In various companies, CIOs, CTOs, and PMOs collaborate closely to collectively oversee and manage various operations. Leveraging CIO task stewardship techniques proves instrumental in elevating client experiences, streamlining operations, and achieving predetermined goals.

Task Management facilitates business leaders in establishing and sustaining alignment across departments, teams, and overarching strategic objectives. It also ensures that business counterparts are connected with technological objectives, enabling efficient execution of complex projects. The CIO Task Management system assists the management office in supporting departmental activities while closely monitoring the organization's overall strategic objectives. Task management for a CIO includes managing significant projects, allocating resources, monitoring project progress, and completing tasks on schedule. Additionally, it provides information officers with a platform to support department heads.

The CIO controls all IT-related operations to ensure optimal functioning and resource utilization by corporate objectives. CIO task management enables firms to achieve desired results within budgeted timescales while providing vital technical and managerial assistance. The CIO ensures that the IT personnel and the firm have the skills and tools to succeed.

4.4 ROLE OF CIO IN CHANGE LEADERSHIP

"Change is the law of life and those who look only to the past or present are certain to miss the future." This famous from John F. Kennedy aligns with the change leadership expectations of a CIO. To keep ahead of the curve, the CIO should develop a plan outlining what the organization needs to flourish in a digital environment. Customer experience, innovation, data governance , cyber security, and personnel management should all be on the table. The CIO may guarantee that the organization is well-prepared to take on new challenges by taking a proactive approach. CIO must develop a plan explaining what is necessary for the organization to flourish, which involves creating a big data strategy, investing in security, and integrating new technologies. They also need to be able to communicate effectively with other members of the executive team, as well as with outside vendors.

CIOs lead initiatives in cloud infrastructure, data analytics, artificial intelligence, and talent acquisition. Simultaneously, they offer crucial support to other executives during the transformative transition into the digital era. Over the years, discussions related to IT have been marked by tension within leadership circles. Consequently, the CIO must consistently address recurring concerns regarding the organization's ability to recognize and adapt to opportunities presented by emerging technology. As the operational and strategic reliance on IT has surged, the IT leader has rightfully solidified their position as an integral executive leadership team member.

In the context of change leadership for CIOs, the study by Langer and Yorks (2018) reveals that CIOs have confronted distinctive challenges in recent years, spanning workforce shortages, trust deficits within their leadership teams, and strained relationships with CEOs. Concurrently, CIOs grapple with the expansive growth of the IT services market and the increasing technological proficiency of their line managers. As IT activities increasingly shift towards outsourcing, questions arise about the ongoing significance of the CIO role and the future trajectory of this position. The role of the CIO is actively adapting in response to technological advancements and transformations in enterprise dynamics.

According to Steve Hall, partner and head of technology research at ISG, effective change leadership for CIOs involves a transformative process. CIOs can assume leadership positions in technology-centric divisions or leverage their IT departments to build the digital infrastructure essential for a smooth shift towards hybrid cloud environments and innovative work methodologies. Steve Hall emphasizes that effective CIOs are undergoing a metamorphosis—assuming leadership in technology-centric divisions or utilizing IT departments to champion the digital infrastructure essential for navigating the shift toward hybrid cloud environments and cutting-edge work practices.

The article published by Joia and Correia (2018) states that CIOs are assuming increasingly crucial roles in collaboration with suppliers and experts, driven by the escalating demand for sophisticated change initiatives. CIOs employing agile methodologies find themselves tasked with responsibilities extending beyond project management. Their duties now encompass fostering consumer connections and adopting an entrepreneurial mindset centered on disruption and innovation. In the contemporary landscape, CIOs must integrate and leverage emerging technologies such as Blockchain and IoT, fundamentally reshaping corporate processes. Staying abreast of technological advancements is paramount for CIOs to comprehend the impact of their actions on organizational success. CIOs must also focus on developing strategies to bridge the gap between IT and the business. They must create IT solutions that are tailored to the specific needs of the organization. Finally, they must ensure that their IT teams are adequately trained and prepared to manage the changing technology landscape.

4.5 CIO ROLE IN STRATEGIC PARTNERSHIP

"Coming together is a beginning, staying together is progress, and working together is a success." This famous quote from Henry Ford has excellent relevance in the CIO's strategic role. In today's intensely competitive corporate market, strategic thinking is a must-have ability for CIOs. Companies are looking for executives who understand consumer behavior, developing product lines, sales techniques, and how digital technology can be leveraged as strategic factors to increase profitability. When competing for top-tier roles, demonstrating this business acumen is critical. The success of a CIO is dependent on two essential factors: their ability to properly manage and secure their organization's data and their ability to stimulate innovation. However, what catapulted them to success in the past may now jeopardize their future triumphs. CIOs must stay agile and update their strategy as technology advances and new threats emerge.

In business, achieving dominance often requires unwavering dedication, persistent effort, and, at times, bold initiatives. However, relying solely on such traditional approaches has limitations in the digital age. In today's digital context, business is more like a talent-centric battlefield than a conventional weapons fight. The cultivation of a connected culture is critical to success in this sector. While hard work and good problem-solving remain vital in business, many entrepreneurs look for quick and easy answers to their problems. Real success requires patience, concentration, and persistence. Finding the root of a problem is essential to treating it successfully; this can be challenging, but it is a prerequisite for creating a workable action plan. CIOs must acknowledge that there are no easy IT fixes for challenging business issues; diligence is essential.

De-Tuya *et al.* (2020) emphasize that contemporary CIOs are crucial in spearheading a cultural shift that embraces data. When companies look for a CIO, they want someone who can learn on the job and understand how different parts of the organization work together in complex ways. Additionally, staying abreast of evolving technology and its applications in the business landscape is imperative. The CIO's role extends beyond mere technology management; they bear the capacity and responsibility to lead organizational change. This entails a commitment to fostering a culture and behaviors conducive to being data-driven, open to continuous learning, and digitally-centric. CIOs no longer play a supporting role; instead, they require a holistic approach, similar to other senior executives, especially in strategic alliances, as they gain these enhanced competencies.

4.6 CIO ROLE IN DRIVING AGILITY

"The greatest danger in times of turbulence is not the turbulence; it is to act with yesterday's logic.". This famous quote from Peter Drucker is significant in today's business, where agility plays an important role. Nambisan *et al.,* (2017) highlight the critical relevance of flexibility and agility as desirable abilities in the business sector in their 2017 research. To satisfy these challenges, companies recruit CIOs from a variety of backgrounds. The dynamic interaction of a competitive landscape, changing consumer expectations, and technology improvements are redefining the corporate landscape, forcing firms to stay ahead. Technology has become a vital component for firms seeking to maintain their competitive advantage, and the goal of the IT department is developing as a result. Businesses must capitalize on the most recent technologies and trends to remain at the forefront of their respective industry. In this fast-changing environment, businesses that can swiftly recognize change, adapt their operational procedures, and react to it will succeed.

As organizational transformation accelerates, CEOs increasingly recognize the need for heightened agility and adaptable IT infrastructure. In this digital era, innovative working methods are crucial for fostering adaptation and responsiveness. Across all sectors, companies depend on both mature and cutting-edge IT to enhance communication with clients, suppliers, and staff, ensuring competitiveness and growth. Digitization is a fundamental aspect of the contemporary business paradigm, influencing supply chains, operations, marketing, transactions, and interactions with current and future customers. In driving agility, CIOs must reassess their roles, emphasizing restoring the CIO-business unit leader connection and streamlining IT efforts beyond the CIO's traditional authority. Rather than focusing solely on managing technological investments, CIOs should take a strategic approach, overseeing the delivery of current IT services essential for the organization to achieve its goals, compete effectively, and adapt to market changes.

The role of the CIO is constantly evolving, marked by heightened complexity in both challenges and opportunities. To effectively navigate these dynamics, CIOs should establish an internal escalation process, enabling them to leverage specialized knowledge within their organizations as needed. However, there are situations where surpassing predefined categories becomes necessary to reach optimal solutions. Operating or overseeing technology-related initiatives alone is no longer sufficient for CIOs. A successful CIO acts as a catalyst for organizational change, skillfully integrating both human and technological elements in the modern landscape. Moreover, they prioritize creating an environment where individuals are empowered to take calculated risks, explore innovative ideas, and embrace technology for automation within their enterprises.

The rapid ascent of Software-as-a-Service (SaaS), Platform-as-a-Service (PaaS), and Infrastructure-as-a-Service (IaaS) has reshaped the landscape of technology acquisition and utilization within IT departments. For CIOs driving agility, the imperative is to navigate away from protracted, CapEx driven contracts. Continuous assessment of partnerships is vital, recognizing that some endure for years while others falter in their infancy. In the context of CIOs driving agility, what distinguishes successful from unsuccessful partnerships extends beyond the surface. It encompasses the depth of service, the level of commitment, and the effectiveness of communication. Indeed, a prosperous partnership hinges on reciprocal engagement in its success, with communication, compromise, and collaboration as pivotal elements. These factors collectively ensure that all parties work harmoniously toward a shared objective.

4.7 CIO ROLE IN CRISIS MANAGEMENT AND RESILIENCE

"The true test of leadership is how well you function in a crisis." This famous quote of Brian Tracy aligns with any leadership role, including CIOs. Technological developments, consumer

expectations, and worker assumptions challenge the IT department and CIOs. Handling such a crisis is critical for a CIO.

The onset of the coronavirus pandemic has redefined the expectations placed upon CIOs, necessitating a modernized change plan tailored to accommodate a fundamentally new work environment and prioritize employee safety. They actively collaborate with leaders across organizational departments, serving as facilitators of digital transformation and addressing the challenges arising from evolving work conditions. The focus of their role has shifted from mere efficiency enhancement to the proactive acceleration of progress, with a newfound responsibility for leading and guiding digital transformation endeavors.

The CIO plays a pivotal role in crisis management, particularly in navigating the complexities of technology and information systems during challenging times. Here are critical aspects of the CIO's role in crisis management:

Risk Assessment and Preparedness: The CIO should assess potential risks to the organization's technology infrastructure. Risk assessment includes identifying vulnerabilities, evaluating potential disruptions' impact, and developing crisis preparedness strategies.

Disaster Recovery Planning: The CIO should lead the development and implementation of robust disaster recovery plans. These plans outline the procedures and technologies necessary to recover IT systems and data during a disruption, ensuring minimal downtime and a swift return to normal operations.

Business Continuity: The CIO should ensure that the continuity of critical business functions is central to the CIO's role. Business continuity involves establishing measures to maintain essential IT services during a crisis, allowing the organization to continue operating even in challenging circumstances.

Communication Infrastructure: The CIO should oversee the organization's communication infrastructure; ensuring communication channels remain operational during a crisis. Communication includes facilitating remote work capabilities, enhancing collaboration tools, and maintaining secure communication channels.

Data Security and Privacy: Protecting sensitive data is paramount during a crisis. CIOs implement and reinforce security measures to safeguard information, prevent data breaches, and ensure compliance with privacy regulations, even in high-pressure situations.

Incident Response: In a crisis, the CIO leads the IT department in executing the incident response plan. Incident response includes identifying the root cause of disruptions, implementing immediate solutions, and communicating effectively with internal and external stakeholders.

Technology Innovation for Crisis Solutions: The CIO should leverage their technological expertise to innovate crisis solutions. Technology innovation might involve implementing new technologies, such as artificial intelligence or data analytics, to enhance the organization's ability to respond to and recover from crises effectively.

Continuous Monitoring and Evaluation: The CIO should continuously monitor the IT environment for potential threats and vulnerabilities. Post-crisis, they conduct evaluations to identify areas for improvement, implement lessons learned, and enhance the organization's overall resilience to future crises.

Resource Management: The CIO should be capable of managing IT resources during a crisis. Resource management includes optimizing the use of existing technology, assessing the need for additional resources, and ensuring the availability of necessary support for the IT team.

Strategic Planning for Resilience: The CIOs are responsible for developing and implementing strategic plans that bolster the organization's resilience. Strategic planning for resilience involves assessing potential risks, developing contingency plans, and ensuring the IT infrastructure can withstand disruptions.

Technology Infrastructure and Security: The CIO should oversee the design and maintenance of the technology infrastructure, including data centers, networks, and cloud services. In times of crisis, they must ensure the security and integrity of the organization's digital assets, safeguarding against cyber threats and data breaches.

Agile and Adaptive Responses: Crises often demand agile and adaptive responses. CIOs, in collaboration with their teams, must be agile in adapting technologies to address emerging challenges, whether it is enabling remote work, enhancing cybersecurity, or implementing new tools for efficient communication.

Data Analytics for Informed Decision-Making: CIOs contribute to informed decision-making during a crisis by leveraging data analytics. They use data-driven insights to assess the impact of disruptions, identify emerging trends, and guide the organization in making strategic decisions to navigate uncertainty.

Communication and Collaboration: Effective communication is crucial during times of crisis. CIOs facilitate seamless communication within the IT department and collaborate with other business units to ensure a unified response. They play a crucial role in aligning technology initiatives with broader organizational strategies.

Continuous Learning and Improvement: Resilience is an ongoing process, and CIOs foster a culture of continuous learning and improvement within the IT department. Continuous learning involves conducting post-crisis evaluations, identifying lessons learned, and implementing changes to enhance the organization's resilience.

Vendor and Partner Management: CIOs work closely with vendors and technology partners to ensure the reliability of external services. Managing these relationships is crucial for securing support and resources during a crisis and maintaining a resilient IT ecosystem.

In summary, CIOs are at the forefront of crisis management and resilience, leveraging their technological expertise to navigate challenges, ensuring the stability of IT systems, and contributing to the overall organizational resilience in an ever-evolving business landscape.

4.8 CIO ROLE IN NAVIGATING DIGITAL TRANSFORMATION, INFRASTRUCTURE SCALABILITY, AND STRATEGIC LEADERSHIP

The function of the CIO has changed recently; it is now more of a key advisor, collaborator, and facilitator of creative action plans rather than just an innovator and member of the delivery unit. Amidst the ongoing digital transformation within organizations, the responsibilities of CIOs are rapidly adjusting. A crucial element of this evolution involves ensuring the IT infrastructure is scalable to meet the latest digital requirements. CIOs are now tasked with assessing whether their existing infrastructure is conducive to supporting digital transformation and determining its readiness for this strategic shift.

The CIO must evaluate whether the change necessitates an open architecture or an infrastructure update. These considerations can now significantly influence customer interest at the organizational level, driven by technology commercialization, especially in mobile technology. According to Pinho and Franco (2017) in their study article, clients seek consistent and coordinated responses across all stages, including mobile interactions and cloud-based operations. CIOs have evolved into pivotal business enablers, championing the adoption of innovative action plans, while IT has transformed into a distinct entity and service in its own right. As highlighted by Van-

Grembergen and De-Haes in their 2017 study, CIOs and their IT departments must establish a technological ecosystem capable of meeting the organization's requirements while optimizing workforce operations. Achieving this mandate necessitates a reliable IT infrastructure and a well-crafted strategy. In the rapidly advancing landscape of technology, CIOs must develop an agile and adaptable IT strategy that leverages contemporary tools such as AI, machine learning, and robotics to craft practical solutions tailored to their business needs.

According to Van-Grembergen and De-Haes (2017), IT's function expands beyond being the source of innovation inside an organization to driving revolutionary business changes and serving as the control center of a forward-thinking corporation. Organizations that do not understand this notion now risk becoming outdated tomorrow. CIOs have a direct impact on strategic decisions and product development. It is now possible for CIOs to interact with a customer's genuine voice and viewpoint, strengthening their position and power inside their value chain. CIOs also serve a vital function as trusted partners in addition to their various responsibilities, such as spearheading organizational transformation, streamlining operations, and enhancing corporate performance through cutting-edge technology.

The digital transformation age is spreading throughout sectors, altering strategies and needs while necessitating increased intellectual leadership and resources. This paradigm change transforms the conventional C-suite and creates new corporate titles and functions, such as the Chief Security Officer, Chief Digital Officer, and Chief Data Officer. Organizations involved in digital transformation initiatives fundamentally restructure existing organizations rather than only introducing innovation. Additional digital developments are altering the position of the CIO, with technology being considered a critical business component rather than merely a support tool. This shift emphasizes the increased relevance of IT and the role of the CIO in driving sales success.

Embracing the idea of the customer journey or customer-centricity is critical in order to succeed as a CIO in this changing environment. The customer journey framework offers a structured approach to comprehending individuals' progression through the various stages of the purchasing process, from initial awareness to consideration, consideration to choose, and, ultimately, the decision to purchase. This framework is valuable for analyzing consumers' positions in their buying journey and understanding their specific needs at each phase. Customer-centricity requires concerted and systematic effort to standardize the customer experience from the moment they become customers. An in-depth understanding of an organization's complete user experience, from the first interaction to conversion, retention, and advocacy, is possible by adopting a customer journey viewpoint.

4.9 CIO ROLE IN THE DIGITAL AGE

According to Urbach and Ahlemann (2018), the function of the CIO has altered dramatically with the advancement of technology in the digital age. The digital age is a playground of possibilities, where imagination is the architect of the future, so CIOs are under increased pressure to facilitate the adoption of new technologies and drive revenue development through cloud systems, mobile apps, data analytics, and social media. However, these developments bring significant difficulties to the conventional IT area. CIOs must set up and manage data systems and provide a safe and dependable infrastructure while minimizing expenses. CIOs must effectively combine the responsibilities of technical leaders and business boosters in today's marketplace. While digital improvements offer new frontiers, they also present unique issues, necessitating novel solutions for traditional IT concerns such as application integration, execution, cost management, and security.

The digital age has brought new political and organizational challenges, such as managing an extensive portfolio and relationships, modernizing legacy IT frameworks, making technology adoption decisions, harmonizing new systems with legacy ones, implementing governance, cost control, and dealing with talent shortages. According to Nwankpa *et al.* (2021), while not all CIOs are naturally business builders, some organizations respond to the changing landscape by developing a new job called the CDO. The CDO is in charge of developing and implementing a digital strategy. However, as digitalization spreads, the functions of the CIO and CDO may merge.

To perform the CIO's position effectively in this dynamic environment, a mix of creative thinking, creativity, political acumen, and the ability to traverse the rapidly changing technical landscape becomes critical. CIOs are now looking for ways to improve their enterprises, shifting away from the traditional focus on building and maintaining IT infrastructure and automating business processes. IT teams are increasingly focused on generating income, improving the customer experience, and using data-driven insights.

In their comprehensive analysis, Drechsler *et al.* (2019) underscore the pivotal role of CIOs in the digital age, where technology-driven digitization has become a prevailing norm across diverse sectors. CIOs are central in steering organizations towards higher efficiency, gaining deeper customer insights, and innovating new business models. Early adopters of digitalization, such as the media, marketing, and retail sectors, continue to set the benchmark for successful integration. Modern industries, such as oil Industries, use CIO skills to improve exploration and production efficiency by combining mobile devices and analytics. CIOs led the charge in manufacturing by implementing digital modeling, simulation, and intelligent structures, accelerating production processes, improving energy efficiency, and reducing operational costs. In essence, the CIOs' strategic involvement is instrumental in ensuring that businesses thrive in the dynamic landscape of digitization, fostering innovation and efficiency across various sectors.

In the digital age, CIOs play a pivotal role in reshaping industries. Within financial services, CIOs are driving the automation of end-to-end procedures, resulting in cost reduction and enhanced risk management. In healthcare, CIOs leverage mobile devices and analytics to advance research, improve health outcomes, and streamline costs. Likewise, within E-Governance, CIOs leverage the potential of the internet, big data, mobile technology, and sensors to elevate public safety and enhance services for customers or society. The ongoing reduction in technological costs and the widespread acceptance of sophisticated tools like social media and mobile devices are accelerating the digitization trend. In this transformative landscape, CIOs find a unique opportunity to shape the trajectory and implementation of digital strategies within their enterprises. Successful CIOs navigate this digital era by blending vision, creativity, political acumen, and the ability to navigate a rapidly evolving technological landscape, propelling their organizations into the digital future.

4.10 THE FUTURE OF THE CIO ROLE

As technology continues to reshape industries, the role of CIOs in the future is not just about managing IT but about leading the charge in shaping a future where innovation is the norm. The function of the CIO is experiencing significant change. What was formerly solely a technical profession has now evolved into technical and business duties. The CIO's primary responsibility is to ensure that the department prioritizes documentation and procedures that improve business operations. To accomplish this aim, the CIO should investigate business process automation and the implementation of an enterprise content management strategy. This method allows the CIO to devote more time and resources to other activities, underlining the importance of the IT department in any firm. A strong emphasis on documentation and protocols in the IT department guarantees quick project completion, risk reduction, and organizational order.

Robert Kiyosaki states, "*Your future is created by what you do today, not by what you do tomorrow.*" This quote aligns with technology and business as modern enterprise's future heavily relies on the IT department and the CIO. Job responsibilities develop in response to changing business demands as technology moves organizations forward. The recent transition to remote work amid a crisis highlights the inextricable link between IT and business. Organizations seeking to develop future CIO talent must understand the role's shifting nature. CIOs are increasingly strategic partners to a variety of different C-level executives.

In their research paper, Jones *et al.* (2020) anticipate that the CIO and CMO roles may consolidate into a unified position known as the "*Chief Marketing Technology Officer*," blending expertise in both IT and marketing. Expectations suggest that in the foreseeable future, CMOs will allocate an increasing amount of their time to technology management, surpassing the time dedicated by CIOs to the same endeavor. Consequently, CIOs must enhance their marketing skills and comprehensively understand marketing and other business processes to meet expanding job demands. Additionally, CIOs collaborate closely with CISOs, CEOs, CFOs, and other stakeholders.

Knowing how different departments operate puts CIOs in a position to support divisions across the board, leading them toward COO duties. The growing range of titles associated with the CIO position reflects the changing digital environment. As technology and automation play increasingly important roles, there is a growing need for CIOs adept at leading digital transformation initiatives (Madakam *et al.*, 2019). Strong change management skills and the ability to plan, carry out, and supervise digital transformation projects will put CIOs in great demand. According to Denford and Schobel (2021), a prosperous future CIO must work with senior leaders to develop a plan for digital transformation, encourage a digital attitude, improve operational effectiveness continuously, and put the customer's needs first. In the future, CIOs will be information officers and pivotal leaders steering organizations through the currents of digital change and transformation.

According to research from Gartner's CIO Agenda titled *"Securing the Foundation for Digital Business,"* the percentage of enterprises that have achieved digital scale has risen from 17% to 33% in the past year. This trend is impacting the management of IT and CIO practices within organizations. In a similar survey, 49% of respondents reported that their organization's business model had transformed, with 55% transitioning from project delivery to product delivery. Urbach *et al.* (2018), in their research paper, state that the role of the CIO, which was previously focused primarily on IT operations and mitigating technological risks, has recently undergone a significant transformation.

This shift in the CIO's job requires a shift in skills and capabilities, making the post available to those with technological experience and inventive thinking. La-Paz (2017), in his research paper, states that CIOs must hone their leadership abilities as their organizations expand digitally. Organizations proactively embracing digitization have several opportunities for growth and innovation in the digital environment. Customer expectations drive the need for agility, emphasizing the importance of demonstrating progress as soon as feasible.

In the evolving landscape, businesses tend to prefer CIOs equipped with robust business acumen and adept team-building skills while retaining the essential foundation of technical knowledge. The future role of CIOs involves seamless collaboration with business stakeholders, leading to remarkable accomplishments. For instance, a synergistic partnership between a CIO and marketing teams in developing CRM software can elevate consumer insights and refine marketing strategies. Similarly, aligning with sales teams and leveraging predictive analytics enables precise demand forecasting and improved inventory management. Engaging with HR to create employee engagement tools fosters a more productive workforce. These collaborative efforts illustrate how CIOs can strategically employ technology to enhance productivity, stimulate creativity, and encourage cross-functional cooperation, ultimately leading to outstanding organizational performance.

Gartner's research states, "*A purpose-focused approach encourages greater collaboration between IT and business partners as everyone works toward a single goal to achieve results.*" According to Guarda *et al.* (2021), future CIOs must take a more inventive approach to product creation and execution to achieve important roles in startups or senior leadership positions in significant businesses. The CIO role's future is dynamic and bright, defined by various themes that impact its progress. Organizations and CIOs must both stay adaptive as the digital world evolves.

4.11 CIO'S ROLE IN SUSTAINABILITY AND GREEN IT

The accurate measure of technological progress lies in how efficiently it treads on this Earth. Green IT is the compass guiding us toward a responsible and sustainable future. Green IT is the deliberate endeavor to design, deploy, and manage IT systems and activities to minimize environmental effects. Green IT includes energy efficiency, resource conservation, trash reduction, and appropriate electronic device disposal. Organizations may reduce their environmental impact while saving money and increasing their corporate social responsibility by incorporating Green IT into their plans. Green IT is not a constraint but a catalyst for innovation, pushing us to rethink, redesign, and rebuild our technological landscape for a greener tomorrow. CIOs are well positioned as technology leaders inside their businesses to promote and support the implementation of Green IT practices.

The following are some critical features of the CIO's involvement in sustainability and Green IT:

Implementing Energy-Efficient Technologies: CIOs should encourage using energy-efficient hardware and software. Virtualization technology, for example, can enhance server use by eliminating the need for extra physical hardware and cutting energy consumption.

Environmental Effect Assessment: CIOs should conduct in-depth analyses to comprehend how their IT activities affect the environment. Assessing data centers, servers, and equipment's energy use, carbon emissions, and resource usage is part of this.

Data Center Efficiency: Modern data centers consume significant energy. CIOs may spearhead initiatives to construct and run data centers with an eye toward energy efficiency, leveraging improved cooling techniques, renewable energy sources, and efficient power distribution.

E-Waste Management: It is essential to dispose of electronic trash (e-waste) responsibly. CIOs can guarantee that obsolete IT equipment is recycled or disposed of in an ecologically responsible way, lowering the environmental effect of IT hardware disposal.

Sustainable Procurement: CIOs may work with procurement teams to find environmentally friendly IT equipment and components, considering variables like energy efficiency, recyclability, and using environmentally friendly materials.

A sustainability and Green IT pioneer, Google serves as an outstanding case study. The organization has substantially invested in renewable energy sources to fuel its data centers. Google has committed to procuring renewable energy to offset its entire energy consumption, a goal it has already achieved for its data centers. This commitment contributes to a reduction in carbon emissions and underscores the IT industry's leadership in environmental initiatives. Google's data centers are built strategically with efficient, cutting-edge cooling systems and customized hardware to maximize energy efficiency. Their forward-looking approach illustrates how CIOs can champion sustainability initiatives while maintaining high-performance IT infrastructure.

CIOs play a critical role in promoting Green IT and sustainability practices inside their enterprises in an era where environmental sustainability is a worldwide issue. CIOs can help the environment and the bottom line by utilizing technology to decrease energy usage waste and encourage responsible buying and disposal. Google's sustainable data centers are an inspirational example of how CIOs can lead the way to a greener, more sustainable future in the IT sector and beyond.

4.12 CIO ROLE IN DIGITAL ETHICS

Digital ethics is the collection of ideas and norms that regulate technology's moral and responsible use. It entails making decisions emphasizing individual well-being, preserving privacy, and promoting equity in technology development and implementation. Digital ethics include data privacy, cybersecurity, AI ethics, and the influence of technology on society. "*Ethics is the soul of the company.*" This quote from Anne M. Mulcahy, former CEO of Xerox corporation, aligns with the digital ethics a CIO must practice. CIOs are essential in creating digital ethics inside their firms, ensuring that technology is appropriately designed, deployed, and used.

CIOs are at the forefront of their businesses' technological adoption and innovation. As such, they play an essential role in promoting and preserving digital ethics in the following ways:

Technology Impact Assessment: CIOs should conduct assessments to examine technology adoption's social, ethical, and environmental effects. The technology impact assessment allows the CIO and businesses to make better decisions.

Data Privacy: CIOs must advocate for robust data privacy procedures that ensure consumer and employee data is acquired, kept, and utilized by privacy rules and ethical standards.

Ethical Technology Development: CIOs must ensure they deliver technology solutions with ethics in mind. The CIO gets involved in assessing the potential impact of technology on individuals, groups, and society as a whole.

Ethical hacking and cybersecurity: Ethical cybersecurity approaches entail guarding against cyber dangers while adhering to ethical standards. CIOs should spearhead efforts to protect sensitive data and promote appropriate cybersecurity practices.

AI & Machine Learning Ethics: CIOs should consider bias, fairness, and transparency when adopting artificial intelligence and machine learning systems. They should reduce algorithm biases and enhance openness in AI decision-making processes.

Microsoft is an excellent example of an organization devoted to digital ethics and ethical AI practices. The business has developed explicit rules for the proper development and application of artificial intelligence. Fairness, accountability, openness, and privacy are among these ideals. Microsoft's CIOs and technology leaders collaborate with ethical teams to examine the possible societal effects of AI technologies. For example, when creating face recognition technology, Microsoft chose to perform an honest evaluation, which resulted in the decision to limit the sale of this technology to law enforcement agencies and to implement tight standards to avoid exploitation. Microsoft's dedication to digital ethics and responsible AI practices exhibits leadership and highlights how CIOs may influence technology development in ways consistent with ethical principles.

In digital ethics, the primary duty of the CIO is to ensure that the organization uses technology for its benefit. CIOs can help design a technological environment emphasizing ethics and social well-being by fostering ethical technology development, data privacy, responsible AI practices, and transparent cybersecurity measures. Microsoft's responsible AI policies are an inspirational example of how CIOs can develop digital ethics throughout the tech sector and beyond, eventually contributing to a more accountable and ethical digital future. CIOs can also promote ethical and responsible data practices among their employees by implementing ethical data governance and providing clear guidelines for data handling and usage. They can also help to create a culture of ethical and responsible technology adoption in their organizations, educating their employees on ethical issues and encouraging them to think critically about the impact of technology on their work and society.

CHAPTER 5
BUSINESS-IT ALIGNMENT FOR CIOS: AN EXPLORATION OF THE MEANING, DIFFICULTIES, AND ADVANTAGES

INTRODUCTION

The relationship between business and technology has become inseparable in the ever-changing digital world, setting the stage for business-IT alignment.. For CIOs, achieving this alignment is crucial to the success of their organizations and goes beyond merely being a strategic requirement. This chapter delves into the complexities of business-IT alignment, examining its fundamentals, justifications, and the range of domains it covers. Comprehending the subtleties of business-IT alignment necessitates a thorough analysis of the motivations underlying this collaboration. We examine the underlying causes that drive companies to align their IT and business goals, illuminating how this alignment is a trendy practice and a tactical requirement for survival in the cutthroat corporate environment.

As we go deeper into the chapter, we analyze the numerous areas where business-IT alignment has a revolutionary impact. Every aspect, from strategic planning to technology integration, supports aligning business goals with IT capabilities. However, synchronization also brings hurdles, and here we discuss the common issues that businesses run into while trying to achieve smooth business-IT alignment. However, there are big rewards mixed in with the difficulties. We examine the advantages of a successful business-IT alignment, from increased customer satisfaction and organizational agility to increased operational efficiency and creativity. These advantages highlight the significant influence that a positive business-IT partnership can have on a firm's general performance and expansion.

We also discuss the ramifications of business-IT alignment, highlighting its profound impacts on an organization's resilience, agility, and competitiveness. Understanding that attaining alignment is a customized process, we ascertain a CIO's fundamental characteristics to facilitate and effectively maintain business-IT alignment in their company. We will review the complex web of business-IT alignment in the following pages, providing CIOs with knowledge, tactics, and helpful guidance on successfully traversing and conquering this crucial symbiosis in the fast-paced world of contemporary business.

5.1 WHAT IS BUSINESS-IT ALIGNMENT FOR THE CIO?

When business and IT strategies are coordinated, business-IT alignment is activated, which, in turn, increases the value of an organization. Business-IT alignment is a continuous process rather than a one-time occurrence, as the gap between business and IT alignment is determined by how closely IT projects follow business requirements. According to the study paper by Sieber M. *et al.* (2022), the main goal of business-IT alignment is to close and eventually remove this gap. This alignment has various phases or stages, each adding to the increased value the business produces. Through the perspective of business-IT alignment, an organization may most effectively realize optimal returns on its IT investments.

Our world is increasingly interconnected, and technology is essential to many aspects of our lives, including data storage, corporate operations, education, and communication. Its impact is felt in personal and professional domains, encouraging connection between different businesses and integrating different technology components. The American football player Terrell Owens once said, *"Aligning expectations with reality prevents disappointment,"* which is a good statement for CIOs that applies to balancing business and technology. When a CIO ensures the meticulous alignment of business and technology, the outcome is organizational satisfaction and tangible success in business operations.

The CIO must know the organization's business objectives and top priorities. Understanding the organization's mission, vision, and strategic goals falls under this category. Here are some critical aspects of Business-IT alignment for a CIO:

Governance: The CIO has to set up administrative procedures to guarantee that IT activities and investments are per business priorities. Governance could encompass the use of steering committees, ongoing evaluations, and project management approaches that give precedence to business alignment.

Strategic Planning: The CIO is critical in creating an IT strategy that complements the business plan. Strategic planning entails figuring out how technology might be applied to support and facilitate the accomplishment of corporate goals.

Communication: Effective communication is essential for the success of a business. The CIO must be able to explain to business stakeholders the benefits of IT efforts and vice versa. Translation of technical jargon is required for effective communication.

Prioritization: The CIO must prioritize IT initiatives based on their potential to deliver business value. Prioritization means focusing resources on projects closely aligned with the organization's strategic goals.

Resource Allocation: A CIO should be able to decide how to distribute IT resources (money, staff, and technology) so that they support the most critical business goals. As business priorities vary, this can necessitate reallocating resources. Some CIOs take the approach of categorizing them as priority 1,2,3, etc. Some CIOs categorize them based on the MoSCoW method in which priorities are categorized as Must have, Should have, Could have, and Will not have.

KPIs: Defining and monitoring KPIs that gauge the effect of IT on the business is what metrics and KPIs are all about. KPIs include metrics relating to cost reductions, revenue growth, customer satisfaction, and other factors.

Collaboration: A CIO should promote interaction between other business divisions and IT, including developing a collaborative culture and involving business leaders in IT decision-making.

Risk Management: A CIO should manage risk management in his department and should identify and reduce business-impacting risks related to IT activities, which cover operational, compliance, and cybersecurity risks.

Flexibility: The CIO must be versatile and capable of modifying IT strategy and priorities by changing business requirements.

Technology Evaluation: Regularly evaluating and reporting on the effectiveness of IT efforts and their effects on the organization is known as performance measurement, and this data helps improve continuously and make the necessary corrections.

In conclusion, business-IT alignment is critical for CIOs from a strategic standpoint. It ensures that IT expenditures and initiatives are closely related to the organization's business goals, maximizing the benefits technology can offer the business. In today's technology-driven corporate environment, a strong alignment between IT and the organization is crucial for fostering innovation, enhancing efficiency, and preserving a competitive edge.

5.2 REASONS BEHIND BUSINESS-IT ALIGNMENT

Businesses must prioritize business-IT alignment to ensure that IT connects with the more significant business objectives and strategy. Companies must constantly adapt and innovate to stay competitive in today's industry. The CIO, frequently occupied with maintaining the organization's legacy systems, may find this a demanding assignment for many organizations. The CIO must identify ways to do the new while changing the old to innovate and change successfully. Fortunately, a few crucial tactics can make this happen. The requirement for a CIO to manage and oversee these deployments varies as more organizations adopt new technologies.

The modern CIO needs to know how to interact with outside suppliers and consultants who can accomplish it for them rather than needing in-depth expertise to manage every system inside. The CIO must also determine what new technologies can boost corporate performance. Another vital role that the CIO should play is starting and improving IT by effectively balancing IT and business. When an organization's people's goals, values, and thoughts are in harmony, it functions more effectively. If this balance exists outside the organization, the C-suites, including the CIO, must create it going forward. Alignment is an ongoing process, not a singular event; it requires constant communication, adjustments, and a collective commitment to a shared vision.

According to Kitsios F & Kamariotou M. (2016), achieving business-IT alignment requires actively coordinating IT efforts with the goals and standards established by an organization's business operations. This concept is well known as a valuable method for identifying IT upgrades that will help the business the most while avoiding pointless spending. Companies can optimize the ROI of their IT investments when they align with specific business objectives. Business-IT alignment, a critical factor in the success of IT initiatives, establishes a structure for efficient resource allocation and adaptation to evolving business needs. This alignment harmonizes an organization's IT function with the standards established by its business operations. Any organization seeking to enhance its IT services' effectiveness and cost-efficiency should consider this principle.

Below are the compelling reasons to prioritize and foster business-IT alignment:

Improved Decision-Making: A CIO must provide the organization with fast, reliable data and insights via IT systems, which enable data-driven decision-making, and will lead to improved decision-making. Enhancing the organization's flexibility and responsiveness to alterations in the business environment is very important for a CIO.

Strategic Alignment: A CIO must ensure that IT initiatives and projects align with its strategic goals and objectives. By using IT as a strategic asset, the organization can respond to changes in the market and pressure from competitors.

Innovation and Growth: A CIO must promote business-IT alignment and innovation by giving the required tools and resources for new ideas and projects in the technology sector.

Cost Optimization: A CIO must align IT investments with business strategies to enable more effective resource allocation and lower wasted spending on initiatives that do not advance strategic objectives.

Enhanced Productivity: A CIO should utilize IT to automate and simplify corporate operations can boost productivity and efficiency. With IT business alignment, the corporation can explore new markets, goods, and services through digital transformation.

Competitive Advantage: A CIO should utilize IT to obtain a competitive edge in the market through new product development, top-notch customer support, or operational effectiveness.

Scalability and flexibility: A CIO should ensure that systems and IT infrastructure can grow to accommodate the business's evolving needs, whether these changes result from expansion or unanticipated challenges.

Risk Management: Reducing technology, data security, and compliance risks by coordinating IT with business needs and regulatory requirements. The CIO must ensure that the organization defends from cyber threats and data breaches by ensuring that IT investments are secure and robust.

Customer Experience: A CIO should improve customer experience by utilizing IT to deliver seamless digital interactions, collect consumer feedback, and customize services. A CIO should be delivering the services based on digital accessibility and convenience demands from customers.

Communication and Collaboration: A CIO should foster improved IT and other business unit collaboration and communication to ensure everyone is on the same page and pursuing the same goals.

Talent Development: A CIO should attract and keep top talent—necessary for successful alignment—the IT department should foster a culture of collaboration and ongoing learning.

KPI-based Results: A CIO should create metrics and KPIs to monitor the effects of IT projects on the organization's operations will allow for data-driven accountability and ongoing improvement.

In conclusion, business-IT alignment is essential for CIOs because it helps firms employ technology as a strategic enabler, minimize costs, manage risks, and spur innovation and growth in a business environment that is changing quickly. By integrating IT with the overall business strategy, CIOs can ensure that technology investments yield real value and competitive advantage.

5.3 AREAS OF BUSINESS-IT ALIGNMENT

Aligning business and IT goals entails integrating IT with organizational structures, strategic objectives, and overarching business objectives. This integration brings IT and the organization together and guarantees accurate business results. The organization is advancing in the same direction and at the required rate to complete its mission. Business and IT must be aligned for any firm to prosper in the contemporary digital age. Companies can boost their business agility, a key component of successful business alignment, by aligning their business and IT processes. Teams can achieve a common aim through business alignment, which is typically the achievement of a business goal. Not only does this make it easier to implement enterprise-wide strategies, but it also will enable organizations to transform themselves and drive more innovation. Aligning technology department goals with enterprise-wide strategy is essential for achieving effective business alignment.

By using best practices and strategies, this unification aids firms in achieving their objectives and enhancing customer service. According to studies cited in a Forbes article, businesses that successfully integrate IT with the organization see increases in revenue of 20% and cost savings of 10%. Organizations must foster a culture that encourages IT and other departments to work together on common objectives to reap these benefits. Establishing key performance indicators to track advancement toward these goals is crucial to synchronizing businesses and accomplishing shared objectives. When business and IT are aligned, companies may embark on a new strategic path advantageous to the organization and its clients.

Two crucial work components that can be optimized are marketing and product development, which require coordinating numerous systems and activities. Starbucks had great success aligning its IT strategy with its business plan. Mobile ordering and payment accounted for a sizable percentage of transactions, which improved customer convenience. Increased awareness of the company's loyalty program helped retain customers, and better IT-business alignment enhanced supply chain efficiency and inventory control. Organizations must create a culture where IT and other departments collaborate to accomplish shared goals and objectives to reap these benefits. Combining IT and business methods to achieve common goals is known as *"Business and IT Alignment"*. Business strategy and IT must be in harmony to use the technology at hand best. This alignment depends on IT leaders and business teams developing solid relationships. Objectives can be met by incorporating IT roadmaps into workgroups and coordinating organizations appropriately. Using KPIs and roadmaps increases the transparency of how technological resources are used.

CIOs play a critical role in achieving business-IT alignment by focusing on essential areas inside the enterprise. For IT projects to effectively support and propel the organization toward its strategic objectives, alignment across these vital aspects should be fostered. The following are the main focuses for business-IT alignment for CIOs:

Governance and Compliance: The CIO should establish robust IT governance mechanisms to guarantee that IT choices and projects adhere to internal policy and regulatory requirements. A CIO should develop a culture of risk management and compliance inside the IT division.

Strategic Alignment: CIOs should ensure that the organization's overall business strategy and objectives connect with IT strategies and efforts. A CIO should work together to define IT's function in attaining strategic goals with top executives and business leaders.

Innovation and Digital Transformation: The CIO should explore opportunities for digital transformation, encourage IT innovation, and collaborate with business divisions. A CIO should encourage a culture of experimentation and continuous improvement.

Technology Architecture and Infrastructure: The CIO considers creating and upholding an IT infrastructure that enables the scalability, security, and flexibility to satisfy business expectations. A CIO should modernize and optimize the IT infrastructure to save money and boost efficiency.

Operational Alignment: The CIO must guarantee that routine IT operations and processes align seamlessly with the business's operational needs, enhancing both efficiency and effectiveness. A CIO should streamline IT service delivery is essential for promptly and effectively meeting the demands of the business.

Financial Alignment: CIOs manage IT budgets and expenses according to the organization's financial goals. A CIO should quantify the impact of IT investments on the bottom line to show their worth.

Project Portfolio Management: The CIO should manage and prioritize IT initiatives to complement the organization's strategic objectives. A CIO should evaluate the portfolio frequently to adjust to shifting organizational needs.

Data Management and Analytics: The CIOs should help in decision-making and ensure data governance and analytics initiatives align with corporate objectives. A CIO should promote data-driven initiatives to improve goods, services, and client interactions.

Vendor and Partner Management: The CIO should align vendor ties and relationships with the demands of the business and its objectives. A CIO should analyze and choose technology providers that support the goals of the organization.

Cybersecurity and Risk Management: The CIO is expected to work with corporate executives to evaluate and reduce IT-related risks, including security concerns. A CIO should ensure security measures adhere to the organization's regulatory standards and risk tolerance.

Talent Development and Management: The CIO should develop an IT workforce with the knowledge and abilities to meet organizational goals. A CIO should work to match the organization's workforce planning and development objectives with IT talent management methods.

Customer and User Experience: The CIO should work together with business units to improve the user and customer experience with the help of technology. A CIO should give customer feedback priority and make sure IT initiatives meet user expectations.

Change Management and Communication: The CIO should effectively inform all organization-wide stakeholders of IT changes and objectives. A CIO should lessen interruptions and opposition to IT-driven changes, adopt change management techniques.

Measuring and Reporting: The CIO should establish metrics and KPIs to monitor the effects of IT projects on the organization's operations. A CIO should continually update senior leadership and stakeholders on IT performance and alignment efforts.

CIOs can guarantee that IT is a strategic facilitator for the organization, contributing to its success and competitiveness in the constantly changing business environment by proactively addressing these business-IT alignment issues.

5.4 BUSINESS AND IT ALIGNMENT PROBLEMS

CIOs are very concerned about the mismatch of business and IT since it can lead to several problems and challenges that impede an organization's growth. Business-IT alignment challenges and issues develop when organizations seek to integrate their IT and business strategies. By ensuring that the technology employed by the organization supports its entire mission and goals, this alignment strives to achieve business goals. The organization uses IT to increase productivity and market competitiveness, boosting financial performance.

According to a recent study, 94% of CIOs believe that their teams must prepare for the future. Furthermore, only 49% of CIOs believe they have the power to make choices that significantly affect the entire business. These figures highlight how crucial it is for CIOs to actively address the problems they face. To close the gap and effectively articulate the value of IT efforts, CIOs must proactively engage with the C-suite and other vital stakeholders. It is crucial to illustrate the strategic importance of technology and how it could affect the organization's success as a whole.

Understanding business needs and concerns is one of the main obstacles to business and IT alignment. Many misaligned enterprises want assistance communicating technology management challenges to their business partners in a way that makes sense. This lack of understanding can create a significant barrier to achieving business goals. Michael Hyatt says, "*In organizations, misalignment is the silent killer. It saps energy, slows execution, and erodes trust*". The "*Alignment Trap*" poses a potential threat, as concentrating solely on achieving alignment could impede the IT department's ability to reach optimal IT performance. Merely aligning IT with the business may result in suboptimal outcomes without considering other vital factors.

Patrick Lencioni states, "*A lack of alignment can turn the best strategy into a series of disconnected actions that lead to nowhere.*" A poorly understood or erroneous IT alignment strategy may result in clarity and comprehension, but it may also cause organizational and business processes to be out of alignment. Business executives may need to be informed about their companies' technological possibilities or IT problems. This ignorance can be a roadblock for many firms looking to match business strategy and IT infrastructure. Utilizing effective business management frameworks that assist in bridging the gap between technology and organization needs is crucial for overcoming these difficulties. Agility, operational effectiveness, and a strategic approach that integrates technology with the organization's objective are necessary for achieving this alignment.

Successful IT alignment supports business strategy and ensures IT resources align with other business operations. It can be challenging to achieve this alignment, however. Stressed management consultants and executives frequently require assistance coordinating their goals with those of other units, leading to inconsistent systems, procedures, and behaviors. Researchers and consultants promote a strategic strategy that combines technology with the organization's objective to overcome these obstacles. Proper business IT alignment is crucial for shared goal achievement, organization transformation, new revenue streams, and enhanced customer service. However, organizations require assistance in coordinating business and IT. One of the significant challenges is defining KPIs that can measure the benefits to the organization and its customers.

Matching an organization's technology requirements with its objectives presents another complex problem for IT business alignment. To tackle these challenges, experts advise using a strategic approach that combines technology and mission. Any corporation must balance its IT and business strategy, which takes time and effort. It calls for organizational restructuring, business change, and strategic alignment to achieve maximum efficiency. Unfortunately, many firms struggle to integrate IT with their business operations due to poor departmental communication, a lack of staff ability, and organizational misalignment.

There needs to be more than technology skills to achieve alignment; interpersonal skills are also crucial in the commercial world. The organization may rotate its IT staff to enhance mutual understanding of jobs and organization knowledge. As advised by consultants and researchers, overcoming these difficulties calls for a strategic strategy that unifies technology with the organization's objective. However, a lack of organizational changes within the IT industry might result in problems and issues with business-IT alignment. Other essential business lines can grasp how to structure their IT successfully with the support of close departmental coordination and top management.

According to a research paper published by Puspita (2021), most firms concur that closer business and IT collaboration could optimize their service and product delivery. The technology operates in a very different manner from conventional business structures. Stereotypes contribute to the spread of untrue notions about how IT and business interact. Because they think IT is too complex to understand, non-IT personnel may need to know that IT is involved in fundamental revenue-generating activities like sales, marketing, customer service, Etc.

Below are some typical business and IT alignment problems that CIOs may encounter:

Resistance to Change: Business divisions may resist IT-driven changes if seen as disruptive or out of step with their objectives. This opposition can impede alignment attempts and slow down IT initiatives.

Siloed Departments: Silos between IT and other business divisions can restrict communication and sharing of knowledge and resources, making it difficult for the organization to work cohesively.

Lack of Clear Communication: Communication problems between business executives and IT teams can lead to misunderstandings, a lack of alignment of priorities, and a failure to transform business objectives into workable IT strategies.

Lack of IT Governance: Scope creep, budget overruns, and initiatives that fail to produce the anticipated business value can result from inadequate governance and supervision of IT projects.

Inadequate Skills and Resources: The organization's capacity to successfully implement its IT strategy may need more IT personnel or resources.

Mismatched Priorities: It can squander resources and lose possibilities for innovation and growth when the strategic business and IT priorities are out of sync.

Technology Complexity: IT may need help to react quickly to shifting business needs due to complex and out-of-date IT systems, which can cause delays, higher costs, and a lack of agility.

Unclear Metrics and KPIs: It can be challenging to gauge the effects of IT projects on the business without defined KPIs and metrics, which makes it challenging to show alignment.

Short-Term Focus: Making IT decisions that prioritize current demands above long-term strategic alignment may be forced by pressure to achieve quick results.

Vendor and Outsourcing Challenges: Poorly managed vendor relationships or outsourcing contracts may lead to IT solutions that fall short of expectations or must align with organization goals.

Legacy Systems and Technical Debt: The ability of IT to adapt to evolving business requirements may be constrained when legacy systems are cost-effective to maintain and inadequately integrated with modern technologies.

Compliance and Security Risks: The organization may be subject to legal, regulatory, and security issues if IT standards do not align with compliance requirements or cybersecurity standards.

Lack of Business Understanding in IT: IT teams may find it difficult to provide solutions that are genuinely in line with business needs if they do not have a thorough understanding of the operations and goals of the organization.

Changing Business Environment: Rapid changes in the business environment, such as changes in the market or economic interruptions, can make it difficult for IT to stay in line with changing business priorities.

The formation of clear governance structures, a dedication to open communication, aggressive leadership from the CIO, and a focus on creating a culture of collaboration and continual improvement between IT and the rest of the business are all necessary to address these alignment issues. CIOs must continuously evaluate and modify their plans to ensure that IT successfully manages the organization's changing needs.

5.5 BENEFITS OF BUSINESS-IT ALIGNMENT

In the corporate realm, CIOs recognize the pivotal role technology plays. Leveraging information technology strategically can afford businesses a substantial competitive edge. In the swiftly evolving landscape of technology, companies should select specialized tools that align with their objectives and industry. Since technology is leveling the playing field, small businesses must stand out. A company's ability to establish its unique position and generate revenue, save costs, expand its market, automate processes, allocate workers more efficiently, cut overhead costs, and enhance customer service can all be achieved through the strategic use of technology.

CIOs understand, though, that technology cannot replace human resources. For overall performance, cooperation between the IT and HR departments is essential. By coordinating their goals, this teamwork guarantees that staff members are happy, efficient, and skilled at utilizing technology to their maximum advantage. Businesses can achieve sustainable growth and success through this synergistic strategy, as technology smoothly complements and enriches the personnel. In this arrangement, the CIO acts as the company's conductor, enabling the seamless integration of technology across the enterprise and enhancing all aspects of its architecture.

The CIO's function is crucial in today's tech-driven world since technology is ingrained in almost every area of our daily lives. Through their leadership and technological know-how, CIOs enable enterprises to thrive in an interconnected world and leave a lasting impression on their respective industries. Numerous significant advantages result from this alignment, including improved customer satisfaction, agility and flexibility, operational efficiency, and cost optimization. To sum up, to gain a competitive advantage, increase customer happiness, nurture agility and adaptation, improve operational efficiency, and minimize costs, enterprises must strategically integrate technology with business objectives. The company's success in the digital era depends on the CIO's leadership in guiding this alignment.

The organization gains from improved customer satisfaction and loyalty when customer interactions are consistent and realistic. Instead of constantly developing new solutions, CIOs play a critical role in managing system alignment of business goals through standardization and reuse of mature components to pursue organizational agility. By reducing system variety and scalability issues, this strategy improves organizational agility and allows the organization to react quickly to shifting market demands. Operational effectiveness is crucial for CIOs; however, establishing additional connections with vendors, customers, and service providers may be necessary to ensure continuous development.

IT and IS (Information Systems) must be well-aligned with the demands of these interactions to achieve effectiveness. CIOs should consider more extensive organizational alignment requirements in addition to iterative development for cost reduction efforts. Lack of coordination might result in higher capital expenses and inconsistent solutions that are challenging to support. On the other hand, alignment makes standardization and consolidation easier, which reduces costs. Additionally, alignment planning encourages CIO-led firms to assess their systems' efficacy regarding various variables, such as legal, compliance, and regulatory needs. Increasing alignment supports the organization's overall risk management strategy by managing risks and improving insight into possible threats.

In summary, CIOs are crucial to achieving organizational objectives for improving customer service, agility, operational effectiveness, and risk management. CIOs may promote positive change, enhance customer experiences, streamline operations, and achieve cost savings by putting alignment first and cultivating solid connections.

5.6 BUSINESS IT ALIGNMENT IMPLICATIONS

According to author James C. Collins, "*Building a visionary organization requires one percent vision and 99 percent alignment*". Successful integration of IT with the overall mission and strategy of the organization can result in improved performance, financial stability, and market competitiveness. Effective communication among departments is vital for the success of alignment implementation. Regular review of the integration management process is necessary to ensure it aligns with the organization's objectives. IT is a tool that businesses use to achieve their goals, and consequently, maintaining a strong alignment between IT and business is of utmost importance.

According to John C Maxwell, "*Great leaders are willing to sacrifice their interests for the team's good. They understand that alignment and teamwork are more important than individual success*". IT and business strategies must be synchronized to collaborate effectively and efficiently on shared goals. This alignment requires robust communication between business and IT leaders and linking multiple business units. Additionally, agility is essential because it enables businesses to streamline operations and swiftly respond to market changes. Business IT alignment is necessary to meet corporate requirements, improve customer service, and guarantee the adoption of suitable IT solutions. Regular reviews are required to ensure that IT and business are in sync. Although IT solutions can facilitate organizational transformation, careful planning and attention to KPIs are essential.

By coordinating their business and IT strategies, firms can increase their agility by maximizing their revenue sources. Maximizing revenue can be accomplished by coordinating business strategy with IT objectives, which have various advantages, such as achieving organization goals, increasing earnings, and increasing productivity. The benefits of this alignment may take some time to manifest, but they are well worth the wait. Modern technology is essential for enabling firms to align their strategies and benefit from them. Organizations can enhance quality by prioritizing IT-business alignment.

Procter & Gamble, a multinational consumer goods organization, sought assistance in aligning its business and IT objectives to stimulate development and innovation across its diverse brands. To increase agility and efficiency, P&G understood how critical it was to integrate its business and IT divisions. The corporation completely reorganized its IT department by forming cross-functional teams and collaborating closely with different business units. This shift made it necessary to connect IT initiatives to clearly defined business objectives, such as enhancing consumer interaction and supply chain management.

P&G achieved remarkable results by fostering a superb connection between business and IT. For instance, the firm created a Demand Signal Repository (DSR) that integrates sales, inventory, and point-of-sale data to give real-time insights. P&G was able to adapt quickly to market shifts and streamline its supply chain operations. Business-IT alignment activities increased revenue, lower expenses, and higher customer satisfaction. Impacts on business and IT alignment are crucial because they specify how IT and business strategy interact. Managers in industry and IT can collaborate to accomplish shared objectives. This coordination's primary goal is to ensure that IT supports and carries out business activities efficiently. The benefits are relevant to the corporation and its various departments for the coordination between business units and IT.

CIO to review the practices, plans, procedures, shared knowledge, and crucial performance metrics of the IT and business departments to ensure alignment. Achieving enterprise IT alignment has several implications that organizations must consider. Above all, the framework must link business demands with IT goals, ensure technology layers meet current IT requirements, and identify reoccurring patterns. Another impact of employing conventional EA frameworks is the dissemination of corporate information, which enhances strategic agility.

5.7 ESSENTIAL TRAITS FOR A CIO ENABLING BUSINESS-IT ALIGNMENT

To effectively facilitate business-IT alignment, a CIO must be exceptionally strategic and aware of corporate goals and technical capabilities. Strong communication abilities are also essential since they enable the CIO to act as a liaison between IT specialists and business executives, promoting cooperation and guaranteeing that technological projects are in perfect sync with the company's overall goals. A CIO must exhibit the following qualities to carry out this responsibility effectively:

Intellectual Honesty: A successful CIO should exhibit intellectual integrity by giving direct responses, even when they may not be well received. Making decisions without the influence of one's prejudices or outside influences requires using correct data and strong reasoning.

Cultural Fit: A CIO must be a great cultural fit for the business. The CIO can match their approach and conduct with the organization's culture by comprehending and embracing its values, conventions, and objectives. Cultural fit encourages more profound connections with coworkers and stakeholders, fostering teamwork and effective communication.

Holistic Perspective: Successful CIOs can see the larger picture and have a holistic perspective. CIOs may make well-informed decisions that benefit the organization by considering their actions' potential ramifications and consequences across various dimensions.

By exhibiting these qualities, CIOs contribute significantly to organizational alignment, improved performance, and increased competitiveness. Alignment is essential to accomplish organizational objectives and ensure a successful and long-lasting business strategy. CIOs help organizations succeed in a constantly shifting business environment with strategic insight and leadership. Practical communication abilities are of utmost importance for CIOs. They must communicate their thoughts, ideas, and choices to all technical and non-technical stakeholders. CIOs may ensure that their organization's initiatives are aligned, understood, and supported by effective communication.

In conclusion, an effective CIO should possess several crucial traits. They should demonstrate intellectual integrity, match the organization's culture well, have a global outlook, and have excellent communication abilities. These qualities enable CIOs to drive the effective alignment of information and technology resources with the broader business strategy, make informed decisions, create strong connections, and do so. As a result, CIOs play a pivotal role in steering the organization toward success, fostering innovation, and embracing the transformative potential of technology.

CHAPTER 6
HOW CIO CREATES SYNERGY: INCREASING BUSINESS-IT ALIGNMENT TO UNLOCK VALUE

INTRODUCTION

In today's dynamic organizational context, innovation and long-term success are contingent upon the interdependence of IT and business. This chapter gives readers a thorough overview of the problematic area of business-IT alignment, highlighting its challenges, intricacies, and revolutionary potential to improve businesses. We dissect the elements required for a successful alignment between IT operations and business strategy, viewing these attributes as the cornerstone of a seamless integration that fosters corporate expansion.

Nonetheless, there are obstacles in the way of a successful alignment. In this chapter, we investigate the extensive ramifications of aligning business and IT, offering a thorough viewpoint on the impacts that ripple across an organization, influencing its operational environment and strategic orientation. The central focus of this investigation is value generation within the framework of the Business-IT alignment paradigm. It demonstrates how the collaboration of technology and business improves operations and stimulates innovation, efficiency, and, eventually, value creation.

The chapter lays out strategies for achieving successful business-IT alignment, moving from theoretical considerations to practical insights. These strategies work as pillars, providing businesses with a road map to successfully negotiate the complex terrain and realize the full advantages of a well-coordinated business-IT alignment. The alignment journey encompasses distinct stages, each presenting unique opportunities and challenges. The goal is to comprehensively understand companies' evolutionary paths toward achieving optimal business-IT alignment. Governance systems are examined as vital tools to steer the alignment process toward strategic objectives, ensuring planned and sustainable change. Navigating the complex landscape of IT-business alignment requires a multidisciplinary approach.

This chapter delves into practical strategies companies can employ to maintain constant synchronization between their IT and business processes. Exploring the latest advancements in IT-business alignment, we emphasize the importance of cultivating a forward-looking mindset for businesses to evolve and thrive in an ever-changing environment. Join us on this captivating journey through each chapter as we dissect the business-IT alignment process, uncovering its future implications crucial for the success and adaptability of businesses in the digital age.

6.1 KEY SUCCESS FACTORS FOR BUSINESS-IT ALIGNMENT

Success is the accomplishment of an aim or purpose. It is the achievement of a goal, the attainment of a desired outcome, or the favorable outcome of an endeavor. Success factors are the elements or conditions that are crucial for achieving success. They are the key components, characteristics, or variables significantly contributing to accomplishing goals. Effective communication, collaboration, strategic planning, governance, change management, and ITSM are crucial success criteria for a CIO's business-IT alignment. By concentrating on these aspects, the CIO can ensure that IT efforts support organizational success and that technology expenditures align with business goals.

Industry analysts explain that a good CIO's career is built on a foundation of both failed and successful attempts. Even if failures offer priceless teaching moments, it is just as crucial for CIOs to have a portfolio of accomplished projects. These accomplishments demonstrate their capacity to finish essential projects that influence the bottom line and keep them current in their industry. All CIOs want to see projects through to completion, be recognized for their work, and effectively lead and manage teams.

However, how a CIO handles projects that stray from the intended course is the real test of their effectiveness. What takes place if an endeavor fails? Can a CIO still be considered adequate in these situations? A sensible CIO will build a portfolio including failed and successful ventures. Every CIO should take failures seriously and view them as chances for development and enhancement. CIOs need an incident response plan to prepare for unforeseen issues and efficiently manage expectations. It is crucial to watch what works and what does not. To prevent worst-case situations, plan and anticipate possible problems. The secret is to persevere in facing difficulties and learn lessons from failures.

Discussions on company failures are typically lacking, even though many people are happy to share their accomplishments. Accepting failure is essential for professional and personal growth, yet people may be reluctant to admit their mistakes out of shame. Regrettably, making excuses for mistakes made can result in them happening again. In this situation, the CIO's role is critical and demands a firm recognition that failure is just a mismatch—a misalignment that can be fixed with ongoing learning and flexibility.

According to a research report, making informed judgments about IT investments is crucial for accomplishing strategic goals in today's dynamic corporate environment, according to Parida (2020). A key facilitator in this process is the practice of service portfolio management within a business. Before implementing new services, it is crucial to show a strong business case that substantiates a clear return on investment instead of embracing them solely because it is the norm in the sector. Service portfolio management becomes indispensable when carefully balancing customer expectations with the financial commitment required by the business to develop and deliver services.

The service strategy assumes a pivotal role for CIOs as it involves a comprehensive assessment of the effectiveness of IT services in alignment with stated plans and desired objectives. By strategically identifying areas needing adjustment, the CIO ensures increased efficacy through ongoing evaluation and monitoring. Business relationship management (BRM), a potent tool for CIOs, makes it easier for clients and the IT service provider to communicate strategically and tactically. By comprehending the client's unique business requirements, BRM equips CIOs to forge and maintain a solid commercial relationship with clients. Additionally, BRM synchronizes business objectives with service provider operations, empowering CIOs to deliver outcomes that successfully address the organization's changing requirements. Service Level Management (SLM) for CIOs guarantees that all current and upcoming IT services align with set and attainable goals. This thorough procedure entails an ongoing cycle of deliberations, decision-making, documenting, reviewing, and reporting on IT service goals and accomplishments.

In addition to this, the following factors also help a CIO in doing business-IT alignment:

Common Aims and Purposes: A CIO should set shared targets and goals that the business and IT departments can strive toward. By doing this, it is ensured that IT initiatives directly assist the overarching organizational goal.

Support and Involvement of Leadership: It is imperative to have strong leadership support, particularly from the C-suite and senior executives. Initiatives aimed at achieving IT-business alignment need to be actively supported by leaders.

Clear Communication: Business executives and IT executives must communicate openly and transparently. Each party must comprehend the other's objectives, difficulties, and priorities.

Strategic Planning: Align IT projects with overarching company strategy through strategic planning. Plans and initiatives related to IT should have a direct impact on accomplishing business goals and improving organizational performance.

Cross-Functional Collaboration: A CIO should encourage cross-functional cooperation between the IT and different business divisions. Cross-functional teams have the potential to improve comprehension, streamline communication, and produce IT solutions that are more successful.

Technology Investment Strategy: A CIO should create a plan for your technology investments that considers business priorities. Give top priority to investments that help the organization achieve its goals and provide measurable returns.

Vendor management: A CIO should skillfully handle connections with IT vendors to guarantee that outside services and solutions meet the company's wants and advance its commercial objectives.

Data Governance and Security: A CIO should establish strong data governance and security protocols to safeguard confidential data, guarantee adherence to legal requirements, and promote confidence between business and IT departments.

Continuous Improvement: A CIO should create a culture that is focused on continual improvement. Review and modify IT-business alignment plans regularly in response to user input, evolving business needs, and new technological developments.

IT Governance: A CIO should guarantee that IT activities align with business priorities, adhere to legal requirements, and efficiently manage risks, implement robust IT governance frameworks.

Agile and Adaptive Culture: A CIO should encourage an organizational culture that places a high importance on flexibility and agility. Effective IT-business alignment depends on having the agility to quickly adapt to shifting business requirements.

User satisfaction and involvement: A CIO should prioritize user satisfaction and involve end users in IT decision-making. User-friendly IT solutions are more likely to be adopted and influence business performance.

Performance Measurement and Metrics: A CIO should establish and monitor KPIs that show how well IT efforts achieve their intended business outcomes. Review and modify tactics regularly in light of performance indicators.

Change Management: When introducing new IT solutions or procedures, a CIO should use efficient change management techniques to handle resistance and guarantee seamless transitions.

Aligning and developing skills: A CIO should make sure that IT teams have the know-how to recognize and tackle business concerns. Ongoing initiatives for training and development can fill skill shortages.

6.2 PHASES OF BUSINESS-IT ALIGNMENT

The use of technology to optimize business operations in line with the overall business plan is included in the business and IT alignment stage in the context of the CIO's Phases in IT and organizational alignment. To guarantee that the organization moves forward in a technically aligned manner, this phase entails coordination between technical and business leadership teams. During the business and IT alignment phase, it is critical to understand how IT and business strategy are interconnected. Business leaders, IT, and business teams must work together to improve operational performance and organizational agility. Creating a bridge between these groups makes it easier to create plans that improve agility and dismantle traditional silos. Putting in place a technical framework can help with communication. The first step towards fixing alignment problems is admitting they exist, as we cannot solve what we cannot see.

The business and IT alignment stage is a strategy that connects the goals of the technology department with the organization's business and strategic objectives. Increasing business agility, stimulating innovation, and enabling change are all components of promoting IT business alignment. When the right technology is used with business goals, employees are motivated to contribute to the organization's most important performance indicators. Additionally, it guarantees that IT systems align with corporate goals, improving customer service. To do this, corporate information must be effectively distributed among all departments, and IT personnel must be constantly exposed to new technologies that can improve departmental productivity. Success requires CIOs to break down their corporate goals into more minor, manageable activities.

An organization's operation can only be strategically aligned to meet its various business tasks and objectives if a dedicated effort is made toward business and technology innovations, process improvements, and operational goal alignment. By cooperating, businesses may optimize their technology investments, eliminate obstacles, reduce inefficiencies, and manage operational risk. The IT organization should integrate improvement projects by continuously planning, executing, monitoring, and assessing them. Efficiency can only be produced by holding executive-level meetings, which bring together key industry stakeholders to discuss the organization's objectives and how technology may help them.

IT business alignment requires satisfying business needs and accounting for business outcomes by providing knowledgeable approaches, plans, and methods for fusing IT operations with business divisions. Executives must comprehend the significance of metrics and KPIs to evaluate the effectiveness of their technological systems and processes. By partnering with LLC Services, businesses can access industry-leading knowledge for enhanced technical alignment. The successful operation of any firm depends on the ongoing, never-ending, and usually ignored task of aligning IT with business.

Below are some of the steps followed by CIOs for business and IT alignment.

Identify the organization's Drivers: The CIO determines the business requirements guiding IT in this step. Under what business circumstances is IT enablement necessary? Is the company introducing a completely new product or service? Will it change its practices to acquire another company? It is essential to periodically recognize that these business requirements are dynamic to take appropriate action. The CIO ascertains the organization's drivers by examining its strategies, speaking with business stakeholders, doing a gap analysis, identifying KPIs and KRAs, setting priorities for IT initiatives, creating a roadmap, and communicating the procedure.

Create IT Vision: The IT vision provides projects with clear direction, and the alignment guarantees that IT expenditures provide value for the firm. To satisfy business priorities, this step determines the IT capabilities, which consist of strategy, processes, infrastructure, and organization. The fundamental rules or directives that direct the development of an IT capability are outlined in this vision. Remember that, depending on their presumptions, two people may respond differently to identical expectations. Before answering the IT Capability question, defining these fundamental attitudes and values in a vision is imperative. The procedures a CIO uses to create IT-business alignment include:

- Developing the IT vision.
- Identifying the IT capabilities.

- Defining the IT objectives.
- Aligning IT investments.
- Engaging stakeholders.

Evaluation of Current Alignment: Finding improvement areas and evaluating how well IT and the business are aligned is essential. By assessing the alignment between IT and the business, the CIO can identify areas for improvement and develop a plan to achieve IT-business alignment. The roadmap must be routinely examined and revised in light of shifting goals and the business climate. The CIO assesses the existing alignment by comprehending the business strategy, identifying the business processes, evaluating the IT infrastructure and performance, reviewing the IT investments, interacting with business stakeholders, and creating an action plan.

Find Alignment Gaps: The CIO can create a thorough plan to integrate IT and business processes by examining the disparities between IT and the business. The CIO has to review and adjust the roadmap to ensure that IT investments continue to benefit the business. Comparing the planned or "to-be" IT capabilities with the current or "as-is" IT capabilities is necessary to identify misalignment gaps. Potential fixes can be chosen after the fundamental problems are identified. Achieving IT-business alignment requires identifying areas where the business and IT can work together more effectively. A CIO can find gaps in IT alignment through establishing business objectives, evaluating IT capabilities, communicating with business stakeholders, conducting gap analysis, prioritizing IT tasks, and developing action plans.

IT project priorities: CIOs must prioritize IT projects to match their objectives with the company's. CIOs manage resources, risk, finance, process optimization, and IT project alignment with business goals. By doing this, CIOs may add to the organization's growth and demonstrate their value. The business process optimization, risk management, budgetary allocation, and resource allocation are all impacted by the CIO's project priorities, affecting IT and business alignment.

Review of possible business IT implementations: CIOs may use various business IT implementation techniques to incorporate IT within the company. Some methods include the top-down strategy, Agile methodology, IT governance, business process re-engineering, and business-driven IT. These strategies are tools that CIOs can use to ensure that IT projects closely align with the organization's strategic goals and objectives.

Adjust IT Strategy: CIOs must regularly adjust their IT and business alignment approach to guarantee that IT initiatives stay aligned with the organization's goals and objectives. To change their IT and business alignment approach, they should evaluate their business objectives, monitor IT projects, work with business executives, update IT governance, and introduce new technology. CIOs can achieve this by ensuring that IT projects closely match the changing demands of the company. The CIO should monitor internal and external business environment developments and identify appropriate solutions. According to Moreau (2018), senior management must ensure they do not keep trying failed strategies. Using a sizable budget in an unpleasant circumstance is not a good idea. CIOs who take on these difficult choices benefit from them.

6.3 APPROACHES FOR ACHIEVING SEAMLESS BUSINESS-IT ALIGNMENT

CIOs use a range of strategic techniques to accomplish seamless integration between IT and business operations because they recognize technology's critical role in the success of contemporary organizations. These strategies cover a variety of tasks, procedures, and structures:

Understand the business: IT leaders must understand the organization's aims, goals, and workings. This information enables them to create solutions that meet particular business demands and coordinate IT initiatives with the overarching business plan.

IT as a vision enabler: An organization's overall business plan is amplified and supported by efficient IT departments, which act as facilitators. IT may contribute to the business's success and assist in realizing its vision by comprehending and cooperating with the business plan.

Communicate the value of IT: The CIO should inform business stakeholders about the potential and benefits of IT. IT leaders should do this successfully, and value communication entails demonstrating how technology can spur creativity, boost productivity, and accomplish organizational objectives.

Involve business stakeholders in decision-making: Transparency, cooperation, and shared ownership are encouraged by involving business stakeholders in the decision-making procedure for IT initiatives. They involve business stakeholder's guarantees that technological investments receive the required support and meet business requirements.

Align IT metrics with business outcomes: IT executives should create metrics and performance measures that complement corporate goals. Aligning IT metrics makes it possible to gauge how IT affects the organization and to have fruitful dialogues about its benefits.

Prioritize projects based on business impact: A CIO should prioritize projects based on their potential to produce measurable business advantages. IT may show its worth to the organization by concentrating on efforts that directly result in revenue growth, cost savings, customer happiness, or other important KPIs.

Continuously evaluate and adapt: CIOs should periodically evaluate how well IT initiatives fit with changing business requirements. This constant assessment enables modifications and improvements to ensure IT is responsive and aligned with the organization's shifting needs.

Clear communication about technology: Communication regarding technology should be clear; CIOs should outline the underlying ideas and prerequisites when talking to business executives about technologies like AI. Clear communication enables IT leaders to create a workable implementation strategy by assisting them in comprehending the capabilities and constraints of the technology.

Listening and learning from business counterparts: CIOs should actively listen to their business counterparts and ask them to share their thoughts and goals to learn from them. This cooperative method guarantees that IT projects align with business needs and objectives and helps prevent speculative thinking.

Interpersonal interactions for alignment: Building strong relationships with coworkers in different departments, like marketing or accounting, enables IT employees to understand their difficulties better and collaborate to discover solutions. A CIO should ask the correct questions when interacting with business colleagues to enable effective IT and business alignment.

A CIO should use the following methods for business and IT alignment:

Understand the Business Goals: Before working with business leaders, the CIO should thoroughly know the organization's strategic objectives, market trends, and difficulties. This understanding allows them to make informed inquiries that harmonize IT projects with the overarching business direction.

Listen Actively: A CIO should consider corporate executives' worries, priorities, and ideas. A CIO should pay attention to how they see technology as a tool for attaining their objectives. The CIO will be able to obtain essential insights from this and tailor their inquiries accordingly.

Bridge the Gap: Business executives will have difficulty understanding IT jargon and concepts. A CIO should ask inquiries in plain language that non-technical people can understand. To maintain clear communication and understanding between parties, a CIO should avoid jargon and utilize simple language.

Collaborate and Educate: One of the responsibilities of the CIO is to inform organization executives about the potential of technological solutions. Ask questions that encourage discussions about how technology might help with particular business difficulties, improve business operations, improve consumer experiences, or spur creativity.

Focus on Results: A CIO should focus on the business value and intended outcomes rather than the most minor details. Kindly ask what part IT can play in increasing efficiency, cutting expenses, and achieving a competitive advantage, which will illustrate the alignment between IT initiatives and organizational objectives.

Continuously Learn: A CIO should learn new things constantly because the business and IT landscapes always change. Keep abreast of business trends, new technologies, and best practices. A CIO can encourage meaningful discussions that align IT and more general business objectives by posing the correct questions, listening intently, and encouraging collaboration. A CIO should also strive to stay ahead of the curve by reading industry publications, attending conferences, and participating in professional networks. He should also stay current on applicable laws and regulations to ensure that IT is compliant with all regulations. Finally, a CIO should seek out mentors and advisors to gain expertise and guidance.

6.4 CHALLENGES, STRATEGIES, AND SUCCESS STORIES FOR ACHIEVING EFFECTIVE BUSINESS-IT ALIGNMENT

Recognizing the distinct IT alignment requirements of each organization, CIOs play a crucial role in addressing these challenges and formulating a coherent alignment plan tailored to the specific needs and objectives of the business. They are instrumental in formulating a coherent alignment plan tailored to the specific needs and objectives of the business. The initial steps towards achieving effective business-IT alignment involve acknowledging the unique characteristics of IT alignment within an organization and resolving any areas of misalignment. According to Rasenber (2020), this practical viewpoint provides priceless insights for recognizing possibilities and barriers along the path to alignment. Below are various alignments which a CIO could do in his organization:

Strategic Alignment: According to Hilgetag (2020), strategy-driven efforts are often central to IT and business alignment. Strategic alignment calls for a thorough comprehension of the portfolio of IT projects created to address the needs and preferences of the business community specifically. Strategic alignment includes the actual IT projects and the budget complexities closely related to the company's overall strategy. This strategy-driven alignment emphasizes results, especially when providing IT services.

Operational Alignment: According to Mawela's 2021 study, the IT department must create an operational plan that works harmoniously with its operational protocols to achieve operational alignment. Operational alignment is more focused on the practical completion of tasks than strategy-driven alignment, which is more achievement-oriented, particularly in IT service delivery.

Calendar Alignment: Calendar alignment involves speed, timeliness, and synchronization with the organization's recurring calendar. This element enhances consistency in the timing and sequencing of essential initiatives by ensuring that interconnected organizational activities align, including the budget calendar, IT vision, and strategy.

Economic Alignment: As evidenced by Khatoon's (2020) and Martini's (2018) studies, economic alignment becomes increasingly essential when IT continuously suggests projects and allocates funds to different groups. This strategy makes sure that everyone in the company has the same understanding of expenses. IT cost management is different from other departmental cost management in that it requires careful thought out how budgeting, monitoring, and reporting activities match up with a CIO's viewpoint and presentation of expenses.

Cultural Alignment: AiZhan (2018) in his research claims that cultural alignment needs to be sensitive to the organization's general perspective on technology, handle technological issues, and consider the character and suitability of IT staff members as essential members of a larger community. The distinct characteristics of each organization and its departments contribute to a corporate identity that might take time to articulate. However, the CIO can observe and negotiate these cultural dynamics from a distance because of their astute viewpoint.

Converging organizational goals with IT is essential for success in the dynamic world of modern business. Attaining smooth alignment between IT and business is a big issue, especially for CIOs who are in charge of organizing this collaboration. A strategic alliance between IT and business operations is more critical than ever as firms rely more and more on technology to spur innovation, efficiency, and growth. In this chapter, we look into the key tactics that enable CIOs to connect IT and business, ensuring that IT projects are not only in line with but also connected to the organization's overarching objectives. CIOs create the path for a harmonious partnership between IT and business departments, driving the organization toward sustainable performance and increased value creation through proactive cooperation, effective communication, and strategic decision-making.

CIOs can use frameworks that make integrating IT with business objectives easier to improve IT management and shape the organization's future course. The solutions cycle framework is a popular methodology that provides valuable information for matching technology solutions to organizational strategy. By implementing this method, CIOs may effectively manage their IT portfolio and guarantee that it remains aligned with the overarching business strategy. Improving transparency in the use of IT resources requires the use of roadmaps and KPIs. Because of increased openness, organizations are better equipped to make educated decisions about future technology investments.

CIOs can use a wide range of technology tools and solutions to help facilitate the transition of business and IT alignment. Using online brainstorming tools, for example, encourages ideation and makes it possible for team members to share and choose creative ideas together. Data analytics tools allow CIOs to examine customer interactions in detail and spot trends and new business opportunities. CIOs must develop a multi-cultural mentality and match IT personnel with the organizational culture to accomplish business-IT alignment. Every organization has different requirements for IT alignment, just as all person's fingerprints are different. As no two hands have the same fingerprints, are there different IT alignment settings?

Depending on specific conditions and organizational nature, misalignment may be influenced by one or more factors like strategic alignment with business, cultural alignment, multi-cultural alignment, resource alignment and structural alignment.

Indra Nooyi, the former CEO of PepsiCo, underlined Information Technology's role in fostering innovation and organizational success. To achieve seamless business-IT alignment, Jody Davids, PepsiCo's CIO, concentrated on comprehending the organization's objectives and engaging with business executives.

A CIO's initiatives ensure that technological solutions smoothly mesh with the organization's overall business objectives when pursuing business-IT alignment. Without considering the company plan, merely implementing technology solutions might result in inefficiencies and improper distribution of crucial resources. Alignment barriers must be found and eliminated for IT to properly guide the company toward its strategic objectives and fully utilize technology's potential for process improvement.

The technology decisions a CIO makes can have a long-term impact on the business. Finding the appropriate course of action might be challenging, especially when seeking clarification on best practices. Since each CIO operates differently, there has yet to be a clear answer to this question. Consulting with experienced peers or seeking guidance from other CIOs in various organizations can be a valuable resource. They might surprise the CIO with their willingness to share their insights. Building connections with other CIOs through networking helps obtain support and achieve future success. It is important to remember that there is no one-size-fits-all solution, but seeking assistance can expand the CIO's knowledge and enhance the CIO's decision-making abilities.

6.5 BUSINESS-IT ALIGNMENT, GOVERNANCE, AND TRANSFORMATION

Technology plays a pivotal role in business-IT alignment, governance, and transformation in the contemporary service-oriented economy. It is a crucial factor that sets service providers apart. In today's competitive market, successful businesses embrace technology to improve customer engagement, differentiate services, and streamline processes. A CIO must ensure that technology investments support the organization's objectives and use technology to provide top-notch services. A CIO demonstrates careful attention by listing potential issues and possible solutions. With this, a CIO can implement initiatives and professionalism, two highly valued qualities.

When a CIO reports to the C-suite, it is much more critical to approach the C Suite with solutions rather than concerns. This strategy demonstrates the CIO's proactive mentality and ability to manage a technology department's challenges successfully. It also exhibits the CIO's strategic thinking regarding how technology may enhance the organization's success. A CIO should establish himself as a valuable asset by continually demonstrating his ability to overcome obstacles, provide improvement suggestions, and integrate technology with business goals. As a result, the CIO will gain a reputation as a reliable partner in promoting technological innovation, operational excellence, and business expansion.

A synergistic combination of process enhancements and technology use generates a value chain. It plays a crucial part in enabling and transforming organizational processes, which boosts productivity and creates value throughout the whole value chain. The ability of IT to deliver real-time information, automate processes, and seamlessly connect diverse business systems is a crucial component of Information Technology's value generation. By eliminating inefficiencies, this integration improves corporate performance. Additionally, IT enables businesses to grow by leveraging economies of scale and exploring new geographical and online market niches. The seamless user experience provided by IT solutions, regardless of location or time of use, further increases business potential.

Effective IT and business function collaboration is crucial to achieving these advantages. IT can develop into a transformative instrument and a long-lasting source of competitive advantage with effective teamwork. By working together, businesses can fully utilize Information Technology's capabilities and strategically integrate them with their long-term objectives. Organizations may use technology to generate innovation, optimize processes, and achieve a significant competitive advantage in the market by appreciating the value that IT delivers and encouraging a collaborative atmosphere. As a result, IT develops into a strategic asset that fosters the success and growth of businesses.

6.6 STRENGTHENING BUSINESS-IT ALIGNMENT FOR VALUE CREATION

A CIO must engage various levers to achieve alignment, with project and program management standing out as one of the most critical. Studies indicate that approximately 83% of initiatives should deliver the expected business value and ROIs. Appropriate frameworks ensure that projects and initiatives intended for revenue generation continue adding value beyond completion. The CIO should analyze an organization's business challenges as a case study and devise solutions. Ideally, every case study should end with important conclusions or suggestions that can be applied to develop long-term approaches to problem-solving.

The CIO has to align Business and IT with the organization's growth plan, integrate technology advancements into services that add value, and maintain secure, seamless business operations. This goes beyond having skilled program and project managers. Improving the traditional centralized IT and decentralized business-IT alignment models is necessary. A modern framework that preserves a centrally managed technological base while promoting decentralized decision-making is essential. The CIO plays a vital role in this process, helping to modify innovation and renovation within the IT organization to meet the evolving needs of the business.

CIOs are responsible for developing protocols, processes, and governance structures to support a culture of quick invention and ongoing development. The IT organizational structure needs to elevate the bar for customer service by quickly converting creative ideas into functional capabilities. In this situation, having an agile system that can react quickly to changes and has well-defined processes and governance that align with company goals is essential for success. In addition to overseeing ongoing operations, the CIO should strategically create a proactive, flexible environment that can easily adjust to changing business requirements.

"The task of leadership is to create an alignment of strengths so strong that it makes the system's weakness irrelevant." This famous quote by Peter Drucker has excellent significance in IT and business alignment. An organization can guarantee that every dollar spent on IT supports its strategic goals and objectives by achieving business-IT alignment. A firm can also benefit from cutting-edge, emerging

technology that could enhance operational efficiency. The CIO must be prepared for three specific risks in the IT business alignment when dealing with it. One is the technical risk the CIO and IT should evaluate to see if the IT system functions correctly. The second is organizational risks, which the CIO should investigate to determine whether system users will adhere to instructions. The third risk is where the CIO should consider the commercial risks and determine whether implementing and utilizing the IT system will be beneficial.

IT teams stepped outside their former boundaries and took on a more strategic role in this rapidly changing environment. They became planners of corporate policies, guardians of funds, and creators of all-encompassing business plans. Their choices had a profound impact that went far beyond the world of servers and cables to the organization's mission. The change took time and effort for many businesses. It took much work to take a step back and ultimately embrace this new strategic vision due to the daily demands of IT operations. Information Technology's function has changed from a reactive support role to a proactive, strategic force essential to the organization's efforts to create value. This shift in focus has revolutionized the way businesses operate, with IT becoming an integral part of the strategic decision-making process. Companies have realized that IT can no longer be seen as a cost center, but as an investment that can drive growth and increase value. This shift has led to the rise of IT as a Service, or ITaaS, which allows companies to better manage their IT operations and ensure their long-term success.

Within the dynamic landscape of corporate IT, these insights serve as stark reminders of the critical role that IT plays in defining and advancing modern companies. They highlight the transformative power of implementing a strategic IT approach in line with larger business objectives and the difficulties that may occur with significant changes. CIOs should note that negotiating the intricacies of the contemporary business environment and promoting value generation require a well-aligned IT strategy.

The core concept revolves around the notion that an organization's business operations inherently contribute value. While IT does not generate value in isolation, it plays a vital role in enhancing the operational efficiency of the business. IT is a fundamental support system for a company's daily operations. Consequently, every initiative undertaken by IT should align with and advance the objectives of one or more business departments. The impetus for IT projects originates from the business, which formulates the plan and establishes the schedule.

One of the biggest retailers in the world, Walmart, had supply chain management issues due to inefficiency, overstocking, and understocking. The CIO of Walmart started an initiative to update the organization's supply chain with cutting-edge data analytics and technology. They set up a system that gathered real-time data from POS terminals and connected it with outside data like weather predictions and traffic statistics. Walmart enhanced the supply chain process, increased forecasting accuracy, and optimized inventory levels. By fusing IT initiatives with corporate objectives, Walmart reduced inventory holding costs by $2 billion and saw an increase in sales of 10% due to better product availability. The supply chain's simplification produced significant operational efficiency and cost savings because of IT and business alignment, resulting in value creation.

6.7 FUTURE TRENDS IN IT-BUSINESS ALIGNMENT

For organizations looking to utilize technology to its total capacity to accomplish their strategic goals, the alignment of IT and business has always been of utmost importance. This synchronization is more important than ever in today's ever-changing digital environment. Several future trends shape the connection between IT and business, and the CIO function is developing to face these issues head-on. Below are the future trends in IT business alignment:

Digital Transformation: Businesses are adopting digital technologies at a never-before-seen pace to remain competitive. The CIO plays a crucial role in guiding this change by promoting the adoption of cutting-edge technologies like artificial intelligence (AI), machine learning, IoT, and blockchain. The CIOs must focus on aligning business and digital transformation to get the correct value.

Data-Driven Decision-Making: Data is becoming more and more essential to modern organizations. CIOs are responsible for managing massive data sets and turning them into the insights needed to make decisions. Adopting vital business intelligence and data analytics solutions is necessary to enable data-driven organizational decision-making for aligning IT with business. Complying with regulations such as the GDPR and preserving data privacy are essential to the collection and analysis of data and will become a key factor for business IT alignment.

Cybersecurity and Risk Management: CIOs must prioritize Cybersecurity due to the frequency and sophistication of cyber threats. They protect the organization's digital assets, client information, and intellectual property. The CIO's responsibilities now go beyond simply implementing technology; they include thorough risk management and aggressive cybersecurity measures. Aligning Cybersecurity and risk management in line with the business has also become a key consideration for the CIOs.

Cloud and Hybrid Environments: More scalability and flexibility are possible as cloud computing popularity increases. Whether using public, private, or hybrid cloud technologies, CIOs are responsible for developing cloud strategies that complement the enterprise's objectives. They must also manage data integration, security, and vendor management difficulties in a multi-cloud context. Aligning cloud and hybrid environments has become a key factor for the CIOs.

Agile and DevOps Practices: To keep pace with the fast rate of technological change, organizations embrace agility and DevOps methodologies. CIOs must dismantle the barriers separating IT from other business units and foster an atmosphere of agility and cooperation. Agile and DevOps practices foster software's rapid development and deployment, aligning IT operations with business needs. CIO should align agile and DevOps practices in line with business.

Customer-Centric Future: Modern organizational tactics focus predominantly on improving the customer experience. In the future, there will be a focused effort to use technology to improve personalization, engagement, and overall customer happiness in CIOs' IT-business alignment. CIOs are strategically using analytics and data to learn more about the preferences and habits of their clients. This abundance of data is essential for matching IT solutions to create more personalized and engaging user experiences.

Sustainability and ESG: Environmental, social, and governance, or ESG, factors are becoming increasingly important when making corporate decisions. CIOs are becoming more proactive in implementing sustainable IT practices as the environment changes. Examples of these activities include using environmentally friendly technology, building data centers with low energy consumption, and lowering the total carbon footprint of IT operations. For CIOs, aligning IT plans with ESG goals is becoming increasingly important. A CIO seeking to create value now requires ESG factors to align with more general business objectives.

Partnerships and Ecosystems: The importance of ecosystems and strategic relationships as innovation accelerators is something that CIOs are beginning to realize more and more. They actively interact with startups, technology vendors, and industry partners to keep a competitive advantage in their respective markets. This cooperative strategy responds to client needs while aligning with current industry developments. Value development critically depends on alliances and ecosystems strategically aligning with corporate goals.

Quantifying IT Value: In the future landscape of CIOs' IT-business alignment, CIOs must demonstrate the return on investment from IT initiatives. CIOs are developing more intricate measurements and KPIs to evaluate the tangible effects of IT endeavors on the organization's overall financial performance. This data-driven approach guarantees that IT aligns with the organization's strategic and financial objectives.

In conclusion, the CIO's job is changing in reaction to these predicted future developments in IT-business alignment. CIOs are becoming more than just guardians of technology; they are strategic thought leaders connecting IT with overarching corporate objectives. They must be skilled at promoting collaboration, managing risk, and spurring innovation, in addition to having a comprehensive understanding of technology and its effects on the firm. The CIO's role in ensuring successful IT-business alignment remains crucial to an organization's success as technology transforms industries.

CHAPTER 7
NAVIGATING THE IT LANDSCAPE: UNRAVELING THE THREADS OF IT GOVERNANCE, STRATEGY, AND LEADERSHIP

INTRODUCTION

The modern CIO function has changed dramatically in our quickly evolving digital landscape. The modern CIO is no longer limited to traditional IT infrastructure and support services; they are essential to an organization's success as strategic and operational leaders. The dynamic and varied duties of the contemporary CIO will be examined in this chapter, particularly emphasizing their operational and strategic objectives. Assume that the CIO is a master conductor who uses a baton to orchestrate the convergence of cutting-edge technologies such as artificial intelligence (AI), generative AI, cloud computing, machine learning, data science, and the Internet of Things. The CIO's impact is greatly expanded by this innovation symphony, putting them in a position to create strategies. As Eddie Shleyner aptly says, *"Your strategy is your game plan, and your tactics are how you will implement your strategy and win."*

CIOs are at the vanguard of balancing business and technology as organizations negotiate the era of unparalleled technological convergence a fusion we call *"Contextual Congruence."* To accomplish this alignment, CIOs must navigate a challenging landscape of tactics, utilizing IT solutions, improving teamwork, and establishing a competitive edge. Encouraging business transformation through strategic IT collaboration and communication is fundamental to a CIO's strategic responsibility. In this chapter we will map out strategic horizons as compass points, and strategically direct organizational plans to ensure that an organization achieves short-term requirements and long-term competitive advantages.

We will also explore how CIOs serve as the environmental monitors of their companies, skilled at gathering and combining outside trends to inform strategic choices. They also act as stewards of technology, balancing cutting-edge technologies with older systems to maximize results and promote compatible technical solutions. A fundamental component of the CIO's job is innovation, which includes developing, nurturing, and working together on technology concepts that support corporate innovation objectives. This chapter will explore the many tactics, obstacles, and successes contemporary CIOs encounter in negotiating the complex terrain of technological convergence.

7.1 WHAT IS IT GOVERNANCE?

The CIO should have the appetite and energy to drive things in parallel. The CIO should have the necessary energy levels in such a way that his mind works to make it possible. In strategic planning, CIOs should consider the essential elements required for success, including financial resources, human resources, and other necessary assets. Identifying the critical success factors and key milestones provides a clear and focused foundation for shaping strategies based on these metrics. CIOs should invest their mindshare into the problem and ensure that their team is also sponsoring their mindshare into the situation. For problem-solving, CIOs should start with a *"Why."* Once this is aligned, the next step becomes much more accessible.

A CIO should ensure that they communicate a compelling value proposition for their team by delving deeply into a topic and developing a firm belief. CIOs must adopt a growth attitude and demonstrate tolerance for the inevitable failures that will inevitably occur, understanding that failures are essential to research and innovation. Recognizing that life is multifaceted, CIOs are more equipped to handle obstacles. Remaining focused is crucial for a CIO as the organization depends on the support of its members (Gartner, 2018).

The high demand for IT specialists stems from their remarkable ability to uphold business operations, especially in times of crisis. However, having well-thought-out plans becomes crucial when IT faces challenges and CIOs encounter difficulties. After the recent global ransomware outbreak exposed vulnerabilities, numerous CIOs faced criticism for perceived shortcomings in their contingency plans. Effectively managing the life cycle of IT resources is not merely an option but a necessity. While challenging days are inevitable for CIOs, it is essential to recognize their humanity and understand that setbacks are a natural part of life. Rather than fixating on disappointments, CIOs should maintain perspective and acknowledge that difficult days are intrinsic to the human experience. By refusing to let personal challenges compromise their professional ethics and interpersonal relationships, CIOs can recover and emerge stronger. Building solid alliances is paramount to the success of a CIO.

7.2 WHAT IS IT STRATEGY?

The CIO is the head of the IT organization and is solely able to assign decision-making authority within the IT department. Every action the CIO makes has ramifications, and they are responsible for them. This duty not only has a great deal of weight but also has an enormous impact. As the head of the IT department, the CIO has enormous authority but also significant responsibility. The CIO primarily oversees and manages the organization's technological stack, including security. Its creation and management fall within the purview of the CIO. Technology option assessment is a significant duty that CIOs are unable to outsource. The CIO's selection of technology suppliers will significantly impact all facets of the company, including productivity, security, and compliance.

Today, strategic partners may assist the organization in achieving its objectives; it is no longer just about keeping the lights on or maintaining computers. The CIO's function is rapidly changing, with information technology taking on a more strategic role in businesses. CIOs should collaborate with business executives to establish an annual service and IT function to be seen as essential executive team members. By implementing an Annual service function, IT can be viewed as a service company instead of just a department that offers technological services.

CIOs should develop an IT Annual Function (ITAF) and a Service Annual Function (SAF) to demonstrate the value of IT. Business executives should be involved in developing SAF, including a thorough evaluation of how IT services meet and fit the organization's needs (Gartner, 2022). Many CIOs find themselves in this situation, and while some choose to imitate the methods or approaches of others, there are more effective ways to address it. CIOs need to be capable of fixing problems. They should not attempt to steal ideas or procedures from other people. CIOs should instead focus on creating their own solutions tailored to the specific needs of their organization. They should also use the resources available to help them evaluate their current situation and identify areas for improvement. Finally, CIOs should be proactive in seeking out new and better approaches.

7.3 THE STRATEGIC ROLE OF IT AND CIO IN AN ENTERPRISE

IT plays a pivotal role in propelling organizational value and enabling game-changing transformation. In the digital age, Information Technology is not just a tool but a strategic driver propelling organizations into the future. CIOs are becoming crucial leaders in creating and implementing strategic business solutions by working closely with board teams. They aim to improve the organization's competitiveness by coordinating IT and business objectives. CIOs know how IT can be a tremendous force for value development. They are crucial in utilizing technology to boost productivity, encourage innovation, and optimize operations. The CIOs facilitate the development and implementation of strategic solutions that tackle organizational obstacles and spur growth by comprehending business objectives and coordinating with IT capabilities.

The CIO works closely with executive and stakeholder teams on the board to ensure that IT projects connect with the larger business plan. CIOs help firms take advantage of the full potential of technology to achieve their objectives by managing the alignment of business and IT strategy. The ultimate goal is to enhance the organization's competitiveness in the dynamic and quickly changing commercial landscape. CIOs foster innovation, facilitate digital transformation, and forge long-lasting corporate advantages by skillfully utilizing IT resources. In the rapidly evolving digital era, CIOs are essential in determining the organization's course and ensuring its success through strategic coordination and collaboration.

From a CIO's perspective, IT plays a critical and extensive strategic role in a corporate operation. CIO should understand that strategic IT integration involves more than just managing systems and technologies—it also entails fostering innovation, productivity, and expansion throughout the organization. It is essential to realize that technology now facilitates organizational change and creates a competitive advantage, acting as more than just a support system. In today's dynamic and constantly changing world, the role of the CIO encompasses more than just managing IT operations; it also involves determining the organization's general course.

CIO should ensure technology is critical to accomplishing our strategic goals by coordinating IT activities with more general business goals. The CIO should spearhead the group's development of a plan that unites technology breakthroughs with the organization's goals, be it improving client experiences, streamlining internal operations, or launching new sources of income. IT has a strategic role that includes developing and executing a cross-departmental digital strategy. It entails working with other C-suite executives to spot technology opportunities to improve business results and proactively resolve issues that might impede expansion. Building an innovative and ever-learning culture where IT experts and nontechnical stakeholders can help shape our digital future is essential to the success of our IT activities.

The CIO should know that his decisions and the technology environment impact the organization's direction. CIOs should support investing in cutting-edge technologies because they can transform markets and produce brand-new products. CIO has to protect the digital assets, guaranteeing data security and compliance and upholding our partners' and consumers' confidence. As a CIO, the strategic job of IT is to be a visionary leader who creates digital strategies, sees potential, and leads the organization toward a future where technology drives innovation and promotes long-term growth. It is about pushing IT as a transformational catalyst that takes our business to new heights and stepping outside the boundaries of a standard support role.

7.4 STRATEGY AS NORTH STAR: THE CIO'S ROLE IN GUIDING ORGANIZATIONAL STRATEGIES WITH TECHNOLOGY FORESIGHT

The CIO becomes the celestial mapper, navigating a path through the expanse of modern business, where innovation is the North Star and modifies the celestial rhythm, with strategy serving as the North Star. Please think of this North Star as a constellation of concepts, a compass that the CIO utilizes to guide them toward company growth while avoiding technological oblivion. Rather than existing in a static position, this metaphorical North Star is a dynamic force that leads the corporation through the dark waters of business strategy. The CIO's role is to analyze the constellations of emerging technologies; much like an astronomer deciphers the night sky. The CIO looks beyond the near future with an unmatched vision, making the connections between the organization's goals and technology advancements.

The CIO finds insights that propel the alignment of strategy and technology as they delve deeper into this cosmic domain. The North Star comprises not just a single light but a spectrum of possibilities, including cloud computing for agile scalability, AI for predictive capabilities, and IoT for interconnected creativity. With the technological information that strategy as North Star provides, the CIO becomes a strategist, using innovation as the primary engine to steer the ship. The guiding topic of the North Star now serves as a framework for integrated strategic choices rather than discrete assessments. The role of the CIO changes from that of a technology steward to that of a strategic visionary who incorporates technology into the company's main objectives. As sailors used the stars to guide them, today's CIO follows the strategic constellations. They take advantage of opportunities, foresee disruptions, and steer the company in new directions.

The core of North Star's strategy is the tale of synergy and alignment. It symbolizes the transformational role of the CIO as a catalyst for strategic change as opposed to merely serving as a technology steward. Like the North Star guides explorers to new lands, the CIO guides the company toward a future where technology acts as a compass rather than merely a tool to reach the unfulfilled goals of business strategy.

7.5 HOLISTIC HORIZON MAPPING: THE CIO'S STRATEGY COMPASS

For a CIO, "*Holistic Horizon Mapping*" is a strategic approach that includes thorough planning, anticipatory analysis, and visualization of the technology landscape over various time horizons. With this methodology, CIOs may foresee new trends, plan for upcoming issues, and match their IT plans with the enterprise's overall goals. Within the vast domain where strategy and technology collide, the contemporary CIO is a strategic navigator with a powerful compass—"*Holistic Horizon Mapping*." This compass can be considered a metaphysical tool that will enable the CIO to see into the future and steer the strategic ship of the organization through the unpredictable waters of technological progress.

At its core, holistic horizon mapping is more than just a technique; it is a concept that looks beyond the present and predicts the organization's course into the future. With this method, the CIO can set a course that keeps up with the rapidly changing business and technological environment. The CIO becomes a visionary architect who sees beyond the near future and draws inspiration from the rise and fall of technology trends, the pulse of consumer preferences, and the ebb and flow of market dynamics. Taking this compass with him, the CIO sets out on a strategic quest. Analyzing the exterior scene with the same attention to detail as an explorer in an unexplored area, they interpret the signs and patterns that portend the arrival of new technology.

The compass becomes a knowledge repository through market research, talks with corporate executives, and constant observation. Guiding the CIO through the intricate dance of disruption and innovation assists them in making decisions that align with the grand symphony of the organization's objectives. The potential of Holistic Horizon Mapping synthesis is known to the CIO throughout this strategic voyage. Integrating technology into organizational goals is crucial rather than attempting to comprehend it in a vacuum. To propel the company forward, the CIO integrates various technologies, including cloud computing, IoT, AI, and others. The idea behind Holistic Horizon Mapping is to combine commercial objectives with technological advancements to encapsulate the essence of strategic synergy.

Holistic horizon mapping redefines the CIO as a visionary leader who guides the organization's future instead of just looking after its IT infrastructure. Using this strategic compass, the CIO directs the organization's course, utilizing the shifting winds to steer toward unexplored areas. The CIO never wavers in the face of innovation's ups and downs, steering the ship through a sea of change and using holistic horizon mapping's capability to chart a profitable course.

The modern CIO is a strategic leader possessing a powerful compass: a comprehensive horizon map in the vast domain where strategy and technology meet. Consider this compass a magical tool that helps the CIO predict the future and steer the organization's strategic ship over the turbulent seas of technological advancement. More than just a technology, holistic horizon mapping is a way of thinking that projects the organization's future direction by seeing beyond the here and now. Using this method, the CIO may develop a plan considering how business and technology constantly change. The CIO may develop into a visionary architect by seeing beyond the near future and gaining inspiration from the waves of technological innovation.

The compass becomes a repository for information amassed via ongoing market research, discussions with significant industry participants, and observation. It guides the CIO through the problematic dance between innovation and disruption, assisting them in making decisions that support the company's objectives. The importance of holistic horizon mapping becomes evident as the CIO moves forward on this strategic route. It involves more than just comprehending technology on its own; it involves incorporating it into the larger framework of corporate goals. The CIO weaves a technological tapestry that develops the company using cloud computing, the Internet of Things, artificial intelligence (AI), and other technologies. By combining corporate goals with technical breakthroughs, Holistic Horizon Mapping successfully conveys the concept of strategic synergy.

Through comprehensive horizon mapping, the CIO changes from a guardian of the IT infrastructure to a forward-thinking executive of the organization's future. With this strategic compass, the CIO steers the organization toward new opportunities by harnessing the winds of change. Waves of innovation come and go, but the CIO never changes. As they steer the ship across the vast ocean of change, they use the power of holistic horizon mapping to chart a successful course.

7.6 CIO STRATEGIC & OPERATIONAL GOALS

The organization's strategic goals, which represent the organization's projected future, are linked to strategic planning. They, therefore, relate to the objective and vision of the business. The organization's mission statement describes its goals and the circumstances behind its creation. Williams *et al.* (2019) claim that the vision represents the organization's goals for the future. Strategic goals are created based on a previous analysis of the organization's internal and external scenarios. Internal values include an organization's business model, points of differentiation, capacity for innovation, and intellectual capital. When analyzing a business issue, the CIO and the IT department should investigate which organizational procedures, technologies, or other factors have failed. IT executives should make better decisions on how to close the gaps in the organization by carefully examining the failure. To change IT from a cost-centered business line to one that supports IT, CIOs should establish strategic roadmaps that take IT into account for future business. The "*modern CIO should have a journey of analysis, and he should be able to decipher the root cause of organizational setbacks.*"

After leadership meetings or workshops, some CIOs employ debriefing and reverse questions to assist them in better communicating the strategic roadmaps and solicit team feedback on improving the IT strategy. Gaining the team's support for upcoming roadmaps and strategies and fostering greater collaboration are benefits of the debriefing and reverse questions. An executive, such as a CIO, should monitor how their organization's IT issues are handled and delegated to different staff members. They should also keep an eye on the interactions between management and their team of IT specialists. Finally, the CIO should take on the "Chief Problem Solver" role and observe from the sidelines while the team tackles the issue. A CIO should give the situation and watch how it is handled from behind, so a CIO should always put the team on top.

Competitors, the nation's economic situation, industry policies, the legal system, and other external factors can all impact operations. The SWOT analysis, which stands for Strengths, Weaknesses, Opportunities, and Threats, is a valuable tool CIOs use to assess their companies and develop strategic objectives. It illustrates the areas that need to be modified to achieve better results. When the paradigms of competition, market demand, and business and technology requirements change, the CIO and their plans should be like a leaf, fluttering with the wind. The CIO should have the attitude to reinvent the organization wherever the wind takes the organization. The CIO should consider ways to steer the organization's direction toward IT.

According to Bellisario et al., operational goals are related to how the company runs and handles its procedures (2021). Each employee in the organization receives a set of operational indicators to track and apply to the organization's strategic objectives. Ensuring the achievement of the medium and long-term objectives is greatly aided by a working plan that aligns with the strategy. The table below shows the key differences between the strategic and operational goals of the CIO.

Strategic Goal	Operational Goal
Doing things differently	Doing things better
Doing the right things	Doing things right
Long-term (2-4 years)	Short-term (week, month, quarter)
Aligned with mission & vision	Aligned with strategic goals
Gives coherence to the operational goals	Allows achieving strategic goals by giving a workable execution plan
Sustainable advantages	Best practices
Long-term profitability	Short term profitability
Game of top managers	Game of line managers

7.7 SHORT-TERM STRATEGIES FOR IMMEDIATE BUSINESS REQUIREMENTS

To stay ahead of the curve, CIOs must be proactive and consider their clients' needs, not simply their preferences. They also need to consider the unfavorable characteristics of the client and how they could impact their ability to expand in the future. Too often, we grow entrenched in our ways and forget the bigger picture. A CIO can help them succeed in the long run by considering all factors.

Short-term strategy often centers around three to six months, mainly focusing on revenue and profitability. According to Battifarano *et al.* (2019), short-term objectives address pressing demands, such as boosting cash flow or launching a new product. This short-term perspective helps the CIO to get additional money for longer-term goals and satisfy investors who want results from the CIO's organization. Short-term objectives should support the CIO's long-term vision of the organization. New product launches should complement the organization's existing product line and brand. Tactics for increasing cash flow should generate more income without compromising the CIO's principles or detracting from the organization's overarching objective.

Taking on a CIO post is an exciting time with full of technology opportunities. However, it can be challenging to identify which options are most important for short-term strategy among the multitude of options available. Making the best decisions requires setting priorities for actions based on actual needs rather than just perception. One of the main priorities is to identify and mitigate any potential dangers quickly. Using technology to automate processes and get information quickly can improve decision-making intelligence.

CIOs must concentrate on lowering risk and getting information fast. The main emphasis is making wise decisions that immediately impact the organization's objectives. It becomes critical to use IT resources efficiently while closely monitoring how cutting-edge technology supports organizational development. CIOs need to be able to distinguish between cutting-edge inventions and innovations that improve the company's performance. Adopting a viewpoint that promotes the development of the business model guarantees that short-term plans align with the company's changing requirements.

Here are some short-term strategies that CIOs can implement to achieve immediate impact:

Customer-Focused Digital Initiatives: The CIO should Initiate focused digital campaigns to improve customer satisfaction and involvement. This could entail the creation of user-friendly mobile applications or quickly deploying customer-centric features on digital platforms.

Rapid Implementation of Productivity Tools: The CIO should choose and implement productivity solutions that improve teamwork and expedite internal procedures. Software for managing projects, communication devices, and online platforms for cooperation could all fall under this category.

Elastic IT Infrastructure: The CIO should establish an elastic and scalable IT infrastructure to handle varying workloads. This guarantees that performance will not be compromised and that the company can react swiftly to fluctuations in demand.

Quick Response to Market Trends: The CIO should monitor market developments and promptly adjust IT strategies to exploit new opportunities. This could entail quickly creating new features, goods, or services to meet changing consumer demands.

Cost Optimization and Efficiency Measures: The CIO should determine where performance can be sacrificed without minimizing cost. This could be part of renegotiating contracts, maximizing software licensing, or simplifying IT operations.

Quick Wins in Data Analytics: The CIO should determine which data analytics applications are the easiest to implement. The CIO should implement quick-win analytics projects to assist the organization in making decisions quickly by providing actionable insights.

Enhanced Cybersecurity Measures: The CIO should immediately update security protocols, add multi-factor authentication, and train staff members on specific security awareness topics to fortify cybersecurity defenses.

Cloud Optimization: The CIO should evaluate the current cloud infrastructure of the company and make necessary cost and efficiency adjustments. This could entail renegotiating contracts with cloud service providers, optimizing load balancing, or rightsizing resources.

Agile Development and DevOps Practices: The CIO should be Implementing DevOps and agile approaches will speed up software development cycles. This may result in quicker releases, shorter time to market, and more flexibility in meeting client demands.

Elevate IT Service Delivery: The CIO should improve service management to improve IT service delivery. This entails enhancing service reliability, reducing resolution times, and streamlining IT support procedures.

Partnerships and Alliances: The CIO should examine forming strategic alliances or collaborations with startups or technology providers to enhance the organization's capabilities swiftly. This may entail integrating solutions from outside sources to address pressing business demands.

Employee Training on New Technologies: Employees should receive focused instruction on using new tools or technology that can instantly impact their productivity. This guarantees a seamless changeover and quick uptake of new systems.

By focusing on these short-term strategies, CIOs can demonstrate the immediate value of IT to the organization, fostering a culture of agility and responsiveness.

7.8 LONG-TERM STRATEGIES THAT MAY PROVIDE A SIGNIFICANT COMPETITIVE ADVANTAGE

When developing long-term plans to gain a competitive edge, a CIO needs to decide which conflicts are worthwhile. It is essential to understand that not all IT problems require a quick fix and that not all problems are mission-critical. A thorough grasp of the company and its goals is necessary to match IT with the demands and goals of the business. To avoid departmental disputes and improve collaboration, IT should investigate the underlying causes of issues rather than reactively fixing them.

Although the word "*strategy*" has spread widely, regular planning has given way to strategic thought. Managers write product/market strategies, functional leaders build comprehensive plans, and senior executives set strategic purposes. This development frees managers from the complexities of the planning process to concentrate on broad concerns affecting long-term success. Proactive leaders recognize the value of readiness, as demonstrated by Kyrylov *et al.'s* focus on proactive planning in 2020. The CIO must provide clarity through well-stated objectives and essential questions that direct talks toward fruitful outcomes, whether in board meetings or vendor discussions.

The CIO must encourage creativity in managerial and leadership teams through brainstorming sessions, focus groups, and other initiatives if they want long-term IT fitness. Organizational transformation initiatives are more successful when accompanied by concrete results and monthly brainstorming sessions. An innovative culture is fostered by praising and rewarding ideation efforts in performance assessments, which is essential to the success of any firm. Prosperous conglomerates like Siemens A.G. and General Electric demonstrate a break from bureaucratic stagnation. They have proven the value of well-thought-out, cogent, and quick business plans by embracing entrepreneurial agility and continuously surpassing smaller rivals through technological and commercial innovations. They are positioned as market share and innovation leaders because of this strategic approach, which goes beyond conventional management practices.

Here are some longer-term strategies that can contribute to a significant competitive advantage:

Digital Transformation and Innovation: A CIO should adopt agile approaches to encourage an inventive culture and quick-change adaption. This enables the capacity to experiment with new technologies and respond to market demands more quickly. Create and maintain digital ecosystems by working with startups, partners, and other industry participants. This may result in the development of unique services and solutions that distinguish the company.

Data as a Strategic Asset: A CIO should create strong data governance structures to guarantee data security, compliance, and quality. This establishes the framework for utilizing data as a tactical advantage to facilitate well-informed decision-making. To extract valuable insights from data, spend money on artificial intelligence (AI) and sophisticated analytics. Machine learning and predictive analytics can improve operational effectiveness and allow for proactive decision-making.

Customer-Centric Technology: A CIO should utilize technology to improve client experiences by personalizing content and creating user-centered designs. AI-powered chatbots, CRM systems, and other tools may be used. A CIO should invest in digital marketing tools to reach and interact with customers efficiently. A CIO should also use data analytics to comprehend consumer behavior and preferences for focused marketing campaigns.

Cybersecurity and Risk Management: A CIO should use cybersecurity safeguards to take preventative action against emerging risks. This entails conducting routine security audits, educating staff members, and keeping up with emerging security technology. A CIO should create a thorough risk management plan that considers both external and internal variables. This entails evaluating legislative changes, geopolitical threats, and other business-impacting factors.

Cloud Strategy: A CIO should create a scalable and adaptable cloud strategy considering private and public cloud options. Multi-cloud and hybrid solutions provide the flexibility to adjust to shifting business needs. A CIO should encourage a culture of cloud-native development so that the company can take advantage of cloud computing's scalability, cost-effectiveness, and quick deployment.

Sustainable and Responsible Technology Practices: A CIO should incorporate eco-friendly and sustainable methods into IT operations. This entails using green technologies, cutting down on electronic waste, and optimizing energy use. A CIO should ensure that artificial intelligence and other cutting-edge technologies are created and used morally. This entails eliminating prejudices, encouraging openness, and upholding moral principles.

Talent and Culture: A CIO should encourage a culture of ongoing education and training to ensure workers have the digital skills they will need in the future. Encourage inclusiveness and diversity among the tech teams to foster a range of viewpoints and creative problem-solving.

By aligning these longer-term strategies with the organization's overall business objectives, CIOs can position their companies to thrive in a rapidly changing digital landscape, gaining a sustainable competitive advantage.

7.9 STRATEGIC LEVERAGING OF IT SOLUTIONS FOR ENHANCED COLLABORATION AND COMPETITIVE EDGE

Today's economy demands efficiency, inventiveness, and agility, and businesses are realizing how vital technology is to their success. Gaining a competitive edge now depends on improving organizational communication via clever IT solutions. Using technology to enable seamless communication has moved from a requirement to a strategic requirement in today's rapidly changing digital economy, helping organizations to stay ahead of the curve. The strategic value examines how improved customer service, knowledge exchange, interdepartmental interaction, remote work choices, and real-time communication can alter an organization's competitive landscape and position it for long-term success. Below are the key points that CIOs consider for enhanced collaboration and competitive edge.

Expanding Cooperation: The competitiveness of an enterprise can be significantly impacted by IT solutions that foster internal collaboration. CIO should emphasize that providing smartphones to field service personnel can enhance teamwork and offer them a competitive edge.

Real-time communication: Field support staff can quickly connect with experts in the organization's headquarters using cell phones or other communication devices. Prompt communication improves decision-making, reduces waiting times, and leads to more efficient service delivery.

Knowledge sharing: IT solutions can improve a company's internal knowledge exchange and acquisition. Using a centralized collaborative platform, staff members can document their areas of expertise, debate best practices, and rapidly access pertinent material. Knowledge sharing fosters creativity and productivity by enabling employee cooperation, mutual learning, and less effort duplication.

Cross-functional collaboration: IT solutions can facilitate more effective team or department collaboration within a company. Employees from several departments can collaborate effectively, assign tasks, and coordinate efforts, for instance, with the help of project management software and collaboration platforms. This cross-functional collaboration fosters synergy, enhances problem-solving abilities, and sparks innovation.

Remote work and virtual collaboration: IT solutions are critical to supporting virtual collaboration as remote work becomes more prevalent. Employees may connect from a distance through video conferencing, instant messaging, and file-sharing apps. Remote collaborations enhance work-life balance, expand the talent pool, and boost production by eliminating the constraints of traditional office setups.

Enhanced customer service: IT solutions that facilitate real-world collaboration immediately affect customer care. When employees have easy access to real-time information, they may consult with professionals, communicate effectively, and answer client requests and concerns more promptly and precisely. Improved customer service correlates with increased customer satisfaction, loyalty, and a competitive advantage over rivals.

In conclusion, IT solutions encouraging organizational teamwork led to better cross-functional cooperation, communication, knowledge sharing, and customer service. In today's fast-paced business environment, organizations can set themselves apart from rivals and obtain a significant competitive advantage by utilizing technology to facilitate seamless cooperation.

7.10 ELEVATING CUSTOMER INSIGHT: STRATEGIC UTILIZATION OF DATA ANALYSIS FOR ENHANCED CUSTOMER ENGAGEMENT

From a CIO's standpoint, harnessing data analysis's power to elevate customer insight is a strategic advantage and a fundamental imperative in today's digitally-driven business landscape. CIO should recognize that data is not merely a byproduct of operations; it is a goldmine of invaluable insights that can guide us towards delivering unparalleled customer experiences and forging lasting connections. CIO should understand that data analysis is not an isolated endeavor but a comprehensive approach that permeates every aspect of our organization. We gain a deeper understanding of customer behaviors, preferences, and needs by strategically utilizing data analysis techniques. Understanding the customer requirements enables us to tailor our products, services, and interactions in ways that resonate with our customers personally.

The process of turning raw data into meaningful insights is called strategic data analysis use. The CIO should supervise his staff's use of modern analytics technology to make sense of the massive amount of data we get. The CIO can use this data to predict customer preferences, anticipate their needs, and even spot potential issues before they arise. This makes the clients happier and positions the organization as an active collaborator on their journey. The CIO should also know that data analysis is an ongoing process that calls for flexibility and constant development. Encouraging data-driven decision-making throughout the entire organization is the responsibility of the CIO. The CIO should ensure that divisions collaborate to share ideas and comprehensively enhance the comprehension of our clientele. By doing this, a CIO can construct a thorough picture of the customer's journey and produce seamless experiences beyond specific touchpoints.

As CIOs navigate the world of data analysis, data security and privacy are significant concerns, ensuring that we use customer information intelligently and lawfully. The CIO should implement strict security procedures that protect customer information while enabling us to use it fully in collaboration with the legal and compliance departments. From a CIO perspective, leveraging data to create empathy is critical to strategically applying data analysis for improved customer understanding. It entails getting to know our clients well, anticipating their needs, and offering experiences that resonate with them. A CIO has to weave data analysis into the company's core to create enduring relationships built on relevance, trust, and value. The methods listed below are used to undertake strategic data analysis.

Improving customer insight: Alshurideh (2019) asserts that gathering and analyzing data can provide a competitive advantage by improving understanding of customer requirements and preferences. By leveraging advanced analytics technology, businesses can create targeted offers and messages that encourage customer satisfaction and loyalty. Organizations can gain a competitive edge by raising consumer awareness through increased data gathering and analysis.

Data Gathering: Numerous sources, such as surveys, social media, website traffic, customer interactions, and more, can provide businesses with a wealth of information. This information could include demographics, previous purchases, surfing patterns, evaluations, and preferences. Through systematic data collection, firms can generate a comprehensive understanding of their clientele and their needs. This understanding can be used to refine marketing strategies, create targeted campaigns, and develop new products and services. Additionally, businesses can use data analysis to identify trends and opportunities to better compete in their industry.

Data Analysis: With analytics tools and approaches, organizations may use vast amounts of data to uncover patterns, trends, and insights. Businesses can discover helpful information about customer preferences, buying habits, and market trends using data mining, predictive modeling, and segmentation analysis. By using this information, businesses may create focused plans and make data-driven decisions that enable them to fulfill client requests efficiently.

Personalized Offers and Messages: Businesses may create customized offers and communications by better understanding customer preferences and needs. By tailoring their products, services, and marketing messages to particular customers or client segments, businesses may offer more focused and relevant experiences. Personalization boosts customer satisfaction, engagement, and loyalty by cultivating a sense of understanding and value.

Customer Journey Optimization: Analyzing client data allows for the identification of pain points and opportunities for improvement across the customer journey. By mapping customer touchpoints, businesses can gain additional insight into how customers interact with their brands at different stages. Businesses may address customer issues at every touchpoint, enhance user experiences, and streamline processes with this expertise. Businesses may boost customer satisfaction and loyalty by providing a seamless and rewarding customer journey.

Predictive Analytics: Businesses can anticipate the behavior and preferences of their customers by utilizing advanced analytics approaches such as forecasting and predictive modeling. Predictive algorithms and historical data analysis can help businesses find upselling and cross-selling opportunities, estimate customer needs, and enhance inventory control. Businesses may make proactive decisions using predictive analytics, which helps them meet client needs and deliver pertinent and timely offerings.

Continuous Improvement: By applying data-driven insights, organizations can continuously improve the products, services, and experiences they provide to their customers. Through monitoring key performance indicators, data analysis, and customer feedback, companies can identify areas for improvement and take proactive measures to resolve them. Through continuous improvement based on consumer insights, organizations may sustain high levels of customer satisfaction, stay competitive, and adapt to customer needs.

In conclusion, gaining a better understanding of their customers through data collection and analysis enables companies to develop customized experiences, messaging, and offers that increase client happiness and foster loyalty. Using powerful analytics tools may help businesses better understand the needs and preferences of their customers, giving them a competitive edge.

7.11 CIOS STRATEGIC IT COMMUNICATION AND COLLABORATION

"Success is the sum of small efforts, repeated day in and day out," This quote by Robert Collier also has excellent significance in IT

leadership. The strategic function of IT has developed beyond technical support in today's dynamic business environment to become a potent driver for organizational change. It has become clear that IT communication and collaboration are essential to an organization's capacity for innovation, adaptation, and success. The importance of smooth interactions between organizations and customers, stakeholders, and cross-functional teams has increased, making efficient IT communication and collaboration a strategic lever of previously unheard-of importance.

The following are the main factors a CIO considers while transforming a business through strategic IT cooperation and communication.

Introduce new business models: Businesses can strategically use IT to alter their business paradigms. For instance, a company that has always sold its goods in physical stores can use IT to launch an online store. Consequently, the company can reach a larger audience, save delivery costs, and provide customers with a more convenient service. The IT department is crucial to developing and managing communication networks for both small and large enterprises (Cohen *et al.,* 2018).

Proper and effective communication: One of the most noticeable aspects of the twenty-first century is how easy it is to communicate, which is highly advantageous to businesses. In this day and age, contacting a firm is usually easy and quick. To prosper, a company needs to understand its customers' needs, shopping habits, and satisfaction levels. Timely and efficient communication is essential for meeting customer expectations, fixing issues, and providing solutions. Technology is indispensable because it enables businesses to communicate instantly and globally with millions of customers. Adequate and proper communication is one of the most important aspects of a strategic IT department in a corporation. IT workers must effectively interact with a variety of stakeholders to guarantee that IT initiatives align with business objectives and that stakeholder requests are recognized.

Here are some key points related to the strategic role of IT in communication:

Business Requirements Gathering: IT experts work directly with business stakeholders to understand their requirements and translate them into workable solutions. Effective communication is needed to understand company demands, gather and clarify requirements, and ask the right questions. IT teams find it easier to deliver solutions that complement the goals and objectives of the company when there is practical communication.

Technical Guidance and Education: IT specialists often instruct and guide nontechnical organizational stakeholders in technological concerns. They have to make complex technological concepts understandable to nontechnical individuals. Effective communication facilitates collaboration and guarantees the successful implementation of IT solutions by bridging the gap between technical jargon and business requirements.

Project Management and Collaboration: IT professionals usually participate in initiatives with cross-functional teams. Effective team communication is essential for cooperation, coordination, and project management. Clear communication makes it easier to set expectations, assign resources, manage deadlines, and ensure everyone is focused on completing the project.

Change Management: IT initiatives sometimes involve new technology systems, methods, and workflows. IT professionals must notify all parties that these changes may affect them effectively. Outlining the benefits, addressing concerns, and providing support and training during the transition are all part of change management. Effective communication makes it easier to handle resistance to change and enables the seamless adoption of new practices and technologies.

Vendor and Supplier Management: IT professionals often deal with vendors and providers when searching for technology solutions and services. Effective communication is essential for contract negotiations, service level agreements (SLAs), and ongoing relationship management. Clear communication is critical to managing conflicts, establishing expectations, and ensuring vendors offer the required services and support.

User Support and Training: IT workers may provide training sessions and user support to enhance users' understanding of technological systems and applications. Effective communication is essential for troubleshooting user difficulties, giving clear instructions, and delivering easily understandable training materials. Effective communication boosts output and user pleasure.

IT Strategy and Alignment: IT professionals educate senior management and other pertinent parties on the organization's IT strategy and roadmap. Effective communication is essential for securing resources and support, guaranteeing that IT expenditures benefit the organization, and integrating IT initiatives with business goals.

In summary, the strategic role of information technology inside an organization depends on clear and effective communication. IT professionals must communicate with various stakeholders, including project teams, vendors, business users, and higher management, to understand their needs, provide technical guidance, manage projects, address issues, and align IT efforts with organizational goals. Strong communication abilities enable IT professionals to build rapport, promote cooperation, and successfully implement IT solutions.

7.12 BEYOND IT: THE STRATEGIC LEADERSHIP OF THE CONTEMPORARY CIO

The role of the CIOs has expanded to include managing corporate data, coordinating business needs, and navigating the wide range of developing technologies available in the market. It is about more than just supervising crucial IT infrastructure. Furthermore, the modern CIO now plays a more significant part in strategic vendor management due to the proliferation of managed services and external technological solutions. This change emphasizes how crucial the CIO is becoming as a strategic leader who can use cutting-edge technologies to propel the organization's success and growth.

A new trend is emerging where companies use outside vendors to adopt a best-of-breed strategy. CIOs are now putting together groups of business-savvy specialists who work closely with corporate stakeholders to enable this transition. The main objective of a CIO is to match the business's changing needs with the marketplace's technology. In this dynamic environment, the CIO builds a comprehensive solutions architecture. The enterprise data layer is prioritized in this design, guaranteeing that executives and other essential stakeholders can quickly access timely and reliable information. Facilitating quicker and better-informed decision-making processes is the ultimate goal.

The modern CIO is critical in promoting business agility and facilitating efficient decision-making by cultivating this close collaboration between IT and the business. Cross-collaboration calls for an in-depth knowledge of business and technological processes, enabling the CIO to promote innovation throughout the organization, ease smooth integration, and improve user experiences. Businesses frequently view IT as an enigmatic and unresponsive system, and IT departments frequently assert that they require additional resources to meet business demands (VANCE, 2019). They support IT in allocating resources in a way that best meets needs by helping organizations articulate their technical requirements.

IT departments frequently require additional resources to satisfy business demands, and many firms view IT as a confusing and unresponsive system (VANCE, 2019). The CIO's function becomes vital in this challenging situation since they link the two. The CIO is essential in helping businesses express their technology needs clearly and in assisting IT in assigning resources to meet those objectives. Despite the inherent challenges, organizations still rely on the CIO as the primary facilitator in this process. However, it is essential to recognize that closing this gap is difficult. Unfortunately, many CIOs continue to put execution ahead of other duties.

The emphasis on execution in IT presents a difficult conundrum: how to prioritize projects while taking into account the constraints of IT budgets and budgeting processes, effectively distinguish between "*needs*" and "*wants*," weigh the benefits against the costs, and distinguish between "*tactical*" and "*strategic*" initiatives. CIOs must treat the PMO process as three separate but related components to guarantee its success. In the PMO process, the team must thoroughly assess every project, ranking each based on its alignment with the organization's goals and strategic value. Secondly, they should establish a productive project execution procedure, considering budgets and resource availability. Ensuring the efficient execution of projects, timely completion of tasks, and achievement of desired outcomes within the designated boundaries are of utmost importance. Finally, although necessary, the project evaluation process should be regularly addressed.

The CIO needs to rapidly understand the parallels between managing an IT professional services organization and supervising an IT department to carry out these duties efficiently. This understanding allows them to manage risks, project portfolios, and resources while ensuring they align with corporate objectives. Employing solutions offering integrated IT intelligence to handle these concerns effectively becomes essential. The CIO acts as a change agent by proactively implementing policies and processes that enable the organization to prioritize and triage project requests efficiently. They also concentrate on efficient resource management and allocation, regardless of whether the resources are in-house or off-site. A thorough, integrated, top-down governance approach is essential to addressing these issues. With this solution, the CIO is compelled to manage the IT company rather than focus on specific initiatives or objectives.

CHAPTER 8
STRATEGIC NAVIGATION IN THE IT FRONTIER: GUIDING THE CIO'S JOURNEY THROUGH EVOLUTION, SYNERGY, AND SUCCESS

INTRODUCTION

In this chapter, we explore the story of strategic evolution in the context of CIOs, taking you on a tour that charts the development of CIO strategies from the past to the present and beyond. This chapter acts as a compass, pointing readers toward the complex growth of the CIO strategy. In this chapter we explore the complexities of aligning IT and business objectives, dissecting the fundamental components of strategy creation, and demystifying and developing a strategy specific to the opportunities and difficulties that CIOs confront. All of this is done through the viewpoint of the CIO.

The story goes beyond theoretical models and into the real world, examining how CIOs improve fundamental business procedures to increase the strategic value of information technology. We acquire knowledge about the intricate landscape of IT governance, skillfully navigating its strategic, tactical, and operational facets.

This chapter offers us a comprehensive look at strategic alignment for organizational success from the distinct viewpoint of a CIO. The chapter continues with an in-depth look at developing a vision for an efficient data strategy—a road map for data empowerment emphasizing CIOs' crucial role in using data as a tactical advantage. Achieving technical excellence requires good roadmaps for navigating the complex terrain of IT strategy. We look at the process of creating these roadmaps, comprehending their different kinds, and using them to guide IT activities.

The chapter closes with a thorough examination of planned versus emergent strategy, illuminating the range of possible business paths. We explore the adaptable tactics CIOs use to traverse shifting corporate environments in a world characterized by environmental uncertainty. This chapter guides individuals who want to comprehend, accept, and maneuver through the always-changing terrain of CIO strategies in the exciting nexus of business and technology. We discuss how CIOs can use technology to stay ahead of the competition and win in the ever-changing business landscape. Finally, we explore the different tactics CIOs can use to effectively develop and implement successful strategies.

8.1 CIO STRATEGY EVOLUTION: TRACING THE TRAJECTORY FROM PAST TO PRESENT AND BEYOND

The tasks of IT strategy are vastly overlapping, and it is a continuum. The important thing is that leaders need to be able to collaborate with humility. The CIO should concentrate on developing plans that will enable the IT department to get the most out of its workforce and increase value creation for the company. One of the biggest challenges facing modern brands is meeting the constantly changing needs of consumers, especially in an environment where digital disruptors are changing the game. Analyzing and understanding the client's life cycle amid these interruptions makes the work much more challenging. However, as Oliver (2018) pointed out, handling this complexity is now essential for a brand's overall success.

With emerging technologies like machine learning and the increasing focus on social media, especially visual material, brands now have the tools to create a data-driven model that considers every facet of the brand and the customer life cycle. By leveraging data from previous sales and ongoing operations to create nurturing and ROI plans, brands may improve their scalability and return on investment. In the past, marketers relied on input from customers who returned products or spoke with a service agent directly. Social media feeds may provide brands with immediate insight, including tweets, photos, videos, emojis, and even selfies of customers showing off their latest purchases. Those photos provide incredibly significant glimpses into consumers' sentiments toward products or companies.

The vital role that information management plays in modern businesses and the adaptability of technology executives are reflected in the rise of the CIO. In the early days of information technology, the CIO's primary duty was to ensure operational efficiency. The main goals were automating repetitive tasks, managing data storage, and ensuring internal systems functioned properly. CIOs were often seen as the guardians of the technical infrastructure, keeping an eye on things and mitigating the risks associated with antiquated computing systems. During this time, the CIO's strategic role could have been more prominent, and there was a need for more alignment between IT and business objectives. IT was seen less as a strategic enabler and more as a cost center. However, the seeds of change were sown as technology continued to advance.

CIOs are now essential strategic partners in advancing digital transformation in today's business environment. The emphasis now is on using technology to drive corporate innovation and growth rather than just improving operational efficiency. CIOs are expected to promote an innovative and agile culture by coordinating IT projects with business goals. Important facets of the current CIO approach consist of:

Digital Transformation: CIOs are crucial leaders of digital activities, leveraging cutting-edge technologies like AI, cloud computing, and IoT to enhance business processes and customer experiences.

Data Management and Analytics: With the volume of data growing exponentially, CIOs must put strong data management and analytics strategies into place to extract valuable insights for decision-making.

Cybersecurity and Risk Management: CIOs are at the forefront of creating and implementing comprehensive cybersecurity policies to safeguard confidential data and guarantee business continuity as cyber threats become more sophisticated.

Agile and DevOps Practices: CIOs are implementing agile methods and DevOps approaches to enhance teamwork, accelerate software development, and boost responsiveness to market demands.

New technology and changing company needs will probably influence the course of the CIO strategy. Future trends that could emerge include:

Integration of AI and Machine Learning: CIOs may incorporate AI and Machine Learning more and more into business operations to automate repetitive work and open up new avenues for innovation.

Adoption of Blockchain: As blockchain technology advances, CIOs may investigate its use in supply chain management, maintaining transparency and boosting customer confidence in commercial dealings.

Extended Reality (XR): CIOs ought to look at the potential for augmented and virtual reality (AR and VR) to improve customer experiences, teamwork, and staff training.

Sustainability and Green IT: As the importance of sustainability increases, CIOs may concentrate on introducing eco-friendly IT procedures, maximizing energy use, and acquiring green technologies.

The dynamic interaction between technology and business is reflected in the evolution of the CIO strategy. CIOs have evolved from their initial responsibility of guaranteeing operational effectiveness to their current role as catalysts for digital transformation, making them essential designers of organizational success. Future projections point to a steadily growing role for CIOs as they continue to leverage the potential of new technology to influence the strategic course of their companies.

8.2 CULTIVATING SYNERGY: HARMONIZING IT AND BUSINESS GOALS FROM THE CIO LENS

Promoting collaboration and aligning IT and business goals from the CIO's point of view provides exceptional customer experiences. Businesses worldwide are redesigning their IT environments to be more adaptable, responsive, and collaborative due to the end of the conventional IT era. The transformation of the CIO is a comprehensive process that involves working in tandem with product management, marketing, development, and sales. It is not a discrete occurrence. It requires a deep comprehension of current and future business processes and how technology fits into this revolutionary path. The IT staff must, therefore, design solutions specific to the company's changing requirements.

The CIO in charge of finance and technology advancement and the CIO must work closely with managers and other stakeholders to identify business needs. The primary goal is still profitability, frequently attained by skillfully applying technology. Reliable and up-to-date IT systems are essential for a successful firm. A forward-thinking CIO understands how important it is to improve operations to boost competitiveness and win over senior management and customers. Many companies are modernizing their technological infrastructures as part of a *"technology transformation"* that is now underway.

The CIO needs the CEO's and CXO's support during this transition. The IT team's ability to implement technological improvements can significantly impact the company's performance. In particular, the CIO must know that technology transformation can significantly impact the customer experience. In customer interactions, it becomes imperative to prioritize the consumer's requirements, objectives, and expectations. Around the world, technology is a disruptive force changing businesses and their interactions with customers. Instead of upholding the status quo in IT operations, CIO leadership is changing to become a transformational role.

Academics, consultants, and business executives have all emphasized how critical IT and other business divisions are to align their objectives and schedules.IT has always been the engine of industry growth, and digitalization is changing how people interact with businesses.

According to Darren Topham, the Senior Research Director at Gartner, the significance of IT-business alignment has experienced a noticeable increase. This shift has been recognized by some only in recent times. At first, the IT division prioritized providing necessary services, considering uptime and stability to be crucial success factors. During the twenty-first century, this perspective shifted as C-suite executives collaborated with their technology counterparts to reengineer processes, procedures, and products. As a result, established companies underwent internal changes while startups created new business models. Topham says that while CIOs and their IT departments must continue to provide essential technical support, they must also anticipate how technology will impact the organization's capacity to provide goods and services.

8.3 STRATEGY FORMULATION PROCESS & ITS ELEMENTS

Strategy formulation is the process of figuring out the best course of action to take to accomplish organizational goals and objectives, which will ultimately lead to the realization of the business vision. A CIO's strategy formulation process entails several essential components that work together to create a comprehensive and successful IT strategy that supports the company's objectives. A business process is as strong as its weakest link, just like a chain. Every step must be executed perfectly to succeed. With technology driving rapid change in today's dynamic business environment, the CIO's position has grown beyond technology management to include a critical part in deciding the organization's strategic direction.

The CIOs design a roadmap that seamlessly integrates technology with more general company goals through a crucial procedure called the strategy formulation process. This process is more than a routine activity to match the organization's technological developments with its broader aims. It is a dynamic orchestration that requires a thorough understanding of technology's potential, a great awareness of market dynamics, and a strategic attitude. In today's interconnected world, the CIO's position has changed to become a strategic architect as organizations manage its intricacies. The CIOs are responsible for guiding the organization toward success using technology's revolutionary potential. The strategy formulation process can be used as a roadmap by the CIO to steer the organization toward innovative solutions and guarantee their smooth integration into the organization's DNA.

The following are the critical components of a CIO's strategy formulation process:

Environmental Analysis: To comprehend the company's internal and external environments, the CIO performs an environmental study. Analyzing the environment entails evaluating the business objectives of the firm as well as trends in the industry, the competitive landscape, legal requirements, technical developments, and possible risks and opportunities. The study aids the CIO in determining the primary motivators and challenges facing the IT strategy.

Vision and Mission: The CIO creates a clear vision and mission for the IT department that aligns with the organization's overarching goals. The mission statement establishes the goals and parameters of the IT function, whereas the image describes the ideal future state of IT inside the company. These claims act as a set of guidelines for creating the IT strategy.

Goal Setting: The CIO establishes strategic goals and objectives for the IT department based on the environmental analysis and alignment with the organization's objectives. In addition to addressing important topics like technology infrastructure, digital transformation, data management, cybersecurity, innovation, and user experience, these goals should be SMART (specific, measurable, attainable, relevant, and time-bound).

Stakeholder Engagement: The CIO collaborates with key stakeholders, including senior executives, business leaders, department heads, and end-users, to understand their needs, challenges, and expectations. Engaging stakeholders ensures the IT strategy considers diverse perspectives and incorporates feedback from different parts of the organization. Stakeholder involvement also facilitates buy-in and support for the IT strategy.

SWOT Analysis: To evaluate the internal strengths and weaknesses of the IT department as well as external opportunities and dangers, the CIO conducts a SWOT analysis (Strengths, Weaknesses, Opportunities, Threats). Through this analysis, the IT function can better resolve its deficiencies, build on its strengths, seize opportunities, and neutralize possible threats.

IT Capability Assessment: The CIO assesses the state of the IT, considering the skills, procedures, data management, applications, and technological infrastructure. This assessment helps evaluate the IT activities and investments needed to bridge the gaps between the current and desired future states.

Strategy Development: The CIO develops the IT strategy based on the results of the stakeholder engagement, SWOT analysis, environmental analysis, and IT capacity evaluation. The direction, goals, and initiatives of the IT function are described in the strategy. It covers techniques for talent development, innovation, governance, data management, cybersecurity, digital transformation, and technology adoption.

Implementation Plan: The CIO creates a thorough implementation plan that specifies the precise steps, due dates, roles, and resources needed to carry out the IT strategy. Critical checkpoints, performance indicators, and systems for tracking advancement and making necessary adjustments are all included in the program.

Communication and Alignment: To ensure the IT strategy is well-understood and aligned with the organization's overarching plan, the CIO communicates it to all pertinent stakeholders. To preserve alignment and make sure that the IT strategy stays current and sensitive to changing business demands, communication alignment entails constant communication, exchanging updates, and requesting input.

Continuous Evaluation and Improvement: The CIO sets up systems to monitor the success of the IT strategy and its execution regularly. Monitoring key performance indicators, getting input, performing regular assessments, and making required modifications are all part of continuous evaluation and development. Formulating a strategy is iterative, and the CIO must be prepared to modify and enhance the plan in response to evolving conditions.

Setting organizational goals: A strategy statement can only be completed by establishing long-term objectives. It is common knowledge that strategy usually acts as a means of accomplishing corporate objectives. Objectives stress the state of being there as opposed to strategy. The strategy includes defining goals and how they will be attained. As a result, strategy is a more inclusive term for allocating resources to achieve objectives. Strategic decision-making is simple once the goals and the variables affecting them are established.

Organizational Environment Evaluation: The organization's general commercial and economic environment is assessed in the second phase. A review of the company's competitive position is also included. Analyzing the organization's current product line both qualitatively and quantitatively is crucial. To comprehend their own and their competitors' strengths and limitations, management must determine the components necessary for competitive success in the market. After evaluating its advantages and disadvantages, a company needs to keep an eye on the activities and attitudes of its rivals to spot openings or risks in the supply chain or market.

Establishing Quantitative Goals: In this step, an organization must set precise numerical target values for a few objectives. Quantitative goals enable comparisons and evaluations of possible contributions from other product areas or operational divisions when assessing recurring consumers.

Setting goals about the divisional plans: In this stage, the CIO ascertains the organizational contributions made by each department, division, or product category. A CIO creates a strategy for each subunit based on the analysis made by the IT organization. Planning strategically requires a thorough examination of macroeconomic events.

Performance Analysis: Analyzing performance entails determining and assessing the discrepancy between desired or expected performance and actual performance. The organization must assess itself critically, considering its past, present, and anticipated future states. This critical analysis determines how far the organization's long-term goals deviate from its present circumstances.

Selecting Strategy: A CIO should choose the best course of action by considering organizational objectives, strengths, potential, constraints, and outside opportunities. By incorporating these components, the CIO can create a solid and well-thought-out IT strategy that supports the organization's objectives, deals with pressing issues, and effectively use technology to advance business outcomes.

8.4 STRATEGIC IT SHOWCASE: ILLUSTRATING THE IMPACT OF CIO STRATEGIES

The CIO is critical in ensuring that new technology is adopted and used within the organization's culture. Employees need to be aware of the technology and see it as an advantage to improve efficiency and production. Employee training, management support, and a change management strategy with clear goals and objectives are necessary for a successful implementation. At the moment, every IT function is becoming more sophisticated and convergent. CIOs should concentrate on understanding their present operations to improve their intelligence. Relying on their domain background and staying in their comfort zone will hinder a CIO's change. CIOs should prioritize increasing the intelligence of these functions above changing their domain background.

The process of evolving the CIO function is complicated, impacting several variables from diverse angles. One of the most intriguing and urgent aspects of this discussion is how CIOs should approach the transformation of their role. Paradoxically, it is conceivable that an excessive focus on *"transformative"* activities could inadvertently result in a less transformative role for CIOs. Transformative roles might appear counterintuitive, but if a CIO remains within their comfort zone rooted in their domain background, they may unintentionally bring about a transformation in themselves.

There are many things CIOs need to consider regarding their organizations' future. According to Forrester Research, it depends on who the CIO asks. According to a Forrester poll of technology decision-makers, CIOs spend budgetary money mostly on future investments rather than return on investment. However, line-of-business executives prioritize return on investment when choosing which apps and technology to use. There are many things to consider when debating whether or not a CIO should concentrate on ROI's future. To stay ahead of the quickly evolving technological world, a CIO must retain an end-in-mind mindset. Delivering measurable results and adding value to the company are other critical duties for a CIO.

8.5 STRATEGIC ALIGNMENT FOR BUSINESS SUCCESS: A CIO'S PERSPECTIVE ON BUSINESS DIRECTION

Retaining clients is always preferable to relentlessly seeking out new ones. Moreover, this is a big reason why business strategy is so important. Businesses require plans to succeed, including money management, promotion, and business operations strategies. A business strategy gives an organization a competitive advantage and an organization employs various strategies, such as becoming the cost leader, distinguishing the CIO from the competition, and focusing the CIO's attention on what matters most. Depending on their specific needs, a corporation may utilize a single strategy or a combination of several.

A business that wants to grow might employ a strategy focused on that goal, while one looking to boost profits might look to reduce expenses. Successful businesses regularly review and update their methods and procedures. A robust strategy helps the CIO make sound investment decisions regarding where and how to allocate resources but also aids in prioritizing projects and tasks within the organization. It is crucial to make wise choices when investing CIO resources, both money and time, to attain returns that surpass the average. (Sadjiarto *et al.*, 2020).

8.5.1 KEY PARAMETERS FOR BUSINESS STRATEGY FORMULATION

According to Gartner's research (2022), before formulating a business strategy, one should consider the following;

Setting definite, long-term objectives is essential for CIOs when creating corporate strategies. These objectives must coincide with the main business goals to provide a unified and integrated information management and technology approach. CIOs must concentrate on formulating strategic plans that tackle the organization's pressing issues and set it up for long-term success.

Business opportunity: To capitalize on opportunities, one must first do a thorough analysis of the current situation of the market and project future changes. Make your final decisions only once the CIO has obtained more information. The CIO needs to determine how to address every possible issue resulting from taking advantage of this opportunity.

Innovation: Ensure the services and goods the CIO plans to develop are unique from the competition and aligned with the company's objectives. Remember the launch of Apple's ground-breaking iPod? Customers have since recognized and valued the brand and merchandise of the company. Customers are prepared to spend more on Apple computers and do the same for the company's other products, including the iPhone, iPad, Etc.

Competition: To ensure that the CIO plans remain relevant, closely monitoring the competition is essential. Additionally, consider targeting an untapped or underdeveloped market with minimal or non-existent competition. This strategic move can make it more difficult for new entrants to gain a foothold in the market, allowing the CIO to secure market share, establish the CIO brand, and position the CIO organization favorably.

Economies of scale: The CIO should use economies of scale to lower the company's goods and services cost without compromising its uniqueness. A CIO should offer great assistance and unique features to the business of an organization. Walmart regularly offers discounts on its products to draw customers and increase sales. A CIO can investigate how utilizing state-of-the-art technologies will boost an organization's sales.

Time to market: A CIO should consider how long it will take to get the organization's product or service to market when weighing the "build versus buy" possibilities. It is possible to reduce the overall cost of manufacturing and distributing organizations' products or services by purchasing or outsourcing some components already on the market.

Evaluations: CIOs should routinely review the organization's strategy to ensure it still meets the needs of the market and the company's commercial objectives. Making mistakes cheaply and quickly is better, provided failure costs less than recovery.

Possible risks: A CIO should plan and take preventative measures against risks and failures to ensure the business can thrive despite challenges. A CIO should use the CIO's prior experiences, both good and bad, to shape the present and the future.

Stakeholders: Once the organization's strategy is finalized, it should be disseminated to all relevant stakeholders, including the staff, to ensure everyone can actively participate and comprehend the operational dynamics of the business. Make clear how it relates to both them and the company in general. External stakeholders include partners, suppliers, customers, industry analysts, and investors. For this reason, it is crucial to discuss a different plan with each of these groups. Inform them of the actions taken by the CIO, their rationale, and the impact on the company's expected revenue and stock price.

8.5.2 LEVELS OF BUSINESS STRATEGY

There are three distinct levels of business strategy: the corporate, the business, and the functional.

Corporate level strategy: An organization's long-term strategy for allocating resources and activities is its corporate design. The organization's strategy for the broader market is frequently at the heart of the corporate process. For instance, the leadership of an organization may have to decide which problem needs to be addressed, what goods or services to offer, and how to allocate the resources at hand. Plans at the corporate level are typically created by upper management to help businesses accomplish their primary goals. Business plans should consider the organization's advantages and disadvantages and the risks and hazards of its industry. Businesses can become more successful and competitive by considering the abovementioned aspects.

Business-level strategy: The business-level strategy involves formulating a course of action with the result in mind. Among these goals may be the penetration of new markets or the growth of existing ones. If a business strategy is to be effective, it must be in line with the organization's larger purpose and objectives. It is essential to consider the organization's advantages and disadvantages as well as the opportunities and risks in the industry.

Functional-level strategy: A CIO's primary goal is to ascertain how the company will use its IT resources to accomplish particular goals within a given functional area. In IT, this could entail choices about how best to deploy resources, adopt new technologies, and innovate to improve the efficacy and efficiency of particular business operations. By coordinating IT initiatives with that department's specific needs and goals, this strategic approach seeks to enhance the organization's overall performance. A company's functional-level IT strategy is usually developed and implemented by top-level IT executives, including the CIO. To achieve the particular functional goals, this entails making well-informed judgments on technology investments, resource allocation, and IT solution integration.

All three levels of an organization's business strategy must be in sync to succeed. If this happens, the organization will likely continue or decline due to internal misunderstanding and strife. A well-defined business strategy helps employees at all levels work together to achieve the organization's goals.

8.6 DATA EMPOWERMENT BLUEPRINT: CRAFTING A CIO'S VISION FOR EFFECTIVE DATA STRATEGY

Every organization determines how to engage with, use, and capitalize on its data, whether at the project or enterprise level. Adopting an enterprise-grade data strategy from an integrated perspective can help businesses reduce costs and maximize their investments in IT. Gaining a competitive edge can be achieved by incorporating these insights into company operations (Gartner, 2018). Corporations can improve operations and profitability by leveraging and organizing key business metrics. A company's data strategy is a plan for gathering, preserving, and handling data to support its business goals. The organization's overall business strategy influences data strategy. The chief data officer and business executives create a customized plan based on the organization's needs, and the latter is in charge of carrying it out.

To become data-driven, organizations must have a plan in place for advancing their transformation journey and effectively leveraging data as a corporate asset. This plan should match operational decisions with the methodical and automated, interpretation of data. Creating a data strategy is the first step towards making such a plan possible and improving the organization's Analytics IQ. To increase the caliber and precision of decision-making, this expression characterizes an organization's ability to consistently use sophisticated analytics at every point of interaction, whether mechanical or human.

A data strategy guarantees that every data project follows a reproducible structure and standard operating procedure. It is feasible to describe and rationalize all solution designs that employ data in some way because of 6jthis uniformity, which facilitates effective communication within the business. Many organizations ignore its importance because they think creating a data strategy would *"boil the ocean"* or be an *"infinity project"* with no return. They have to be fixed both times. It is worthwhile to design a data strategy.

It is also an essential phase in the transformation process of any organization. Businesses that implement data strategy ideas usually assign particular responsibilities to be in charge of these policies and procedures. Depending on their operational needs and strategic goals, different businesses have different critical components for their data strategy. The essential elements of a data strategy are as follows:

Business strategy: Understanding an organization's data needs is the first step in developing an effective data strategy. Next, choose the data-use plan that will best satisfy those needs.

Data access: This entails organizing data sets and developing simple dashboards for team usage to maximize accessibility to the organization's team.

Data architecture: The CIO must understand the data storage framework that the organization uses. Choose a location for master data storage, such as a local data warehouse or cloud storage.

Data integration: By combining organizations' data into a single system, the CIO can provide each organization unit access to enterprise data, which businesses use across all divisions and locations and may share and use as needed.

Data management: Establishing business processes and norms for an organization's data management is known as data management or data governance, and it makes data more accessible to access and share. The organization's data architecture treats all data equally. Thus, effective data management reduces decision-making times to make decisions.

Data Sources: Identifying the metadata of data assets, including origin details like file size, creation date, and creator, is crucial. It is essential to ascertain whether the data originates from the organization's records or an external source.

Conversion of data into business insights: The main goal of a data strategy is data analytics. Data analytics uses visualization tools to convert abstract data into observable patterns and explain how the data might help the CIO's business strategy.

8.7 NAVIGATING IT STRATEGY: CRAFTING EFFECTIVE ROADMAPS FOR TECHNOLOGICAL EXCELLENCE

The IT departments oversee technology, software, and architecture to serve internal and external customers. The CIO's role profoundly impacts the organization's effectiveness, growth, and goal achievement. Handling IT operations involves addressing a multitude of enhancement requests that may surpass the practical capacity of the CIO. Additionally, it requires a deep understanding of the users' needs within organizations, going beyond what is explicitly stated in their requests. The landscape is evolving, and there is a growing resemblance to product management.

By adopting a product mentality, future-focused IT executives translate strategic strategies into IT roadmaps. The CIO can use road maps to illustrate the timeline for delivering strategy-aligned projects and solutions and clearly describe the critical areas that must be prioritized to meet corporate objectives. Roadmaps can help the CIO focus on the most critical parts of the business to deliver solutions more quickly, whether serving internal or external clients (or both).

An IT roadmap, or technology roadmap, is a tool for visualizing how IT will develop to support the organization's leading products and the business. An IT roadmap describes the *"why," "what,"* and *"when"* of significant IT investments before the CIO starts the *"how"*—the development and implementation work. Completing complicated tasks, such as dealing with technological debt, infrastructure, and growth-oriented innovation, depends on these roadmaps. A technical roadmap highlights upcoming advancements while showcasing the technology already in use. A technology roadmap also considers the potential end-of-life dates for various technologies. A technological roadmap, for instance, will indicate when support for an existing CRM system will cease and when the new CRM will go live.

A well-thought-out IT strategy roadmap can reduce uncertainty when investigating potential long-term strategic goals. It helps the CIO visualize innovation and change so that the CIO may focus on what matters most in the subsequent stages of IT development. In addition to preparing businesses for expected challenges, IT roadmaps can also aid in dealing with the unexpected. A strategic plan may include moving data storage to the cloud, which offers greater security and resilience against external threats like natural catastrophes (Gartner, 2022).

8.8 DECODING STRATEGY CONSULTING AND PLANNING: NAVIGATING GROWTH AND SUCCESS

Strategy consulting is a service that helps businesses develop plans for handling different business processes. Strategy consultants usually work with C-suite executives and other high-level managers to learn about an organization's goals and objectives and suggest how to reach those goals. By 2025, the market for strategy consulting will reach a value of $101.7 billion, over $46 billion more than its worth in 2019. As long as companies want to increase productivity and cut costs, strategy consulting will likely remain essential to the professional services industry. It can help companies in many ways. *"Hiring strategy consultants can be good for a business in several ways,"* says McKee, a consultant at Bain & Organization.

McKee says that companies hire strategy consultants because they have worked on similar problems in different industries and shown they know how to solve them. *"Their ability to bring frameworks, structure, and best practices to unclear situations, their third-party objectivity, and their ability to validate an organization's own management team's strategy before investing significant resources" can all help a business"*. Other benefits of the business are:

Unbiased perspective: Employees and board members of an organization should be closer to the problems to see how to solve them. Strategy consulting lets leaders see things from a different point of view and get an honest assessment of their processes and goals without any possible conflicts of interest getting in the way.

New ideas: Strategy consultants bring a lot of experience and knowledge to the table, which can lead to new, out-of-the-box ideas for the growth and success of an organization.

Fast results: Business strategy consultants focus on getting the job done and stay focused on other priorities and projects because they have plans and a results-driven approach.

Conversely, strategy planning entails creating a thorough plan outlining how a company will accomplish its objectives. Strategy planning, which comprises concept generation, testing, planning, testing marketing, full-scale execution, and control management, is a subset of the broad area of strategy consulting. A single long-term plan demands a lot of resources, including money. Therefore, every strategy stage needs to be well thought out and planned. The program can prevent going wrong and incurring significant losses with careful preparation.

Although it can last longer, strategic planning typically entails establishing goals for the ensuing three to five years. Business planning differs from strategic planning because the former usually focus on short-term, tactical goals like allocating funds. One can address anything from a few months to a few years in a business plan. What emerges from strategic planning is a strategic plan. It is frequently recorded or displayed in several ways. These plans are simple to share, comprehend, and adhere to for stakeholders such as staff members, clients, investors, and business partners. Organizations often engage in strategic planning to consider the organization's potential impact of shifting market, industry, legal, and regulatory situations. At that point, a strategic plan could be modified to assess any changes in strategy.

8.9 DECIPHERING PLANNED VS. EMERGENT STRATEGY: NAVIGATING THE SPECTRUM OF BUSINESS DIRECTION

Strategy research agrees that making a strategy is somewhere on a continuum from planned to emergent strategies, and most strategies are a mix of these two. There have been different ideas about how to explain the things that affect strategy-making. There is a difference between *"planned strategy"* and *"emergent strategy."* Planned strategy is the strategy set by a formal strategic planning process (the strategy that happens as a business responds to changes in its external environment). If only business strategy were as simple as writing a business plan and putting it into action to reach strategic goals. While careful and thoughtful planning is crucial to success, it is not the only factor. Business success often involves various elements, including effective execution, adaptability, market conditions, competition, Etc. A well-thought-out business plan is essential, but there are other guarantees of success.

A planned strategy is grounded in a formal process for establishing corporate objectives and crafting a business plan that leverages available resources to achieve those goals. Therefore, planned strategy is the standard business planning process in all business textbooks. In summary, a planned strategy arises from a structured strategic planning process, aligns with specific corporate objectives, utilizes traditional planning tools and methodologies (such as SWOT Analysis, the PESTLE framework, and Porter's Five Forces), and is detailed in a formal business plan.

The idea behind the term *"emergent strategy"* was first used by Professor Henry Mintzberg to describe *"a pattern of action that develops over time in an organization without a specific mission and goals or despite a mission and goals.*" Mintzberg said that "*strategy emerges over time as intentions collide with and adapt to a changing reality.*" Emergent strategy is a responsive approach that adapts to events, including external environmental changes. It frequently entails strategic and tactical adjustments and is unrestricted by formal planning tools and methods.

Striking the correct mix between planned and emergent tactics is the actual issue facing CIOs. Planned strategies give direction and stability, but strict adherence might result in missed opportunities or a slow response to changes. However, focusing too much on emergent tactics could lead to disarray and a lack of coherence in the IT environment. Effective CIOs comprehend that a sophisticated strategy is essential to navigate a company's diverse paths. They incorporate adaptability into their planned plans so they can be adjusted when conditions change. This could entail reviewing IT priorities regularly, encouraging a culture of innovation and lifelong learning, and taking advantage of technological advancements to keep one step ahead of the competition.

CIOs use data analytics, AI-driven insights, and state-of-the-art tools to inform real-time and strategic planning decisions. By leveraging technology, CIOs enable companies to proactively respond to changing market conditions, client demands, and emerging possibilities. In summary, modern firms depend heavily on CIOs' ability to interpret the range of business directions. CIOs make sure their companies are both future-ready and adaptable enough to survive in a constantly shifting business environment by deftly balancing planned and emergent tactics. Tracing the range of business directions is a strategic need and a critical skill in this changing climate.

8.10 NAVIGATING ENVIRONMENTAL UNCERTAINTY: ADAPTING STRATEGIC PLANNING FOR CHANGING BUSINESS LANDSCAPES

When circumstances inside a corporate setting constantly shift, it is known as *"environmental uncertainty"*. As a result, the organization needs more significant control over factors outside of its administration. Uncertainty in the environment is a sign of organizational and decision-maker behavior. Additionally, it is a mediator in the relationship between organizational performance and behaviors and structures.

Executives who adopt this old approach run the risk of believing that the world is either specific and predictable or that it is unknown and unpredictable. Managers must conceal that their cash flows may be more reliable when capital planning or budgeting calls for point projections. These systems make it evident that managers must reduce uncertainty to persuade others to adopt their plan. Managers may, however, abandon the analytical rigor of their conventional planning procedures and instead depend primarily on their intuition when making strategic decisions if they believe that the environment is entirely unpredictable. Executives that adopt a *"just do it"* attitude to strategy may place bets on unproven products or markets, potentially resulting in record write-offs.

Risk-averse managers who operate in unpredictable environments need more faith in their gut feelings and seek guidance when making decisions. They do not make critical strategic choices regarding the goods, markets, and technological advancements they should pursue. Instead, they concentrate on internal programming, quality control, and reengineering to reduce expenses. These initiatives are beneficial, but they cannot take the place of strategy. To make wise strategic decisions without knowledge about future developments, the CIO must adopt an alternative strategy that avoids this risky dichotomy.

Managers rarely lack significant strategic knowledge, even in the most uncertain circumstances. They can create several potential results or even a list of specific scenarios. This fundamental concept is crucial because it establishes a organization's optimal path of action and growth process based on the uncertainty it experiences. Here is a methodology for determining the degree of uncertainty associated with strategic choices and modifying strategy accordingly. While there is no way to eradicate the issues that arise from ambiguity entirely, this approach provides the CIO with helpful guidance to enable the CIO to make more assured and knowledgeable strategic decisions.

CHAPTER 9
STRATEGIC LEADERSHIP IN GLOBAL IT MANAGEMENT

INTRODUCTION

The IT industry is spearheading globalization in an era of rapid technological advancement and enhanced connectivity. This chapter explores the complex network of globalization trends in IT, illuminating how the sector changes and affects global operations. Globalization's unrelenting pace has impacted every aspect of the IT industry, including how businesses embrace technology, innovate, and collaborate globally. This chapter looks at how the global IT scene is changing, from the emergence of cloud computing to the pervasiveness of digital platforms. It scrutinizes the dynamics of outsourcing, offshoring, and the cross-border flow of information that characterize the modern IT ecosystem.

There are challenges involved in navigating the worldwide IT landscape. This chapter identifies and examines the numerous opportunities and challenges that firms involved in global IT operations confront. IT leaders face challenges that call for strategic forethought and flexibility, from managing various regulatory frameworks to tackling cybersecurity threats globally. This section highlights how crucial it is for CIOs to be involved in creating a robust global IT strategy, given their vital role in guiding enterprises through the problems of global IT.

Understanding cultural subtleties is critical for effective collaboration in global IT teams. The chapter explores the topic of cross-cultural communication and highlights how crucial it is for IT teams to recognize and value diversity. The complexities of managing IT infrastructure across geographical locations are covered in this part.

Organizations face many legal and compliance concerns when they grow their IT footprint internationally. The legal and compliance considerations that are a part of global IT operations are examined in detail in this chapter. It delineates the legal frameworks that information technology leaders have to negotiate to guarantee moral and legitimate business practices, ranging from data protection laws to intellectual property rights. These instances work as helpful manuals, providing insights into the tactics and methods that have enabled businesses to prosper in the constantly changing global IT environment. Readers gain valuable insights into overcoming challenges and taking advantage of opportunities in pursuing global IT operations through this chapter.

9.1 GLOBALIZATION TRENDS IN IT

Globalization and IT are the two fundamental forces driving us into the uncharted territory of the digital frontier. The IT sector has been significantly impacted by globalization, which has resulted in revolutionary changes that have shaped the sector's environment. Global interdependence of economies, cultures, and technologies is reflected in these trends. Globalization and IT are not just trends; they are the twin engines propelling us into a future where connectivity is the new currency. Globalization and IT have allowed us to break down traditional barriers of time and space, creating a global marketplace where goods and services can be bought and sold in an instant. This has given rise to a new wave of digital nomads, people who can work from anywhere in the world and stay connected with their colleagues, customers, and clients. Furthermore, globalization and IT have opened up new opportunities for collaboration and innovation, allowing us to create products and services that were previously unimaginable. The following are major IT globalization trends:

9.1.1 OUTSOURCING AND OFFSHORING: GLOBAL TALENT POOL & OFFSHORE DEVELOPMENT CENTER CONSIDERATIONS

Businesses outsource IT services to nations with competent workforces to access a larger global talent pool. This lowers costs and increases accessibility to specialist knowledge. To reduce out-of-pocket expenses, CIOs are searching for a broader and deeper global talent pool to find qualified workers in nations where they have a competitive edge. This tactic utilizes areas renowned for their highly skilled and knowledgeable labor force, frequently at a reduced expense compared to wealthy countries. CIOs must consider a global talent pool to effectively manage resources and bring in varied skills and views that can enhance innovation and efficiency in IT operations. Organizations can realize cost savings without sacrificing work quality by utilizing people from nations with lower OPEX expenses. This allows them to deploy resources more effectively and fund long-term growth-promoting strategic projects.

Navigating the global talent pool takes time and effort. Cultural differences, time zone shifts, and language barriers are some factors that CIOs must carefully take into account. Facilitating the integration of global talent into the business requires the establishment of efficient communication channels, the deployment of collaborative tools, and the development of a coherent virtual work environment. Furthermore, it is imperative to thoroughly address legal and regulatory aspects to limit the risks connected with an outsourced workforce. Notwithstanding these obstacles, firms can prosper in a dynamic and fiercely competitive business environment by using the potential advantages of tapping into a broad and reasonably priced global talent pool.

Numerous IT corporations set up offshore development centers to use the labor markets and continuous development cycles. Establishing an offshore development center (ODC) in a nation with competent labor becomes a strategic option for CIOs as they want to maximize operating expenses and improve their organization's development capabilities Offshore development centers give CIOs access to a highly skilled and affordable talent pool, which allows them to perform software development, IT support, and other technology-related tasks at a fraction of the cost of in-house teams or onshore outsourcing. The availability of skilled labor in nations with reduced operational expenses (OPEX) can significantly enhance software development projects' overall effectiveness and scalability.

Nonetheless, several criteria must be carefully considered for an offshore development center to succeed. To ensure adherence to global norms and data protection legislation, CIOs must evaluate the legal and regulatory environment of the selected offshore location. Furthermore, it is vital to proficiently handle cultural subtleties and time zone disparities to ensure smooth cooperation between the onshore and offshore groups. Ensuring the successful integration of the offshore development center into the larger organizational structure and avoiding potential problems need the implementation of robust communication channels, project management frameworks, and security measures. CIOs can use offshore development centers as a potent tool to boost organizational agility, spur innovation, and cut costs by carefully managing these factors.

9.1.2 CLOUD COMPUTING: BORDERLESS DATA ACCESS & GLOBAL SERVICE PROVIDERS

Cloud computing has made data access and storage possible for businesses globally. Cloud computing facilitates the exchange of information across borders and promotes collaboration between teams that are separated by distance. A CIO must exercise extreme caution when navigating the complicated terrain of borderless data access in the context of global infrastructure management. The first crucial aspect is ensuring compliance with various data protection regulations across various jurisdictions. Data handling procedures must be carefully considered to comply with privacy legislation, such as the US's California Consumer Privacy Act (CCPA) and the General Data Protection Regulation (GDPR) in Europe. Furthermore, it is crucial to cultivate a culture of data governance and awareness within the company to reduce the risks related to cross-border data flows and to provide staff members with a sense of accountability for using information ethically.

Optimizing data access and communication throughout a globally distributed infrastructure is the focus of the second concern. A CIO must strategically leverage cloud services, content delivery networks, and edge computing to increase data accessibility and decrease latency. By putting in place a smooth and expandable network architecture supported by technologies such as SD-WAN (Software-Defined Wide Area Network), it becomes possible to transmit data efficiently and guarantee that users anywhere may obtain information quickly. Additionally, the CIO can balance performance, resilience, and cost-effectiveness by implementing a hybrid or multi-cloud strategy and customizing solutions to meet the specific requirements of each geographical area. A CIO can effectively manage a global infrastructure while navigating the complexities of borderless data access by combining technology expertise with regulatory compliance.

Cloud service providers run data centers worldwide and provide scalable and adaptable solutions to meet the demands of organizations everywhere. For Global Service Providers (GSPs), there are numerous factors to consider when managing global infrastructure as a CIO. The CIO must ensure consistent performance and seamless communication across numerous geographical locations. This entails assessing the bandwidth, latency, and network capabilities of the GSPs to ensure that the infrastructure can support the organization's global operations. Data security and compliance have also become critical issues. To protect sensitive data and uphold legal compliance across jurisdictions, the CIO must evaluate the GSPs' data protection policies, encryption techniques, and compliance with foreign standards. It is also imperative that the CIO understands the geopolitical environment because of regulations about data sovereignty and geopolitical upheaval that may jeopardize the infrastructure's security and accessibility.

Scalability and adaptability are essential for a CIO overseeing global infrastructure via GSPs. The infrastructure must be flexible enough to quickly adjust to business strategy, technology, or demand shifts as the organization's demands change over time. The CIO should collaborate closely with GSPs to ensure that the infrastructure is scalable and cheap, preventing unnecessary expenses during periods of low demand. Strategic alliances with GSPs should also support innovation and guarantee that the organization's technological stack stays state-of-the-art in line with its long-term objectives. Creating a robust global infrastructure that can handle the demands of the ever-changing and linked business world requires regular performance evaluations, backup plans, and open lines of communication between the CIO and GSPs.

9.1.3 COLLABORATIVE DEVELOPMENT: OPEN-SOURCE COMMUNITIES & REMOTE COLLABORATION TOOL CONSIDERATIONS

The rise of open-source software development has been spurred by globalization, as individuals from all backgrounds work together on projects. This cooperative strategy generates a wealth of shared information and speeds up invention. Managing global infrastructure within open-source communities poses unique challenges and considerations for a CIO. A critical component is that open-source technologies must be strategically integrated and leveraged across many geographic areas. Open-source communities typically have a global network of contributors, each with unique working methods and cultural quirks. It is up to the CIO to manage this variety and foster a cooperative and harmonious workplace. Successful implementation requires an understanding of the local context and the integration of regional insights into decision-making processes. Managing global infrastructure also entails considering local legal and regulatory factors making sure that open-source solutions abide by industry norms and local regulations.

Moreover, a CIO managing global infrastructure in open-source communities needs to place a high priority on good communication and teamwork. Active participation and contributions from a wide range of stakeholders are essential for the success of open-source initiatives. The CIO ought to cultivate a welcoming environment that promotes information exchange and cooperation between team members dispersed across various time zones. Implementing platforms and technologies that allow for smooth communication, like project management software, collaborative coding platforms, and video conferencing, is essential. Furthermore, by creating explicit policies for community involvement, documentation, and reporting, the organization can ensure that its global infrastructure supports its strategic objectives and uses the open-source community's combined knowledge. A CIO overseeing global infrastructure in the dynamic environment of open-source communities must delicately balance the autonomy of local contributors with the requirement for a cohesive vision.

IT teams use various tools to interact across national boundaries, including instant messaging, project management software, and video conferencing. This makes it easier to coordinate projects and communicate in real time. The choice and application of remote collaboration tools are critical factors for a CIO in charge of global infrastructure. First and foremost, a close inspection of these tools' security and compliance aspects is necessary. Protecting sensitive company data requires ensuring the selected solutions abide by national and international data protection laws and industry-specific compliance requirements. Due to the infrastructure's global reach, the tools must enable safe file sharing and communication between various geographical locations while providing robust encryption mechanisms to fend off potential cyberattacks. The tools should undergo a thorough security assessment to find and fix flaws and defend against hacks and illegal access.

Second, a CIO overseeing an international infrastructure must consider remote collaboration solutions' scalability and integration potential. The selected technologies must be easily integrated with the current applications and infrastructure, promoting a unified and effective digital environment. Scalability is necessary to support the demands of teams working in various time zones and geographical locations, enabling flexibility and adaptation as the company expands. A thorough evaluation of the information technology's efficacy in diverse network scenarios is essential to guarantee maximum performance globally. Incorporating user experience and training programs is also necessary to ensure seamless adoption and optimize the productivity benefits of remote collaboration technologies. A CIO can strategically leverage remote collaboration tools to enhance global infrastructure management by prioritizing security, scalability, and integration.

9.1.4 GLOBAL SUPPLY CHAIN CONSIDERATIONS: HARDWARE MANUFACTURING, LOGISTICS AND DISTRIBUTIONS

Global supply chains are essential to the IT industry's production of hardware components. Businesses import parts from several nations, creating a complicated web of manufacturers and suppliers. CIOs responsible for global infrastructure management face numerous intricate challenges when dealing with hardware production within global supply chains. First, logistics, transportation, and customs laws become more complicated when manufacturing plants are geographically diversified. CIOs must ensure that the hardware parts cross international borders with the least possible delay while meeting various regulatory requirements. This means establishing reliable tracking and management systems that can handle the complexities of international shipping, customs processes, and various import/export laws. CIOs should also prioritize cybersecurity measures because they know how much more exposure happens in operations due to their global nature. The digital infrastructure supporting hardware manufacturing operations must be secured to protect sensitive data, intellectual property, and the chain's general integrity.

Furthermore, hardware manufacturing in global supply chains becomes even more difficult due to the quick speed at which technology is developing and the constantly changing industry requirements. CIOs must keep up with the most recent advancements to guarantee that manufacturing processes remain productive, economical, and aligned with industry best practices. This entails establishing partnerships with technology suppliers, keeping up with new developments, and implementing adaptable infrastructures that can consider modifications to production processes or hardware specs. The challenge is striking a balance between maintaining the stability of the manufacturing process and integrating cutting-edge technologies to obtain a competitive edge. CIOs are crucial in creating an agile IT strategy that permits innovation while limiting risks associated with potential interruptions, ensuring that hardware production processes can readily adopt changes without incurring any delays.

Information Technology items will reach consumers globally through effective logistics and distribution networks. It takes an integrated supply chain to satisfy the demands. Logistics and distribution greatly influence global supply chains' effectiveness and success, which raises several issues for CIOs overseeing the supporting infrastructure. The requirement for reliable and networked information systems is a crucial factor. A CIO is responsible for ensuring that cutting-edge technological solutions, like data analytics tools, real-time tracking systems, and supply chain management software, support the logistics and distribution networks. These technologies make accurate inventory level monitoring, expedited order processing, and prompt supply chain disruption or demand change reaction possible. A more robust and flexible global supply chain can also be achieved by integrating cutting-edge technology like artificial intelligence and Internet of Things (IoT) devices, which can improve visibility, automate procedures, and optimize decision-making in real-time.

CIOs in charge of global infrastructure must give careful thought to cybersecurity. The potential of cyber assaults is becoming a major worry as logistics and distribution activities grow more digitally oriented. Strong cybersecurity measures must be put in place by

CIOs to safeguard private information and guarantee the integrity of the chain of supply. Identifying and countering such cyberattacks entails putting encryption techniques, multi-factor authentication, and continuous monitoring systems into place. To ensure the global infrastructure is safe and compliant, the CIO must keep up with changing cybersecurity risks and compliance laws in various jurisdictions. A proactive and all-encompassing strategy for cybersecurity is essential to protect the integrity of the supply chain, uphold consumer confidence, and reduce potential financial and reputational risks related to data breaches or interruptions.

9.1.5 DATA PRIVACY AND SECURITY: CROSS-BORDER REGULATIONS AND CYBERSECURITY CHALLENGES

The role of a CIO overseeing global infrastructure is impacted by the complicated challenges of data privacy and security in the context of cross-border regulations. The first challenge facing the CIO is the variety of global data protection regulations, each with unique compliance needs and subtleties. It becomes challenging to harmonize various laws to provide a coherent and uniform approach to data privacy. The CIO must create a plan with scalable solutions to adjust to the changing global privacy landscape and ensure compliance with the tightest standards. It is vital to build up strong encryption standards, access controls, and secure data transfer protocols to protect private information while it travels between multiple legal states.

Cybersecurity issues exacerbate regulatory complexity and add to a CIO's obligations to oversee global infrastructure. Due to the interconnectedness of today's digital economy, businesses are susceptible to a wide range of cyber threats, ranging from ransomware incidents to highly skilled attacks. The CIO's top priority must be implementing state-of-the-art cybersecurity solutions, such as threat intelligence, intrusion detection systems, and continuous monitoring. Developing a cybersecurity-aware corporate culture and ensuring that staff members in various locations are knowledgeable about potential risks and alert in identifying and averting them is also essential to building a robust cybersecurity framework. To proactively guard against changing risks in the dynamic global cybersecurity scene, the CIO must keep ahead of emerging cyber threats, work with cybersecurity experts, and regularly update the organization's defenses.

9.1.6 CULTURAL SENSITIVITY: USER EXPERIENCE DESIGN AND LOCALIZATION

For a CIO managing global infrastructure, cultural sensitivity in user experience design and localization is critical. Understanding and honoring cultural quirks is crucial in user experience design to develop user interfaces and interactions that appeal to a wide range of user bases. A culturally sensitive approach includes identifying differences in iconography, preferred colors, communication styles, and element positioning on a digital interface. For example, different colors may have different cultural connotations, and a popular design in one area may not be in another. To promote a sound and inclusive experience for everyone, a CIO overseeing global infrastructure must ensure that the user experience design complies with the cultural expectations of users across diverse geographic areas.

In the localization context, the CIO must back efforts to localize technology to particular regions and languages. Localization entails modifying software, applications, and information to satisfy a specific location's linguistic, cultural, and legal constraints; it goes beyond simple translation. Localization plans that consider regional preferences, legal considerations, and linguistic differences must be overseen by a CIO. Working with cross-functional teams of linguists, designers, and legal specialists is necessary to ensure that the technological infrastructure perfectly fits the cultural context of every target market. The CIO can improve global infrastructure's acceptance and overall efficiency across varied user communities by prioritizing cultural sensitivity in user experience design and localization.

9.1.7 RAPID TECHNOLOGICAL ADOPTION: GLOBAL TECH TRENDS AND CROSS-BORDER INNOVATION

The rapidly evolving global technology landscape has made speedy technological adoption crucial for CIOs managing global infrastructure. The rapid advancements in artificial intelligence, cloud computing, and the Internet of Things have accelerated innovation to the point that a proactive and deliberate approach to technology integration is required. CIOs must look for new trends to transform company operations, boost productivity, and provide a competitive advantage. The capacity to quickly incorporate breakthroughs into the current infrastructure is essential to preserving a robust and technical ecosystem prepared for the future.

Cross-border innovation increases the potential and problems. Working with global partners becomes essential to leveraging the variety of viewpoints and combined experiences that spur innovation. Flexible frameworks for technology deployment, interoperability, and safety measures are needed to integrate cutting-edge technologies globally. To guarantee that technology adoption is in line with the particular requirements and difficulties of every location within the global infrastructure, CIOs must also cultivate an environment of adaptation within their teams by encouraging ongoing learning and cross-cultural cooperation. In this era of rapid technological evolution, the success of CIOs hinges on their ability to lead organizations through the complexities of global tech trends and cross-border innovation.

In conclusion, the globalization of the IT sector is a dynamic, continuing process that is reshaping how technology is created, used, and consumed around the world. Businesses need to adjust to these developments to remain competitive in a global marketplace that is becoming more varied and linked.

9.2 CHALLENGES OF INTERNATIONAL IT OPERATIONS

CIOs in charge of global IT infrastructure need help managing foreign IT operations. One significant challenge is the variety of laws and compliance requirements among nations, necessitating careful navigation to guarantee conformity with disparate legal frameworks. Furthermore, it might be challenging to coordinate teams that are spread across several time zones, which can cause communication breakdowns and project delays. Global cybersecurity threats are likewise getting stronger, necessitating the development of solid solutions to protect sensitive data from changing dangers. The work becomes even more complex when one needs to accommodate regional nuances while maintaining standard technology platforms. This means the CIO must carefully balance decentralized flexibility and centralized control. Here are a few of the significant obstacles that CIOs must overcome to oversee an international IT network:

Cultural and Language Barriers: A CIO faces significant problems navigating the complexities of global IT operations, including language and cultural constraints. These obstacles are formidable and significantly affect international IT initiatives' general effectiveness and triumph. Cultural differences complicate problem-solving techniques, decision-making procedures, and team dynamics. Fostering unity among a heterogeneous workforce with differing work styles and attitudes toward authority is a responsibility that the CIO must do. Ignoring these cultural quirks can cause miscommunication, which impedes collaboration and may even cause IT initiatives to fail. Furthermore, cultural sensitivity becomes critical when implementing IT solutions because user preferences and expectations vary by area, which affects the uptake and success of technology adoptions.

Communication is more difficult when there are language difficulties, which is another crucial aspect of managing IT internationally. Clear communication is essential for effective teamwork, and language barriers increase the possibility of misunderstandings and poor communication. The CIO needs to take the initiative to address language barriers by putting strong communication standards in place, using translation resources, and fostering an atmosphere that welcomes open communication. Overcoming language barriers has a significant impact since it facilitates smooth collaboration, lowers the possibility of mistakes due to miscommunication, and guarantees that all members of the multinational IT team align with the organization's overall objectives and plans. Taking on these obstacles head-on is essential to maintaining effective IT operations and bolstering the company's international performance.

Regulatory Compliance: Regulatory compliance is among a CIO's most critical challenges while overseeing global IT operations. Due to the global reach of IT operations, CIOs must oversee a complex web of regulations and compliance standards across multiple countries and regions. Every jurisdiction may have unique cybersecurity standards, privacy legislation, and data protection laws. Ensuring that the organization complies with these numerous standards becomes burdensome, necessitating a deep understanding of the legal landscape in each operational region. There can be severe repercussions for not adhering to regulatory regulations, such as legal penalties, harm to one's reputation, and erosion of customer trust. The CIO must, therefore, establish robust systems and protocols to monitor and enforce compliance, often requiring close collaboration with legal teams and regulatory experts to stay ahead of evolving regulations.

Furthermore, CIOs overseeing global IT operations are constantly challenged due to the dynamic nature of regulatory frameworks. Regular revisions and modifications to laws and regulations about cybersecurity, IT governance, and data protection exist. Staying current on these changes and modifying IT processes to prevent compliance failures is critical. The CIO must proactively approach regulatory compliance by implementing continuous monitoring and evaluation procedures to identify and manage new compliance responsibilities. This calls for a dedication to continual education and interaction with regulatory organizations to anticipate changes and guarantee that the organization's IT infrastructure fully complies with international standards. Maintaining a smooth and effective IT operation while navigating the constantly changing regulatory landscape is a difficult task that calls for strategic planning, flexibility, and in-depth knowledge of the legal and technology worlds.

Time Zone Differences: The impact of time zone differences is one of the most critical problems a CIO has when managing multinational IT operations. Teams working in different time zones and across many continents result from the global nature of IT operations. For the CIO, this poses a significant obstacle to rapid decision-making, coordination, and communication. Setting up meetings becomes problematic since it can be challenging to coordinate a time that works for everyone on the team. Effective issue resolution is made more difficult by the delayed response times and the requirement for round-the-clock assistance. This difficulty impacts problem-solving speed, but it also makes team members feel disconnected, which could harm the cohesiveness and collaboration of the group.

Time zone differences impact strategic decision-making, team chemistry, and operational effectiveness. CIOs must balance carefully, considering the availability of crucial stakeholders spread across several time zones when making important and unimportant decisions. Asynchronous communication can cause delays in getting approvals, lengthen project timelines, and make it more difficult for the company to react quickly to changes in the market. Furthermore, the proper management of resources becomes a challenging process because the CIO must assign duties based on the availability of knowledge across multiple time zones. Implementing strong communication standards, making strategic plans, and leveraging technology to enable smooth collaboration among widely distributed teams are necessary to navigate these challenges successfully.

Infrastructure and Connectivity: A CIO's responsibilities for overseeing global IT operations include a variety of infrastructure and connectivity-related challenges. The global technological landscapes are diverse and frequently fractured, which presents a considerable challenge. Dealing with legacy systems, regional differences in technological standards, and varied degrees of technological maturity can all be part of international operations. This may result in integration problems, making setting up a uniform and smooth infrastructure challenging. Geopolitical issues and national regulatory variances can also be hindered because they require different systems to be implemented to comply with different legal and regulatory frameworks. This is because compliance standards can vary.

Infrastructure and connectivity issues can significantly affect a CIO managing global IT operations. Delays in communication, lower productivity, and more downtime can all be caused by erratic or unstable connectivity. Complying with complicated regulatory frameworks may result in increased expenses associated with compliance and possible legal liabilities. Furthermore, protecting sensitive data during cross-border transmission becomes a crucial problem requiring strong cybersecurity measures. To meet the expanding and changing demands of global operations, the CIO must also take care of the infrastructure's scalability. Strategic planning, cooperation with regional IT teams, and cutting-edge technology that can close gaps and improve connections globally are necessary to overcome these obstacles effectively.

Security Concerns: Security concerns are among the most significant challenges a CIO encounters while managing global IT operations. A significant obstacle is the intricate regulatory environment that differs between nations. Navigating industry-specific regulations, compliance standards, data protection, and privacy legislation can be rugged. The CIO oversees a unified and safe global IT infrastructure while keeping the company compliant with these laws. Furthermore, the threat landscape is ever-changing due to the increasing sophistication and prevalence of cyberattacks. Coordination of a coherent and effective defense strategy across several sites requires a deep understanding of the global cybersecurity landscape and the ability to implement standardized security measures suited to local peculiarities.

Security issues have various effects on a CIO overseeing global IT operations. A security breach may result in significant financial losses, harm to the company's brand, and legal repercussions if non-compliance is maintained. The CIO must strike a compromise between the requirement for strong security measures and the necessity of enabling cross-border communication and collaboration. This entails implementing thorough cybersecurity procedures, evaluating risks regularly, and spending money on cutting-edge tools like machine learning and artificial intelligence for threat identification. In addition, the CIO must cultivate an organizational culture that prioritizes cybersecurity knowledge and education to address the human component. This is because employees from various locations become vital partners in the fight against cyberattacks. Effectively addressing security concerns is paramount for the CIO to safeguard the organization's digital assets and ensure the uninterrupted flow of international IT operations.

Supply Chain Disruptions: Disruptions to the supply chain are among the numerous problems a CIO managing global IT operations faces. Because IT operations are international in scope, they involve intricate supply chains spanning several countries, each with unique logistical, legal, and geopolitical challenges. Due to its interconnectedness, the supply chain is vulnerable to disruptions from unforeseen events such as natural disasters, uncertain political contexts, and global health crises. A CIO sees these interruptions as a severe danger to the smooth flow of services, software, and hardware required to keep an effective and efficient IT infrastructure. Maintaining a stable supply chain becomes a careful balancing act that calls for ongoing oversight, risk-reduction tactics, and the capacity to adjust to new difficulties quickly.

Disruptions to the supply chain can significantly affect global IT operations, impairing an organization's overall performance and capacity to achieve business goals. Hardware shortages, delays in delivering essential components, or disruptions in service provisioning can lead to reduced productivity, increased downtime, and possible financial losses. CIOs must create solid backup plans, identify alternate suppliers, and use technology to improve supply chain visibility. The work is made more difficult by the requirement to adhere to several international norms and standards, which necessitates a sophisticated approach to risk management and resilience. The CIO must take a proactive and strategic approach to controlling supply chain disruptions to maintain its standing in a highly competitive global marketplace and guarantee the survival of overseas IT operations.

9.3 OPPORTUNITIES FOR INTERNATIONAL IT OPERATIONS

There are numerous chances in the multinational landscape for a CIO to oversee worldwide IT operations. One significant advantage of having access to many talent pools is that the CIO can assemble a team of people with different experiences and perspectives. Another advantage of having a worldwide presence is the ability to benefit from economies of scale through centralized infrastructure and resource efficiency. Cost savings could result from this. International operations bring the CIO into contact with many markets and technological ecosystems, which fosters innovation and keeps them ahead of industry trends.

Furthermore, access to emerging markets opens revenue development and business expansion doors. Thus, embracing global IT operations can put the CIO in a position to take advantage of synergies, spur innovation, and forge a competitive edge. Below are the key opportunities that a CIO uses while managing global IT:

Access to Global Talent: To manage worldwide IT operations, CIOs now have a transformative opportunity to access global talent. CIOs may access a broad pool of qualified experts worldwide in an increasingly linked environment. This international talent pool may significantly improve the efficacy and efficiency of IT operations by bringing a multitude of information, cultural views, and creative ideas. CIOs should take advantage of this chance to create vibrant, diverse teams to successfully negotiate the challenges of today's quickly changing technology landscape.

Moreover, the influence of CIOs having access to worldwide talent goes beyond the immediate benefits of proficiency and cultural diversity. It creates a cooperative atmosphere that promotes best practices, sharing, and cross-cultural communication. CIOs may use a globally distributed team's aggregate intellect to propel innovation and problem-solving efforts worldwide. However, this change also presents difficulties, including juggling time zones, cultural quirks, and legal obligations. CIOs must skillfully navigate these challenges to fully realize the potential of global talent and ensure faultless international IT operations that support company goals and priorities.

Market Expansion: Besides overseeing global IT operations, CIOs are essential in identifying and seizing opportunities for market expansion. Maintaining development and competitiveness in the current global corporate environment requires access to outside markets. CIOs are at the forefront of matching technology initiatives with overarching business objectives to enable smooth market entry and expansion. They use their knowledge to spot and profit from new trends, technology, and consumer needs across different geographies. CIOs may design flexible and adaptable IT infrastructures that support market growth plans by having a thorough awareness of various nations' distinct IT requirements and regulatory landscapes. This entails not just technology concerns but also a strategic comprehension of how IT might be utilized to satisfy regional market demands and adhere to various regulations.

CIOs significantly influence global IT operations beyond merely gaining market access; they also shape the entire organizational ecosystem. A thorough awareness of regulatory frameworks, cultural quirks, and geopolitical factors is necessary to administer global IT operations effectively. A cooperative and integrated international IT environment that encourages cross-border collaboration and information sharing is greatly aided by CIOs. This improves the organization's ability to react quickly to market changes while facilitating the smooth flow of data and knowledge. Furthermore, CIOs reduce the risks connected with cross-border operations by putting strong cybersecurity measures in place and ensuring that international data protection laws are followed, which gives stakeholders and customers trust. In other words, CIOs create a strong, networked IT infrastructure and access new markets, which form the cornerstone of successful international business operations.

Cost Efficiency: Organizations can enhance their global technical infrastructure and achieve cost efficiency by managing global IT operations with the help of CIOs. CIOs are essential in planning and executing IT strategies that support the company's overarching objectives while considering global operations' various and frequently intricate needs. CIOs can negotiate bulk purchasing deals, take advantage of economies of scale, and use centralized control and coordination to standardize technology platforms across various locations. This simplifies IT processes and allows for more efficient resource allocation, which reduces costs and unnecessary labor associated with managing many systems. Furthermore, CIOs can harness emerging technologies such as cloud computing and virtualization to create a flexible and scalable IT environment, enabling organizations to adapt to changing business needs on a global scale.

Beyond just financial gains, CIOs' access to cost efficiency in overseeing global IT operations has a significant impact. It has a favorable impact on the organization's overall agility and competitiveness in the global market. CIOs help streamline company procedures, foster better cross-border team collaboration, and expedite decision-making through optimizing IT operations. IT system standardization promotes a unified corporate culture by enabling smooth cross-border communication and data exchange. Furthermore, substantial and groundbreaking projects could receive funding through the profits of efficient resource-saving IT operations. CIOs are essential in reshaping the technology landscape to satisfy the needs of an international business climate's needs, as companies depend more on digital transformation to remain competitive. This helps to drive both strategic growth and operational efficiency.

Global Collaboration and Innovation: Because of their access to global innovation and collaboration, CIOs are presented with an expanding number of opportunities they have never had before in the fast-paced world of modern business. CIOs are essential to coordinating the smooth integration of information technology across many geographic areas as firms grow globally. Connecting with a worldwide network of professionals enables CIOs to take advantage of various viewpoints, technological innovations, and industry best practices. Because of this access, which promotes a culture of ongoing learning and adaptation, CIOs can stay on the cutting edge of technological innovation and deploy cutting-edge solutions that cut across national borders.

The worldwide collaboration and innovation that CIOs have access to have a multifarious effect on multinational IT operations. On the one hand, it makes it easier to design and implement globally standardized IT systems that improve productivity, consistency, and interoperability across various industries. However, it also allows CIOs to customize solutions to fit unique regional demands and regulatory requirements, promoting a balance between local customization and global standardization. With this access, CIOs may quickly embrace disruptive technologies that provide them a competitive advantage in the global market and remain ahead of developing trends. In the end, CIOs that strategically leverage global collaboration and innovation not only maximize IT operations globally but also put their businesses in a position to negotiate the complexity of the global business landscape effectively and creatively.

Scalability and Flexibility: Modern technology's unmatched flexibility and scalability have drastically altered CIOs' jobs in managing international IT operations. The advancements in cloud computing and advanced networking solutions have allowed CIOs to expand their IT infrastructure globally. Businesses can expand globally due to their scalability, as the traditional constraints of physical infrastructure do not limit it. CIOs may quickly provide and deploy resources in several regions by utilizing cloud services, which enables them to adjust quickly to shifting market dynamics and business needs. This increased scalability allows CIOs to match IT capabilities to global markets' varied needs more effectively while optimizing resource use.

Moreover, the degree of flexibility that CIOs possess in overseeing global IT operations significantly influences the agility and responsiveness of their organizations. When combined with cutting-edge management tools, cloud-based solutions enable CIOs to easily coordinate IT resources, guaranteeing that systems can adjust to changing workloads and local demands. This adaptability goes beyond infrastructure and includes deploying various software programs to satisfy specific legal, cultural, or commercial demands. CIOs can implement agile development approaches and roll out upgrades globally to keep IT operations in line with the changing demands of the global business environment. Essentially, scalability and flexibility give CIOs the means to handle the challenges of overseeing global IT operations, encouraging creativity, and allowing businesses to prosper in a changing environment.

Diversification of Risk: In managing global IT operations, CIOs are essential in taking advantage of opportunities and minimizing risks. The deliberate distribution of resources among several locations is a noteworthy possibility for risk diversification. CIOs' capacity to identify and capitalize on expanding markets allows organizations to grow internationally. They can reach new markets and strengthen their business strategy by doing this. Diversification protects against technical, geopolitical, or economic shocks affecting a particular area. Equipped with a global viewpoint, CIOs can strategically arrange applications, data centers, and IT resources to reduce the impact of unanticipated occurrences and maintain business continuity.

In global IT operations, CIOs' access to risk diversification has a significant impact. Organizations may effectively manage and spread workloads, maximize performance, and improve overall system reliability with a well-designed global IT infrastructure. Additionally, by utilizing a variety of global talent pools, CIOs may assemble a competent and adaptable IT staff that can handle regionally unique problems. This encourages creativity and guarantees the company is prepared to adjust to changing regulatory environments. CIOs may also put strong cybersecurity measures in place that are customized to the unique threats that exist in each region, protecting sensitive data and guaranteeing adherence to local laws. In summary, the advantages of risk diversification for CIOs enable businesses to thrive in a rapidly changing global IT environment while mitigating possible issues related to worldwide operations.

A strategic strategy is necessary to balance the potential and challenges in international IT operations, emphasizing risk management, compliance, and cultural sensitivity. Businesses that successfully manage these complexities will have an advantage over rivals in the global IT market.

9.4 CROSS-CULTURAL COMMUNICATION IN MANAGING GLOBAL IT TEAMS

Effective collaboration within IT teams requires cross-cultural communication, particularly in the modern globalized workplace where teams frequently straddle national borders and cultural boundaries. IT teams that effectively communicate across cultural boundaries are more productive innovative, and create a happier work atmosphere.

9.4.1 FACTORS AFFECTING CROSS-CULTURAL COMMUNICATIONS

The following are essential factors to take into account and techniques for overcoming cross-cultural communication barriers in IT teams:

Cultural Awareness: Cultural sensitivity has to be the first focus of a CIO's leadership approach in the dynamic world of global IT management. It is essential for managers of teams that work across continents and with a diverse range of stakeholders to recognize and respect cultural oddities. Cultural awareness encompasses more than just understanding overt cultural practices; it also involves recognizing local differences in work ethics, communication styles, and implicit values. Understanding cultural differences allows a CIO to create a more inviting atmosphere, improve teamwork, and reduce the likelihood of conflicts resulting from misinterpreted cultural norms. By incorporating cultural sensitivity into their leadership approach, the CIO can create a cohesive global IT team that leverages the unique strengths of each member and can quickly adapt to the challenges of a multinational work environment. A CIO must know geographical variations in business procedures, regulatory frameworks, technological infrastructures, and cultural norms.

Language Considerations: Developing consistent communication protocols and documentation in a commonly recognized language supports a global IT strategy by minimizing confusion and streamlining procedures. The CIO must be aware of the diverse linguistic environment within the company because team members may originate from various linguistic backgrounds. Establishing a standard language for official communication is crucial to ensuring that all parties understand the information clearly. Creating uniform communication protocols and documentation in a commonly understood language facilitates process simplification, reduces miscommunication, and supports a unified worldwide IT strategy. The CIO should also be aware of cultural quirks and refrain from using terminology that could be offensive or misconstrued in other locales. This will promote a more welcoming and cooperative workplace.

The rules of simplicity and clarity in language are essential in global IT administration. Because technology is so complex and the IT staff has a wide range of technical expertise, the CIO must communicate clearly to explain complicated ideas adequately. When speaking with non-technical stakeholders, removing technical jargon and simplifying technical aspects might be helpful to improve understanding and goal alignment. Finding the ideal mix between technical accuracy and linguistic simplicity enables the CIO to provide a compelling vision, bring the global IT team together around shared objectives, and improve IT's overall efficacy and efficiency.

Communication Platforms and Tools: Effective communication platforms and technologies are essential for facilitating smooth collaboration and information sharing between geographically separated teams in the context of global information technology management. The organization's goals should be supported by these tools, which should also consider the various communication styles of users and the particular challenges of overseeing a global IT infrastructure. Project management, instant messaging, video conferencing, and collaborative document editing tools are just a few technologies the CIO must carefully select to enable effective communication across global locations.

After identifying the communication tools, the onus ensures that the workforce knows how to use them. Under the CIO's direction, training programs become essential for equipping staff members with the abilities and know-how to use these tools efficiently. To support a coherent global IT environment, this training should go beyond basic technical competency and cover best practices for virtual collaboration, data security measures, and cultural sensitivity.

Active Listening: A CIO managing international IT teams across multiple nations must possess solid listening skills. Good communication is critical to efficient teamwork and project execution in a complex and dynamic environment. To listen actively, one must not only hear what is being said but also comprehend the underlying context, feelings, and subtleties that the speaker is trying to impart. Adopting active listening as a CIO promotes an inclusive and transparent culture among the international teams. It shows a sincere desire to comprehend different viewpoints, which is crucial when interacting with people from different professional and cultural backgrounds.

In global IT management, CIOs can use strong feedback channels to help with active listening. These systems allow international team members to freely share their ideas, worries, and recommendations. Regular team meetings, online town halls, and surveys that let staff members express their opinions on ongoing initiatives, challenges, and organizational tactics might help achieve this. Furthermore, real-time interactions can be facilitated by utilizing contemporary communication technologies and collaboration tools, which helps team members feel connected even when they are geographically apart.

Flexibility in Communication Styles: Adaptability and flexibility of communication style are critical traits for CIOs overseeing multinational IT teams in several countries. Effective communication strategies are only sometimes applicable in the dynamic realm of global business. A CIO must be skilled at modifying their communication style to fit the many linguistic variances, cultural quirks, and everyday working habits in each area. This adaptability encompasses different communication norms, hierarchical structures, decision-making processes, and language obstacles. A CIO can promote an inclusive, cross-border work environment that is collaborative by acknowledging and accommodating these variances.

A CIO must possess adaptability and communication skills to navigate the intricacies of a global IT world. National differences in market dynamics, legislative modifications, and technological breakthroughs might be substantial. A flexible CIO knows the need to change course, integrate new technology, and keep up with changing market trends across geographies. Because of this flexibility, the CIO can maintain a consistent worldwide IT strategy while implementing customized IT solutions that meet local needs. Additionally, by adopting an agile approach, the CIO can effectively manage challenges resulting from shifts in the geopolitical environment, economic fluctuations, and unforeseen disruptions, all of which enhance the resilience and success of the business's IT operations across international borders.

Cultural Sensitivity in Meetings: Meetings must be mindful of cultural variations, mainly when a CIO oversees multinational IT employees. Comprehending and honoring heterogeneous cultural conventions guarantees proficient correspondence and cooperation within the group. It entails recognizing variations in decision-making procedures, communication philosophies, and job expectations. It is critical to foster an inclusive atmosphere in meetings where team members from all cultural backgrounds feel free to voice their thoughts and opinions. The global IT team should feel united, have open communication, and receive training on cultural sensitivity from the CIO.

Meeting manners are essential to preserving professionalism and effectiveness in various teams. Clear rules for online or in-person meetings that prioritize promptness, engagement, and courteous communication must be established by the CIO. The conference experience can also be improved by utilizing technology accommodating various time zones, languages, and communication preferences. It is advisable to occasionally alternate meeting schedules to handle the problem of arranging meetings across several nations. This strategy prevents burnout from regularly unpleasant meeting schedules by guaranteeing that team members from all geographies can participate during convenient hours, supporting equal involvement. By implementing appropriate meeting etiquette and prioritizing cultural awareness, the CIO may cultivate a cooperative and harmonious global IT environment.

Documenting Decisions and Agreements: It is impossible to overestimate the significance of recording decisions and agreements in the complex world of global IT administration, where a CIO supervises teams operating across borders. Written documentation is one of the most essential tools for promoting accountability, clarity, and alignment within distributed teams. A standardized and consistent documentation style is essential in this global setting because of the wide range of cultural and language backgrounds. This style is a universal language, guaranteeing that vital information is accurately and wholly communicated across national boundaries. To guarantee that the entire global IT department agrees, the CIO must set up robust documentation procedures that cover codified decision-making processes and the subtleties of agreements made during virtual meetings.

In a globally distributed IT environment, efficient communication and cooperation depend on a standard documentation format. It provides a structured framework for recording agreements and decisions, making it easier for team members from different nations to understand, refer to, and carry them out. This reduces the possibility of misunderstanding and promotes information exchange and cross-functional cooperation. Furthermore, well-documented agreements and choices act as a historical record in the fast-paced world of technology, providing insightful information for reference and learning in the future. Carefully recording decisions and agreements becomes vital for maintaining operational excellence and advancing a unified global IT strategy as the CIO negotiates the complexities of managing IT staff across borders.

Conflict Resolution: Effective leadership requires resolving conflicts, mainly when overseeing multinational IT teams in many countries. The CIO is essential in resolving disputes quickly to maintain a positive work atmosphere. Conflicts are unavoidable in a global IT setting because of the differences in cultural backgrounds, communication styles, and work habits. It takes a robust interpersonal skill set and a thorough comprehension of cultural quirks for the CIO to resolve conflicts and promote cooperation.

Prompt resolution is necessary to keep small arguments from becoming more significant problems that could ruin team chemistry and project results. Prompt resolution of issues allows the CIO to keep the global IT organization's culture positive, raise morale, and increase overall productivity.

When teams are spread across multiple countries, time zones, and cultural contexts, miscommunication, divergent priorities, or different working methods can lead to problems. A neutral third party intervenes during mediation to help communicate and provide direction for the settlement process. In this capacity, the CIO serves as a mediator to help team members overcome differences and come to an understanding. This strategy helps build a more resilient and cohesive team and resolve current disputes. Through open communication, comprehension, and cooperation, mediation creates a climate in which different points of view are respected. The CIO can build a cohesive worldwide IT team that uses diversity to its advantage rather than as a cause of conflict by using mediation to handle issues. This will ultimately help the company succeed in its technological ambitions.

Building Team Cohesion: Especially for a CIO, fostering team cohesion in a multinational IT setting where teams operate across borders is a complex but vital responsibility. It can be challenging to foster unity and collaboration amongst team members from different regions and cultural backgrounds. The CIO must implement strategic team-building exercises that go beyond geographical limitations to get past this obstacle. Team members can interact personally and professionally by participating in virtual team-building activities, online workshops, and collaborative projects. Prioritizing open communication channels is crucial, and the CIO should use technology to make regular video conferences, online town halls, and other interactive platforms possible. In addition to fostering stronger interpersonal ties, these initiatives help build a coherent workplace where team members feel appreciated and linked even though they are physically separated.

Accepting the diverse viewpoints, abilities, and experiences of people from various countries fosters team innovation, creativity, and problem-solving. The CIO ought to encourage a welcoming environment where diversity is accepted and honored. Training in cultural sensitivity, cross-cultural mentoring programs, and campaigns that honor and value different cultural customs and holidays can all help achieve this. The CIO promotes cooperation and understanding among team members by creating a culture that embraces diversity, which eventually helps to create a more robust and flexible international IT workforce. Emphasizing diversity enriches the work experience of each team member and positions the organization to thrive in the dynamic and ever-evolving landscape of the global IT industry.

Continuous Improvement: Adopting continuous improvement principles is critical to thriving in this complicated environment. Continuous improvement is not just a technique but also a way of thinking that promotes a gradual, methodical approach to process improvement and performance improvement. In global IT management, where laws, regulations, and consumer needs change quickly, continuous improvement ensures that teams constantly review and improve their plans. Using strong feedback loops is a fundamental part of this strategy. Teams from different countries may communicate openly, exchange insights, solve problems, and improve their methods when they have regular and positive feedback systems.

Under the responsibility of a CIO, developing a learning culture is yet another crucial component of efficient global IT management. In this perspective, developing a culture where ongoing learning is integrated into the daily operations of IT teams worldwide constitutes a learning culture that extends beyond official training sessions. To foster a culture that fosters experimentation, curiosity, and information sharing, the CIO is essential. The CIO fosters a continuous learning culture that cuts beyond national borders by promoting cross-cultural exchanges, information-sharing seminars, and mentorship initiatives. In addition to empowering teams to keep up with technology developments, this learning-centric strategy develops a flexible, resilient workforce that can lead innovation in a quickly changing global IT environment.

IT teams may effectively traverse the obstacles of cross-cultural collaboration by prioritizing cultural understanding, encouraging open communication, and putting methods in place that account for different communication styles. In an international workplace, this method not only strengthens team dynamics but also increases IT initiatives' general efficacy and efficiency.

9.5 MANAGING IT INFRASTRUCTURE ACROSS GEOGRAPHICAL LOCATIONS

Managing IT infrastructure across geographical locations requires strategic vision, careful planning, and efficient execution. The CIO, as the main person in charge of the IT department, is essential to ensuring that the company's IT infrastructure facilitates smooth operations and business continuity across various locations. From the perspective of the CIO, the following are essential factors and tactics:

Global IT Strategy: A global IT strategy is essential for information technology to be seamlessly integrated with broader business goals. This is especially true when the CIO oversees teams dispersed across several countries. This strategic strategy promotes efficiency, innovation, and competitive advantage by coordinating technology projects with the organization's goals. In addition to managing a unified IT infrastructure, the CIO is in charge of negotiating the intricacies of various operational, legislative, and cultural contexts in many nations. A deep awareness of local and global contexts is necessary to align global IT strategy with business objectives successfully. This allows the CIO to customize technological solutions that meet local needs and support the organization's overall success on a global basis. This delicate balancing task ensures that technology becomes a potent enabler that drives the business toward its strategic objectives while welcoming the diversity that comes with an internationally dispersed IT environment.

Standardization and Consistency: Standardization and consistency are two fundamental ideas that are essential to guarantee smooth functioning and operational effectiveness in the ever-changing field of global IT management. Creating and upholding consistent procedures, guidelines, and technological frameworks within an organization is known as standardization. A CIO should ensure that different parts of the IT infrastructure function together, promoting interoperability and lowering complexity. Contrarily, consistency emphasizes preserving consistency in procedures and results, reducing variances that can result in errors or inefficiencies. These ideas provide a strong basis for an efficient and dependable IT system.

Technology standards are essential to standardization and critical to a CIO's managing global IT. These standards provide guidelines and specifications that control how technologies are used and implemented, guaranteeing compatibility and interoperability across various systems and environments. A CIO managing IT teams dispersed across several countries needs centralized management. To achieve this, a single governance framework must be established, with technological standards, regulations, and processes managed centrally to ensure uniformity and alignment with the organization's key objectives. A CIO can successfully negotiate the difficulties of managing a global IT landscape by combining standardization, consistency, and technology standards; this promotes collaboration and maximizes the performance of multinational teams.

Risk Management and Compliance: Effective risk management and compliance are essential in the dynamic field of global information technology management because they ensure digital infrastructures' continuous operation and security. Besides the challenges of managing IT teams in several countries, CIOs also have to deal with various regulatory environments and compliance standards. Following local laws, rules, and regulations, such as cybersecurity, data protection, and industry, is what regulatory compliance means. A CIO needs to set a strong compliance structure that considers these variances, ensuring the company stays within the law and reducing the chance of fines and reputational harm.

Simultaneously, risk assessment becomes essential to the CIO's global IT team management plan. To detect weaknesses and potential areas of concern, the CIO must undertake rigorous risk assessments as technology advances and cyber-attacks grow more sophisticated. This entails assessing the possibility and impact of various risks, from geopolitical instability to cybersecurity attacks that could impact the IT infrastructure. The CIO can proactively reduce possible threats, improve the resilience of the organization's IT systems, and prevent financial losses by putting in place a thorough risk management strategy. In this complex function, the CIO ensures that the company's IT operations prosper in the dynamic global environment by acting as a link between technical innovation, regulatory compliance, and risk management.

Global Vendor Management: An essential component of a CIO's job when managing IT operations across borders is global vendor management. The CIO must proactively manage relationships with vendors worldwide in this complicated environment. Forming strategic alliances with vendors becomes essential because it helps the CIO match vendor capabilities and services with corporate objectives. These alliances entail cooperation, common goals, and a thorough comprehension of one another's business processes and transactions. In this particular scenario, the CIO assumes a crucial function in cultivating a mutually beneficial association with vendors, guaranteeing that the IT infrastructure is economical, flexible, and adaptable to the ever-changing demands of an international enterprise.

Effective Global Vendor Management necessitates strategic alliances and close attention to vendor performance. The CIO must establish solid metrics and key performance indicators (KPIs) to assess suppliers' performance, dependability, and overall impact on the company's IT objectives. Regular reviews of vendors' performance highlight areas for improvement, where money may be saved, and potential risks. The CIO can improve the organization's competitiveness in the global market by optimizing the IT ecosystem through proactive monitoring and management of vendor performance. By taking a thorough approach to global vendor management, the CIO can maintain a streamlined, effective, and resilient IT infrastructure while navigating the difficulties of managing IT staff across national borders.

Scalability and Flexibility: In global IT management, scalability and flexibility are critical factors, particularly for a CIO managing teams in several countries. Scalability is the capacity of a system to manage an increase in demand or workload effectively, guaranteeing that its IT infrastructure can grow with the company to meet its changing needs. Scalability is a crucial element of architecture because it enables the CIO to implement solutions that grow with the business and prevent bottlenecks and performance issues. This scalability includes databases, software, system architecture, and hardware. It enables the CIO to make growth plans for the future and guarantees that the IT infrastructure is resilient and flexible enough to change with the times.

Simultaneously, flexibility emerges as a crucial component of worldwide IT operations management. In this sense, flexibility refers to the capacity to modify and adjust IT solutions to satisfy regional demands while maintaining the system's overall cohesiveness. Localized differences in corporate processes, laws, or cultural quirks demand an adaptable IT architecture that permits adaptation within a globally uniform framework. Because of this flexibility, the CIO may create a harmonic IT environment that meets local and global objectives while balancing the need to address local specifics and centralized control. It can be challenging to balance standardization and customization to create a scalable and flexible IT infrastructure that best serves the organization's global objectives.

Network Connectivity and Performance: Performance and network connectivity are essential components of contemporary IT infrastructure, particularly for businesses with international operations. Reliable connectivity enables uninterrupted communication and data sharing between teams, stakeholders, and offices across different locations. Building a robust and secure network infrastructure is critical when a CIO oversees worldwide IT operations with staff in several countries. To reduce downtime and guarantee continuous operations, this involves putting redundant and high-bandwidth connections in place. The CIO must prioritize local demands over global network optimization, considering that various locations may have particular bandwidth requirements, regulatory issues, or connectivity difficulties. The company can improve speed, lower latency, and ultimately improve the global user experience for consumers and staff by taking a strategic approach to network optimization.

A thorough understanding of regional variances is required for global network optimization for local requirements, and connectivity solutions should be tailored accordingly. If particular issues need to be resolved, including network latency, local law compliance, or technology infrastructure adaptation, the CIO must liaise with local IT teams. This strategy contributes to a unified and well-integrated worldwide IT infrastructure and guarantees that every office runs effectively within its specific local context. Network performance and responsiveness can be improved by utilizing sophisticated routing protocols, edge computing, and content delivery networks (CDNs). The CIO may design a network infrastructure that satisfies the various demands of a global firm and lays the groundwork for future expansion by prioritizing dependability, scalability, and flexibility.

Disaster Recovery and Business Continuity: An organization's resilience plan must include business continuity (BC) and disaster recovery (DR) to ensure it can withstand and recover from unanticipated disruptions. The difficulties get complex when a CIO oversees global IT with personnel spread over several countries. Planning for global disaster recovery entails developing a thorough plan considering probable hazards in many geographic areas, cultural quirks, and regulatory variations. The CIO must collaborate with regional teams to develop tailored DR and BC strategies that satisfy local requirements while maintaining a cogent global framework. Regular testing is essential for confirming the efficacy of these strategies, pointing out flaws, and promoting readiness. The CIO's leadership enables the organization to take a proactive stance, promote cross-border communication, and ensure that business may resume as usual as soon as feasible in the event of an unanticipated occurrence.

Remote Monitoring and Management: Effective management of multinational IT infrastructures depends heavily on remote monitoring and management, or RMM, mainly when a CIO oversees teams dispersed over several countries. A key element of RMM is centralized administration and monitoring, which offers a single platform for managing and observing various IT assets from one central location. This method guarantees prompt answers to possible problems by giving the CIO real-time insights into systems and networks' functionality, security, and health. Automated management procedures further increase efficiency by streamlining operations, decreasing manual interventions, and automating repetitive tasks. When a CIO is in charge of managing worldwide IT operations, RMM is essential because it allows the CIO to keep the organization's IT infrastructure performing at its peak, proactively handle problems, and maintain a unified and consistent IT environment across various geographic locations.

Cultural Sensitivity and Communication: Cultural awareness and proficient communication are critical factors for a CIO responsible for overseeing multinational IT teams dispersed throughout several countries. One must possess a deep cultural awareness to negotiate the subtleties of various work styles, communication preferences, and social norms in this dynamic and diverse workplace. The CIO must promote a courteous, inclusive, and diverse workplace culture that honors and celebrates diversity, understanding that cultural nuances are as crucial to effective communication as language. It is imperative to incorporate a variety of communication channels, taking into account variables like time zones and the favored methods of communication in different areas. To overcome geographical barriers and improve the effectiveness of information flow, video conferencing, cooperative online platforms, and asynchronous communication tools become essential. The CIO can create an innovative and collaborative global IT team that thrives on cross-border cooperation by emphasizing cultural sensitivity and using various communication techniques.

Training and Skill Development: Training and skill development become critical success factors in the ever-changing world of global IT management, particularly when managing varied teams in several different countries. Establishing uniform training programs is a top priority for a CIO who oversees global IT operations since it guarantees that all employees acquire and improve skills similarly. This calls for a thorough approach to global talent evaluation, in which the CIO assesses each team's current skill sets and pinpoints areas in need of specialization or development. The CIO can enable their teams to stay updated with new developments in technology and market trends by establishing a culture of continual learning and development, promoting creativity and adaptability. By implementing deliberate training programs, the CIO may close skill gaps, improve cross-cultural cooperation, and strengthen the group's overall knowledge base, guaranteeing the company a competitive advantage in the dynamic field of global IT management.

In conclusion, from a CIO perspective, managing IT infrastructure across geographic locations requires a comprehensive strategy that includes global relationships, standardization, risk management, and cultural sensitivity. The CIO may guide the company in developing a robust and flexible IT infrastructure that meets the many demands of an international company by considering these factors. By developing global relationships, the CIO can create a network of partners that can provide the necessary resources and expertise to ensure the success of the IT infrastructure. Standardization ensures that the same processes and procedures are used across all locations, which helps to minimize costs and provide consistent service. Risk management helps to identify any potential issues that may arise and develop a plan to mitigate them. Cultural sensitivity is necessary to ensure that the IT infrastructure meets the needs of the different cultures involved.

9.6 LEGAL AND COMPLIANCE CONSIDERATIONS IN INTERNATIONAL IT OPERATIONS

There are many legal and regulatory considerations while working in the global IT sector. Organizations must navigate the complicated web of international legislation to safeguard sensitive data, stay out of legal hot water, and maintain morally and responsibly conducted company. Important legal and compliance factors for global IT operations are as follows:

Data Protection and Privacy Laws: For CIOs managing global IT operations, navigating the complicated terrain of data protection and privacy regulations is essential. The European Union has set global standards for strict data protection obligations by implementing the General Data Protection Regulation (GDPR), a basic framework. In addition to ensuring GDPR compliance, CIOs must keep up with the constantly changing global privacy regulations. Handling cross-border data transfers becomes a delicate balancing act that necessitates a deep comprehension of global legal frameworks and regulatory standards. Establishing a culture of privacy throughout international IT teams, utilizing strong data encryption, and putting privacy-by-design concepts into practice are all parts of a proactive approach to data security. To stay flexible in a legislative environment that is constantly evolving and to promote a dedication to moral data handling standards internationally, CIOs must constantly work in tandem with legal specialists to foresee and handle new privacy concerns.

Intellectual Property Rights: It is crucial for a CIO managing worldwide IT operations to navigate the complex world of intellectual property rights (IPR). Patents, trademarks, and copyrights are essential for protecting the company's cutting-edge technologies, distinctive brand, and artistic creations in that order. Achieving adherence to global legal frameworks is crucial, considering the disparities in rules among various regions. The CIO must actively work with the legal and compliance departments to create plans that protect the company's intellectual property and adhere to the many laws governing it in different countries. This entails being thoroughly aware of regional differences in trademark registration regulations, copyright enforcement systems, and patent filing processes. The CIO may safeguard the organization's reputation globally, encourage innovation, and reduce legal risks by cultivating a culture of knowledge and adherence to intellectual property regulations throughout global IT teams.

Cybersecurity Regulations: In the ever-changing global information technology ecosystem, the function of a CIO is closely linked to managing the sophisticated network of cybersecurity legislation, both at the national and industry-specific levels. The CIO oversees an organization's digital infrastructure and operates within international legal and compliance norms to guarantee cross-border data security and integrity. National laws, like China's cybersecurity law and Europe's General Data Protection Regulation (GDPR), provide particular challenges that call for a sophisticated grasp of local quirks. At the same time, it becomes crucial to follow industry-specific guidelines, including those offered by the Payment Card Industry Data Security Standard (PCI DSS) or the International Organization for Standardization (ISO). The CIO must strategically oversee global IT teams, implement robust cybersecurity measures that safeguard vital data, and defend its global commitment to moral and legal behavior to comply with the many laws and regulations.

Export Controls and Sanctions: As a CIO overseeing global IT operations, navigating the complicated world of export controls and sanctions is crucial to guaranteeing seamless operations globally and legal compliance. Managing dual-use technology with both military and civilian applications necessitates a deep understanding of export control procedures to prevent unintended violations. The CIO must establish strong sanctions compliance procedures to prevent the legal challenges accompanying foreign trade restrictions. This entails keeping up with different nations' and international organizations' constantly changing penalties. A proactive approach to compliance is necessary to minimize legal risks and protect the company's brand. This includes ongoing monitoring, personnel training, and thorough risk assessments. A CIO's ability to preserve the integrity of global IT operations depends on their ability to strike an effective balance between pursuing technology breakthroughs and adherence to international regulatory and compliance frameworks.

Contractual and Commercial Laws: A deep understanding of contract and business law is crucial in the dynamic realm of global IT administration overseen by a CIO. Agreements between the CIO and diverse teams operating in different jurisdictions are based on local contract laws. Maintaining adherence to global legal norms becomes critical, necessitating a careful process in drafting agreements that negotiate the complexities of various legal frameworks. The CIO must handle the complexities of conflict resolution while being aware of possible disputes resulting from various corporate, legal, and cultural practices. A comprehensive conflict resolution strategy compliant with international legal frameworks must be developed to ensure smooth operations and reduce risks. The CIO can be positioned as a strategic leader who can promote compliance, minimize legal risks, and facilitate successful cross-border collaboration within the confines of international legal and regulatory requirements by taking a proactive approach to understanding and abiding by contractual and commercial laws on a global scale.

Labor and Employment Laws: The dynamic landscape of corporate operations overseas necessitates that CIOs managing global IT teams traverse complex labor and employment-related legislation frameworks. Local employment laws significantly impact the working conditions and the relationships between companies and employees. CIOs must know the complexities of these rules to ensure that their international IT teams abide by the applicable laws in each nation where they do business. Furthermore, a thorough awareness of global legal requirements and compliance standards is necessary, given the cross-border nature of employment in the present era. CIOs are in charge of developing strategies that consider diverse legal contexts, promote a coherent work environment, and lessen potential risks resulting from variations in labor laws. Effective leadership of multinational IT teams depends on a CIO's capacity to promote compliance, maintain moral principles, and modify plans to fit the many legal environments in which the teams function.

Anti-Corruption and Bribery Laws: When managing global IT, CIOs must navigate complex foreign legal environments. This is especially true regarding Anti-Corruption and Bribery Laws, such as the Foreign Corrupt Practices Act (FCPA) in the US and other comparable laws across the globe. To uphold moral business practices, the CIO is in charge of ensuring that their IT teams follow strict anti-corruption regulations and comply with international laws. Developing thorough *"Third-Party Due Diligence"* protocols is essential, as these initiatives serve as a first line of defense against potential corruption issues related to outside cooperation. The CIO must set up thorough procedures for vetting suppliers, contractors, and partners to determine their adherence to moral behavior, reducing the possibility of unintentional participation in unethical behavior. In addition to protecting the company's reputation, the CIO aims to encourage open and responsible business practices globally by cultivating a culture of compliance and due diligence inside global IT operations.

Accessibility and Inclusivity: To create a digital space that serves a wide range of users, accessibility, globality, and inclusion are top priorities for a CIO managing IT operations. By following the Web Content Accessibility Guidelines (WCAG), digital material can be created and designed with accessibility in mind, giving people with disabilities an easy-to-use experience. The CIO must also handle local inclusivity requirements, considering that various jurisdictions may have varied accessibility-related legislative frameworks and compliance requirements. A thorough grasp of the international laws and regulations governing digital accessibility is necessary to balance these factors globally. The CIO can cultivate an IT ecosystem that satisfies legal requirements and demonstrates a dedication to developing inclusive technology by advocating for inclusivity on a local and global scale.

Consumer Protection Laws: Navigating multinational legal and regulatory environments is a significant job of a CIO in global IT management. Ensuring that consumer data is handled safely and ethically across borders is crucial for upholding consumer protection laws, and this requires the CIO. Clear communication with stakeholders regarding data usage, privacy rules, and cybersecurity safeguards is crucial for transparent corporate practices. Global standards must be followed to prevent deceptive product or service statements through fair advertising practices. Through the active consideration and integration of these components into the global IT strategy, the CIO assumes a crucial role in establishing a reliable and compliant framework that protects consumer rights and promotes a robust and conscientious global digital ecosystem.

Regulatory Reporting and Compliance: A sophisticated approach to regulatory reporting and compliance, incident reporting, and keeping up with regulatory updates are necessary for a CIO to manage global IT operations effectively. A comprehensive plan is necessary to navigate the intricate web of international legal and regulatory obligations. CIOs overseeing international IT teams must establish robust regulatory Reporting and Compliance frameworks to guarantee compliance with diverse regulatory environments, industry standards, and nation-specific regulations. Mechanisms for reporting incidents should be seamlessly integrated to enable quick action in the event of possible disruptions or breaches. Additionally, a proactive approach to regulatory updates is essential; the CIO needs to monitor how international regulations are changing and quickly adjust IT strategy to comply. This proactive strategy protects the company from legal issues and helps worldwide IT teams develop a transparent and accountable culture.

Crisis Management and Response Planning: Crisis management and response preparation are critical for CIOs in charge of international IT operations, especially regarding data breaches. A CIO must strategically coordinate reaction teams across several locations in the connected digital ecosystem of today when cyber threats transcend borders. This means traversing a complicated global legal and compliance web and dealing with technological issues. Data breach response procedures must conform with various legal frameworks, including GDPR in Europe and HIPAA in the US. Legal counsel's assistance becomes essential in helping the company navigate the complexities of data protection laws and potential liabilities. CIOs must collaborate closely with legal experts to develop comprehensive and legal crisis response plans and advance a proactive cybersecurity strategy that safeguards the business and its stakeholders internationally.

Training and Awareness: A CIO's responsibilities in the ever-changing global IT world go beyond technical expertise to strategic management of international legal and regulatory frameworks. To successfully traverse this complicated terrain, training and awareness become crucially important. Employee training programs impart a thorough understanding of the various legal and ethical issues in different overseas jurisdictions and address technical competencies. To create an atmosphere where teams are fully aware of the legal implications connected to international IT operations, the CIO must advocate for an organizational culture that values moral behavior. The CIO may guarantee that IT management complies with global legal requirements by integrating ethical concepts into its core values. This will reduce risks and encourage the development of a moral and legal global IT strategy.

Proactiveness, continuous learning, and a dedication to moral business conduct are necessary for handling legal and regulatory issues in global IT operations. Cooperation between legal departments and IT leadership is essential for the company to stay legal and take advantage of the advantages of a globalized IT environment. IT leaders should collaborate with legal departments to develop and implement risk management strategies to reduce legal and compliance risks. Regular communication between all stakeholders is essential to ensure that everyone is on the same page and that any issues are addressed quickly. Finally, IT departments must stay up to date with the latest regulations and laws.

CHAPTER 10
EMERGING TECHNOLOGIES AND INNOVATION IN THE CIO REALM

INTRODUCTION

The first section of the chapter sets the stage by examining the situation of new technologies. It explains the most recent advancements, such as automation, machine learning, and artificial intelligence, that are changing several industries. CIOs in charge of strategically adopting and implementing new technologies must have a solid understanding of them if their organizations are to remain competitive in the marketplace. The conversation focuses on the CIO's critical position as an innovator and technical architect, highlighting how their choices may spur corporate growth and competitiveness.

The chapter then turns to the significant effects of automation, machine learning, and artificial intelligence on corporate processes. The chapter explores the technologies' revolutionary potential and provides insights into how they might improve productivity, streamline processes, and boost company performance. Following suit, a thorough analysis of blockchain is conducted to reveal its ground-breaking potential for business transformation. CIOs are given a thorough grasp of blockchain by breaking down its salient characteristics and advantages. As the chapter continues, it explores particular use cases and possible changes that blockchain can bring about in various industries, providing CIOs with a road map for negotiating the unexplored areas of technological innovation.

In the last section, the chapter shifts towards the careful balancing act CIOs have to do between innovation and operational stability. The conversation concerns the strategic methods that CIOs may use to manage innovation in their companies and ensure that the pursuit of new technologies aligns with the larger objectives of resilience and stability. CIOs are given the information and resources they need to successfully traverse the constantly changing world of innovation and emerging technologies by synthesizing theoretical insights and practical counsel. CIOs are leading organizational change due to the speed at which technology develops. They are responsible for establishing a future in which innovation is a strategy and a way of life.

10.1 EMERGING TECHNOLOGIES

Cutting-edge technologies build a new world, forging connections between imagination and reality in the landscape of innovation. CIOs must stay abreast of developing technology to maintain their organization's security, efficiency, and competitiveness in the ever-changing digital landscape. CIOs are interested in several critical upcoming technologies.

Below are some of the emerging technologies that the market is trying to adopt:

Artificial Intelligence (AI) and Machine Learning (ML): Emerging technologies such as AI and ML, with their promises of unprecedented efficiency and benefits, have quickly changed various industries. AI, driven by machine learning algorithms, is increasingly used in various applications, such as supply chain management optimization in logistics and predictive analytics in healthcare. While ML algorithms improve finance fraud detection and risk management, AI helps healthcare by facilitating early disease detection and individualized treatment plans. However, there are several obstacles to the broad adoption of these technologies. Significant obstacles include privacy issues, ethical concerns, and the possibility of prejudice in AI algorithms. Furthermore, many organizations need help adopting robust AI and ML systems because of the high computing needs and the demand for experienced individuals. Striking a balance between innovation and responsible deployment is crucial for harnessing the full potential of these technologies in a rapidly evolving digital landscape.

5G Technology: From the standpoint of a CIO, the introduction of technologies such as 5G signifies a fundamental change in how businesses function and utilize connections. The advantages are significant, and CIOs may transform their IT infrastructure with this chance. 5G's fast speed and low latency make it possible for data to transmit seamlessly, which speeds up decision-making and increases overall operational efficiency. 5G offers exciting use cases in the manufacturing, shipping, and healthcare sectors since it allows for real-time control and monitoring. However, the CIO has to face the challenge of implementing this technology. Given the financial outlay necessary for widespread 5G adoption, comprehensive strategic planning is essential, and it is critical to address cybersecurity and data privacy concerns. Another layer of complexity is ensuring that the business's personnel can navigate this technological transformation and enjoy its benefits without sacrificing security. CIOs leading their companies through the revolutionary landscape of 5G and future technologies must balance innovation and risk avoidance.

Edge Computing: From the perspective of the CIO, emerging technologies such as edge computing, with their unique challenges and substantial benefits, herald a paradigm shift in the IT landscape. The main benefit is that data may be processed closer to the source, lowering latency and improving real-time decision-making. This is important for sectors including manufacturing, healthcare, and self-driving cars. By processing data locally, edge computing makes it possible to utilize bandwidth more efficiently while lessening the load on central cloud resources. However, because decentralized processing creates additional vulnerabilities and compliance challenges, CIOs must address security and data governance concerns. Moreover, ensuring smooth compatibility while integrating edge solutions with existing infrastructure requires careful planning. It is crucial to manage the complexity of overseeing a distributed network of edge devices and ensuring their reliability. For CIOs navigating the disruptive edge computing world, finding the correct mix between distributed processing and centralized control remains crucial.

Blockchain Technology: The world of data management and security is being revolutionized by emerging technologies like Blockchain Technology, which presents many advantages to CIOs. Blockchain ensures transaction transparency and trust by being decentralized and resistant to manipulation, which reduces the need for intermediaries and increases operational effectiveness. Furthermore, the blockchain's immutability improves data integrity and offers a solid basis for several applications, including supply chain management and financial transactions. When implementing blockchain technologies, CIOs must seriously consider regulatory compliance, scalability, and interoperability. The revolutionary potential of blockchain technology is demonstrated by its many use cases, such as smart contracts and decentralized finance. However, enterprises must manage the challenges and risks of integrating this technology into their current infrastructure and the constantly changing regulatory landscape. Therefore, CIOs must embrace blockchain technology and carefully reduce related risks if they want to properly exploit it to drive innovation and competitiveness for their organizations.

Cybersecurity Innovations: From the standpoint of CIOs, cybersecurity advances represent a vital frontier in the constantly changing universe of digital threats, presenting considerable benefits and problems. Modern technologies like machine learning, artificial intelligence, and sophisticated encryption methods have enabled enterprises to identify and address cyber threats accurately and quickly. These advances improve the overall security posture by automating repetitive operations, enhancing the effectiveness of the incident response, and supplying real-time threat intelligence. Since these solutions are proactive, CIOs benefit from keeping one step ahead of dangerous actors. Care must ensure smooth compatibility and reduce interruptions while integrating new technologies into the current infrastructures. The use cases protect sensitive data in banking, healthcare, and vital infrastructure and cut across multiple industries. Despite their benefits, CIOs need more qualified cybersecurity specialists, the quick speed at which technology develops, and the possibility of false positives in automated threat detection systems. CIOs trying to protect their companies from the constant barrage of cyberattacks must continue to walk a fine line between innovation and risk management.

Augmented Reality (AR) and Virtual Reality (VR): Virtual reality and augmented reality are revolutionary technologies that bring unique benefits and issues for CIOs. Augmented reality superimposes digital data on the physical world by adding contextual information in real-time to improve user experiences. CIOs know AR's potential to increase customer engagement, staff productivity, and operational efficiency. Conversely, virtual reality submerges viewers in a computer-generated environment, promoting creative training courses and online collaborative areas. Benefits from these technologies include better decision-making, better training, and immersive customer experiences.

Nonetheless, CIOs must consider the necessity of a solid infrastructure, data security, and system integration. Use cases come from various industries, such as virtual product displays in retail and healthcare simulations. High initial expenditures, continuous maintenance, and the requirement for personnel with specialized expertise are some of the challenges. CIOs must balance the complicated obstacles and the possible benefits of integrating AR and VR into their technological ecosystems to guarantee a successful and long-lasting deployment.

Robotic Process Automation (RPA): For CIOs, RPA has become a game-changing technology since it streamlines and automates several repetitive business tasks. The main benefit is lower costs and more productivity because software robots are very good at quickly and precisely carrying out rule-based tasks. As a result, human resources can now concentrate on higher-value projects. RPA is well-liked by CIOs because it integrates seamlessly with current systems, removing the need for significant IT overhauls. Customer support, invoicing processing, and data entry are common use cases. However, CIOs must balance factors like ensuring robust security measures, handling possible job displacement issues, and carefully choosing which functions may be automated. Careful planning is necessary to enhance RPA's efficacy and return on investment because of obstacles like scaling challenges, maintenance complexities, and ongoing monitoring requirements. CIOs must intentionally deploy RPA and regularly optimize it to fully leverage it in fostering a more agile and competitive business environment.

Quantum Computing: The CIOs can benefit significantly from the revolutionary field of quantum computing at the confluence of computer science and physics. Nevertheless, the complexity involved should be noticed. The revolutionary advantage of quantum computing lies in the potential to solve intricate problems ten times faster than classical computers, particularly in simulations, cryptography, and optimization. The idea of quicker data processing stimulating innovation in the banking, healthcare, and logistics industries excites CIOs. However, there are many factors to consider, such as the fact that quantum technology is still in its infancy and that scalable, practical quantum computers are still being developed. CIOs have to face the difficulty of incorporating quantum technologies into applications and IT infrastructure that are already in place. Use cases like advanced machine learning and drug discovery show promise while being in their infancy. Nevertheless, CIOs must overcome the technology's volatility and error-proneness to utilize quantum computing while guaranteeing data security and dependability. CIOs must balance embracing the quantum revolution with a realistic assessment of its current limitations and strategically position their enterprises to do so.

CIOs must manage the changing landscape as technology develops, balancing innovation and risk management and ensuring that new technologies complement their companies' strategic objectives. CIOs must have a flexible mindset, collaborate with colleagues in the industry, and engage in ongoing education to guide their enterprises effectively through the digital transformation period.

10.2 CIO'S ROLE IN ADOPTING AND IMPLEMENTING EMERGING TECHNOLOGIES

The CIO is crucial for an organization's acceptance and use of emerging technology. Businesses must stay ahead of the technological curve to stay inventive and competitive in today's quickly changing digital landscape. As the executive in charge of IT management, the CIO is crucial in guiding the company through the challenges of implementing and integrating emerging technologies.

Strategic Vision: A CIO's ability to strategically accept and apply emerging technologies is critical for managing the quickly changing digital transformation landscape. An innovative CIO understands how vital technology is to the success of their company and plans forward by coordinating new developments in technology with the overarching goals of the business. This vision includes identifying and incorporating state-of-the-art technologies and fully comprehending how these breakthroughs can boost productivity, encourage creativity, and provide an edge over competitors. As part of the CIO's strategic vision, the company will be positioned for long-term success in a constantly evolving digital environment by keeping up with industry trends, foreseeing potential disruptions, and proactively utilizing emerging technology. It also entails fostering a culture of flexibility and ongoing education within the IT staff to guarantee that the company stays responsive to the ever-changing pace of technological advancement.

Technology Evaluation: CIOs must keep up with the most recent technological developments and trends. Their responsibility includes assessing new technologies to ascertain their applicability and possible advantages for the company. This entails carrying out in-depth evaluations, risk analysis, and feasibility studies. One of the most essential parts of a CIO's overall responsibility is the technology evaluation while adopting and deploying emerging technologies. CIOs are crucial in assessing the viability and potential impacts of new technology on the goals and objectives of their organization. This entails conducting in-depth analyses of new technologies, considering security, scalability, compatibility with current systems, and alignment with the overarching business plan. CIOs must keep up with the quickly changing technology world to spot the potential for efficiency and innovation advantages. CIOs may make well-informed decisions and steer their organizations toward strategically adopting and implementing cutting-edge technologies to provide a competitive advantage and promote digital transformation when technology evaluations are executed successfully.

Risk Management: Inherent risks usually accompany the adoption of emerging technology. CIOs must balance the benefits against the negatives, which include concerns about data privacy, security, and potential disruptions to ongoing operations. One of the most critical aspects of their job is creating effective risk management plans. CIOs are essential in helping firms navigate the risks and challenges of adopting innovative technologies. The effective adoption and deployment of these state-of-the-art systems depend heavily on the risk management component of a CIO's duties. CIOs are responsible for proactively identifying, evaluating, and mitigating potential risks, including cybersecurity threats, compliance with regulations, and difficulties integrating new technologies. CIOs must balance innovation and risk mitigation, cultivate a resilient culture within their organizations, strategically match technology initiatives to business goals, and stay current on industry developments to make decisions that support the enterprise's long-term viability and competitiveness. CIOs may successfully guide their companies into the future of technology by taking advantage of opportunities and avoiding potential hazards with a thorough risk management strategy.

Budgeting and Resource Allocation: CIOs are essential when allocating funds for technological projects. The business must allocate resources effectively to ensure that it invests in the right technologies to support its strategic goals. Managing the funds for talent acquisition, infrastructure, and research and development is part of this. A crucial component of the CIO's duties is resource allocation and budgeting, where strategic choices are made to maximize available funds and technology. By coordinating the budget with the organization's overarching objectives and priorities, the CIO guarantees that financial resources are allocated to projects that propel innovation and digital transformation. To facilitate the effective integration of developing technologies, resource allocation entails the prudent distribution of human capital, technical infrastructure, and other essential resources. The CIO is better able to lead the organization toward technological excellence and foster resilience and adaptation in a dynamic digital environment when they place equal focus on resource allocation and budgeting.

Collaboration with Stakeholders: Cooperation between department heads, external partners, and other C-suite executives is necessary to adopt developing technology successfully. CIOs are responsible for fostering agreement among important decision-makers and effectively communicating the value proposition of new technologies. A CIO's function requires close collaboration with stakeholders when adopting and implementing emerging technologies. The CIO acts as a liaison between the organization's strategic objectives and the possibilities presented by innovative solutions. The CIO can learn essential things about business requirements and difficulties by interacting with stakeholders, including department heads, IT teams, and outside partners. This cooperative strategy guarantees that new technologies complement the organization's overarching goals, improve operational effectiveness, and reduce risks. The CIO may design a coherent strategy that embraces innovation and optimizes the benefits of emerging technology for the expansion and competitiveness of the company by encouraging open communication and comprehending the viewpoints of different stakeholders.

Talent Acquisition and Development: The CIO is responsible for assembling and managing a knowledgeable IT staff that can apply and support cutting-edge technologies. This entails hiring people with experience in data analytics, blockchain, cybersecurity, and artificial intelligence. CIOs must also invest in training and development to ensure their personnel know the newest technologies. The CIO's path to embracing and integrating innovative technology begins with talent acquisition and development. Finding and developing the best personnel becomes a strategic necessity as the CIO leads the company's IT revolution. Finding people who can combine technical expertise with creative thinking is essential for thriving. Furthermore, the CIO needs to prioritize continuous development programs to upskill current teams and ensure they have the knowledge and experience to implement the newest trends successfully. Hiring and training new employees become essential parts of the CIO's job description, including promoting an innovative and flexible culture inside the IT division and keeping up with technology improvements.

Integration with Existing Systems: There is a chance that new technology and legacy systems coexist simultaneously. CIOs must develop integration plans to enable a smooth cohabitation and transition between existing and developing systems. Finding the right balance becomes crucial to preventing interruptions to current company activities. The CIO's abilities significantly impact how well new technology integrates with legacy systems. The CIO's job as a strategic leader is to navigate the tricky terrain of technology adoption and ensure cutting-edge solutions enhance and complement well-established systems. This calls for a thorough comprehension of the business goals, procedures, and IT infrastructure that the company currently uses. To maximize performance, the CIO must coordinate a smooth transition between modern technology and ancient systems, utilizing compatibility and interoperability. This integration, which links technology investments with the overarching business strategy to promote development, competitiveness, and operational excellence, is both a technological challenge and a strategic necessity. In addition to technical expertise, the CIO's role in this process entails a thorough understanding of organizational dynamics and the ability to convince key stakeholders of the advantages of technological development.

Monitoring and Optimization: CIOs are in charge of monitoring the performance of accepted technologies and making adjustments as needed after they are implemented. This entails doing data analysis, taking inputs, and streamlining technology utilization to guarantee that it keeps up with the changing demands of the company. A CIO's technology responsibilities go beyond simple adoption and deployment, including careful monitoring and optimization tactics. The CIO guarantees the smooth integration and long-term functionality of developing technologies, pivotal in the organization's technical progress. Monitoring is a proactive process that evaluates the effectiveness of established systems using real-time data and KPIs. Optimizing simultaneously is adjusting workflows, processes, and resource allocation to increase overall effectiveness and optimize return. An effective CIO understands that integrating emerging technologies into an organization successfully is a journey that requires constant monitoring and adaptive optimization methods to stay ahead of the curve and keep the company in line with the rapidly changing technology landscape.

In conclusion, there are several facets to the CIO's responsibility for embracing and integrating modern technology. It entails talent management, cooperation, risk management, strategic planning, and continuous optimization. An organization can be positioned to fully utilize emerging technology, spurring innovation and long-term growth, with the help of a proactive and imaginative CIO. The CIO must keep up with the ever-evolving technology landscape, understand the business implications of adopting new technologies, and also be able to anticipate and respond to changes in the market. They must be able to lead the organization in developing and implementing strategic initiatives that will ensure the success of the organization. Additionally, the CIO must be able to provide guidance and support to the technical team and ensure that the organization can leverage technology to its fullest potential.

10.3 IMPACT OF ARTIFICIAL INTELLIGENCE, MACHINE LEARNING, AND AUTOMATION

Automation, machine learning (ML), and artificial intelligence (AI) significantly influence many facets of civilization. These technologies are transforming industries, economies, and daily life in ways not even found in science fiction. Here are a few crucial places where their influence is most noticeable:

Economic Transformation: Artificial intelligence and automation have led to the automation of repetitive, routine tasks, raising concerns about job displacement. However, they have also created new employment prospects in robots, AI development, and other related industries. Automation and artificial intelligence have greatly enhanced productivity across various industries by optimizing workflows and lowering error margins. Significant economic shifts have been brought about by the pervasive influence of automation, machine learning (ML), and artificial intelligence (AI) in various industries. As these technologies develop, they accelerate change like work, automating repetitive jobs and enhancing human capacities. This change increases output and changes the nature of traditional jobs, requiring workers to be proficient in digital skills. Increased productivity, cost-cutting, and innovation are changing the economic environment and creating new business opportunities. These developments, however, also prompt worries about the loss of jobs and the requirement for reskilling programs. The long-term economic transformation by AI, ML, and automation will necessitate striking a careful balance between utilizing the advantages of new technology advancements and resolving potential social issues.

Healthcare: Medical diagnosis accuracy is increasing due to the ability of AI and ML systems to examine massive amounts of data. This enhances the precision and promptness of illness diagnosis, leading to better treatment results. Artificial intelligence (AI) accelerates the search for novel pharmaceuticals by analyzing biological data and projecting potential therapeutic candidates. This could reduce the time and cost of bringing these drugs to market. A disruptive era has begun in the healthcare sector with the combination of Artificial Intelligence (AI), Machine Learning (ML), and automation, revolutionizing patient care, diagnostics, and operational efficiency.

AI-powered algorithms analyze large-scale medical data to find trends, forecast the course of diseases, and create individualized treatment regimens. Algorithms for machine learning improve diagnostic precision, making it possible to identify illnesses early and boost patient outcomes in general. Automation speeds up administrative tasks, reduces paperwork, and increases the accuracy and speed of processes. Even though these advancements offer a great deal of promise to improve efficiency and the standard of treatment, they also present ethical conundrums, issues with data privacy, and the need for medical staff to adapt to a rapidly evolving technological environment. The healthcare sector could transform if AI, ML, and automation are developed further and applied responsibly. This would eventually benefit patients and healthcare professionals equally.

Education: Traditional teaching and learning approaches have radically transformed due to the education sector's use of Artificial Intelligence (AI), Machine Learning (ML), and Automation. AI-driven educational technologies have personalized the learning experience by adapting the pace and content according to each student's needs. This enhances comprehension and engagement levels. Large volumes of educational data are analyzed by machine learning algorithms, which offer insightful information about student performance and enable teachers to adjust their methods accordingly. Teachers can concentrate on more engaging and innovative instruction parts when administrative responsibilities are streamlined by automation. However, this technological revolution also brings some difficulties, like the need for educators to become more skilled and handle data protection issues.

Despite these challenges, there has been a significant overall impact, creating a more dynamic and adaptable educational environment that better equips students for future demands. AI is making individualized learning experiences possible by customizing course materials to meet the needs of each unique student. Both learning outcomes and student engagement may benefit from this. Automation makes administrative work at educational institutions more efficient, freeing teachers to concentrate more on mentorship and instruction.

Finance: The financial sector has seen a dramatic transformation with the introduction of Artificial Intelligence (AI), Machine Learning (ML), and Automation, which have ushered in a new era of efficiency, innovation, and risk management. With unprecedented speed and precision, AI algorithms analyze vast amounts of financial data, enabling organizations to enhance their predictive capabilities and make more informed decisions.

Machine learning models have transformed investment strategies, credit rating, and fraud detection by streamlining procedures that formerly required manual effort. Automating has streamlined routine chores, which has decreased operating costs and increased overall productivity. The speed and accuracy of financial services have certainly increased due to these developments, but there are drawbacks, including the requirement for solid cybersecurity safeguards, moral dilemmas, and the possibility of some job types being replaced. Maintaining success requires striking a balance between innovation and appropriate use as the financial sector continues to adopt these technologies. Algorithmic trading, which facilitates quicker and more data-driven decision-making in the financial markets, mainly relies on AI and ML. The security of financial transactions can be improved by using advanced algorithms to identify patterns suggestive of fraudulent activity.

Manufacturing and Industry: The revolutionary paradigm change has profoundly impacted efficiency, productivity, and overall operational dynamics by integrating Artificial Intelligence (AI), Machine Learning (ML), and Automation in manufacturing and industry. AI-powered solutions make predictive maintenance possible, which enhances equipment performance and saves downtime. Large-scale datasets are analyzed by machine learning algorithms, which improve manufacturing processes by making adaptive decisions and gaining data-driven insights. Intelligent robotic systems enable automation, which increases accuracy and economy by streamlining repetitive operations. Furthermore, these technologies encourage supply chain management, quality assurance, and product design. The extensive use of AI, ML, and automation heralds historic breakthroughs, but it also raises ethical and labor reskilling issues that must be carefully considered to ensure a smooth and equitable transition to the manufacturing and industry of the future. Automation and artificial intelligence (AI) are turning conventional manufacturing into *"smart factories,"* where equipment talks to one another to maximize output. Machine learning algorithms save downtime and enable preventive maintenance by predicting when equipment will likely break.

Transportation: The transportation sector has radically changed due to automation, machine learning, and artificial intelligence integration. These innovations have greatly improved transportation's sustainability, safety, and efficiency. AI systems streamline operations and lessen traffic by optimizing logistics, traffic control, and route planning. Predictive maintenance for cars is made possible by machine learning, which reduces downtime and boosts fleet performance overall. Furthermore, automation is essential to the development of autonomous cars, which have the potential to completely transform the transportation industry by reducing human error and enhancing safety. Although these advancements can potentially transform the industry entirely, they also present challenges such as employee displacement and ethical dilemmas. These issues require careful management and control as transportation systems progress. The development of autonomous cars is primarily fueled by artificial intelligence (AI), which has the potential to transform transportation by increasing efficiency and safety. By optimizing traffic flow and lowering congestion, intelligent traffic systems increase the effectiveness of transportation as a whole.

Ethical and Social Implications: Automation, machine learning, and artificial intelligence (AI) are developing rapidly, changing many industries and significantly impacting society and ethics. These technologies may increase efficiency, creativity, and productivity; on the other hand, there are concerns about employment displacement, privacy invasion, and biased decision-making algorithms. The ethical implications of AI and ML are significant because they require responsible development and application to reduce the possibility of unforeseen outcomes. It is essential to balance ethical issues and technological advancement to ensure that these potent instruments benefit society by promoting transparency, equity, and inclusivity in their uses. Policymakers, business executives, and the general public must work together to address the ethical and social issues raised by these rapidly developing technologies to create a future in which automation, artificial intelligence, and machine learning are consistent with human values and the welfare of society. Fairness and equity are raised by the possibility that AI systems would inherit biases from the training data. These problems are being worked on, and more moral AI models are being created. Specific jobs could be automated, while others are being redesigned to emphasize skills like creativity, emotional intelligence, and critical thinking, where robots currently fall short.

Privacy and Security: The widespread adoption of automation, machine learning, and artificial intelligence (AI) has unquestionably revolutionized various facets of our lives. However, it brings significant and intricate implications for security and privacy. The growing reliance on AI and ML for data analysis and decision-making raises privacy concerns because enormous volumes of personal data are gathered, processed, and used. The security of these systems is also called into question by the automation of tasks, as there may be security flaws that could be abused. However, these technologies provide cutting-edge ways to improve security and privacy, like predictive analytics, anomaly detection, and sophisticated encryption techniques. Maintaining privacy and security while taking advantage of automation, artificial intelligence, and machine learning is still a significant challenge in the rapidly changing technology landscape. Data security and privacy issues must be carefully considered as AI becomes more widely used. Protecting sensitive data is essential to avoiding misuse and illegal access to personal information.

In summary, the effects of automation, machine learning, and artificial intelligence are complex and present benefits and problems. As these technologies advance, society must confront moral issues, invest in training and education, and create laws that guarantee these technologies' ethical and inclusive integration into a range of facets of daily life.

10.4 BLOCKCHAIN AND ITS POTENTIAL IN BUSINESS TRANSFORMATION

Blockchain technology has emerged as a disruptive force capable of altering traditional business models and processes. Understanding and leveraging blockchain technology has become crucial for CIOs navigating the complex digital transformation landscape. This chapter explores the potential impact of blockchain technology on companies and its significance from the perspective of a CIO.

10.4.1 BLOCKCHAIN: KEY FEATURES AND BENEFITS

Blockchain is a distributed, decentralized ledger system that makes record-keeping safe, open, and impervious to tampering. In contrast to conventional centralized databases, blockchain functions through a peer-to-peer network in which every user has access to a shared, unchangeable ledger. As a result, a trustless environment is created, which decreases the need for intermediaries and increases transaction security. Here are some of the main advantages of blockchain:

Decentralization: The decentralization of blockchain technology offers several benefits. First, it eliminates the need for a central authority, enabling the creation of a peer-to-peer network where transactions and data are cooperatively recorded and validated. This lowers the possibility of isolated failure points and promotes a more open, democratic system. Second, control is more evenly distributed throughout the network, which improves security. The decentralized nature of blockchain ensures a higher degree of confidence and integrity in the data on the network, making it more resistant to manipulation and hacking as no one party has total control. Decentralization of blockchain technology generally encourages robustness, openness, and security across various applications, from supply chain management to banking.

Transparency: Blockchain transparency removes the necessity for reconciling inconsistent data by guaranteeing that all parties have instant access to a single version of the truth. Stakeholder trust is increased by this contemporaneous visibility because there is a shared, unchangeable record of transactions that cannot be altered without agreement. Due to blockchain's decentralized structure, information cannot be controlled or altered by a single party, promoting an atmosphere that is more trustworthy and democratic. This enhanced confidence is especially beneficial in sectors like banking, supply chain management, and healthcare, where precise and dependable facts are essential for efficient decision-making and teamwork.

Security: The primary benefit of blockchain security is the cryptographic technique and its ability to safeguard data integrity and confidentiality. The information saved on the blockchain is kept safe and impenetrable through cutting-edge cryptographic methods. A crucial component that keeps illegal changes or tampering at bay and fosters a transparent and reliable transaction environment is the immutability of records. Because blockchain technology is inherently resistant to manipulation, its entire security posture is improved, making it a reliable solution for many sectors and applications.

Smart Contracts: Blockchain contracts, also known as smart contracts, help to improve business operations. These self-executing contracts boost productivity by automating the execution of pre-established business regulations or processes and eliminating the need for human oversight. Because smart contracts are blockchain-based, they function in an environment that is transparent and impervious to tampering; this lowers the possibility of errors and guarantees the legitimacy of contract execution. The automation and optimized processes of blockchain contracts will save time and improve the reliability and trust of corporate transactions.

10.4.2 BLOCKCHAIN POTENTIAL BUSINESS TRANSFORMATIONS

Blockchain's introduction of transparent and decentralized ledger systems can completely transform company operations. This technology lowers the possibility of fraud and increases transaction trust by enabling safe and impenetrable record-keeping. Blockchain can be used for financial transactions as well as supply chain management. It can reduce costs, simplify processes, and encourage innovation in several industries. The potential changes that blockchain could bring about in business are listed below:

Supply Chain Management: Blockchain-powered supply chain management transforms the market by offering improved transparency and traceability along the whole supply chain. Blockchain gives stakeholders unprecedented visibility into every process stage by enabling real-time tracking of items from manufacturing to final delivery through decentralized and immutable ledgers. This increased openness guarantees increased accountability, drastically lowering the possibility of fraud and counterfeiting. The immutable nature of blockchain records makes the supply chain more trustworthy and dependable, ensuring that the uploaded data is unchangeable and untampered. This novel strategy promotes a more reliable and secure global supply environment in addition to optimizing operational efficiency.

Financial Transactions: There are many advantages that blockchain technology offers for financial transactions. First, it eliminates the need for slower and more error-prone traditional banking systems by employing distributed and decentralized ledgers to facilitate faster and more secure cross-border transactions. Furthermore, blockchain lowers reliance on intermediaries like banks and clearinghouses, which results in significant cost reductions. Disintermediation eliminates the need for several permission levels and streamlines operations, improving transaction efficiency and economic effectiveness. Blockchain's openness and immutability help in increasing auditability and compliance.

The blockchain provides a reliable and auditable financial trail since every transaction is verifiable and cannot be changed after the fact. Increased openness between participants and regulatory agencies promotes trust. Moreover, blockchain's decentralized structure reduces the possibility of fraud and cyberattacks. The blockchain's built-in consensus mechanism and cryptographic security features make it highly resistant to manipulation and unauthorized access, improving the overall security of financial transactions. Blockchain is a game-changing technology in the financial sector because of its advantages over other payment methods, such as speed, security, cost savings, transparency, auditability, and decreased reliance on intermediaries.

Identity Management: The innovative technique of blockchain-based identity management ensures secure and decentralized identity verification. The immutability and transparency of blockchain technology enable individuals to establish their identities confidently. Securely storing all user data on the distributed ledger eliminates susceptible centralized repositories, thereby preventing fraud and identity theft. Furthermore, blockchain empowers people by granting them more control over who has access to their data. Users can improve privacy and lower the danger of illegal access by sharing only certain parts of their identity with others through cryptographic keys. This decentralized identity management solution promotes a more secure and egalitarian digital ecosystem by shifting the power from centralized authorities to individual users. Because of this, blockchain supports user sovereignty in managing their data and offers a reliable option for identity verification.

Smart Contracts in Legal Processes: Smart contracts, which use blockchain technology to automate and streamline contract execution, have entirely changed legal processes. Blockchain-based smart contracts allow agreements with established rules and conditions to self-execute, eliminating the need for human intervention. Because of this automation, legal transactions become much less dependent on intermediaries, opening the door to more economical and effective procedures. Smart contracts improve the speed and correctness of legal procedures by utilizing the immutability and transparency inherent in blockchain technology, resulting in a safe and unchangeable record of agreements. Blockchain's decentralized structure fosters confidence between parties because every stage of the contract's lifespan can be verified and tracked. Incorporating blockchain technology into smart contracts represents a revolutionary development in the legal sector, promoting a smoother, safe, and open contractual environment.

Data Security and Privacy: The blockchain revolution has wholly transformed data security and privacy by introducing decentralized storage and control methods for sensitive information. Blockchain's distributed ledger technology ensures that data is not kept in one area, lowering the possibility of data breaches or illegal access. Implementing a decentralized strategy improves the security of sensitive data by removing a potential point of failure for hackers. Furthermore, blockchain technology has dramatically enhanced data integrity by producing an unchangeable and visible transaction record. The blockchain's tamper-resistant feature provides additional security against fraudulent conduct, which guarantees that once information is recorded, it cannot be altered or erased without the consent of the network.

Users have more authority and control over their data in this new environment. Using smart contracts and cryptographic keys, people can decide under what conditions and with whom they can share their information. This promotes a sense of trust and ownership over personal data and improves user privacy. The emergence of blockchain technology has resulted in a paradigm change in data security by giving users greater control, improved integrity, and decentralized storage. Due to its revolutionary influence, privacy and security have become more critical in the digital age.

10.5 CIO'S APPROACH TO INNOVATION MANAGEMENT

An organization's CIO significantly impacts how it manages innovation, particularly in light of the rapidly evolving business landscape and technological advancements. Maintaining competitiveness, promoting growth, and adjusting to shifting market conditions depend on innovation. An examination of the CIO's strategy for managing innovation is provided below:

Strategic Alignment: The CIO plays a crucial role in achieving strategic alignment in the global IT and innovation management framework. The CIO must adeptly align IT objectives with overall business goals in the rapidly evolving technology field, considering the numerous demands and challenges associated with global operations. A proficient CIO recognizes that innovation involves implementing state-of-the-art technologies and cultivating an environment that stimulates original thought and flexibility. A global CIO's approach to innovation management includes spotting new trends, assessing how relevant they are to the organization's objectives, and coordinating the rollout of game-changing technologies that boost competitive advantage and operational effectiveness globally. His strategic alignment guarantees that the IT projects support the organization's long-term growth and goals and immediately meet the demands of different locations. According to the CIO, innovation projects must align with the overarching business strategy. This entails being aware of the company's objectives, difficulties, and market trends. By working with other C-suite executives, the CIO can find opportunities to gain a competitive edge through innovation and technology. Technology and innovation can create a strategic advantage.

Technology Landscape Assessment: How a CIO in charge of global IT operations approaches innovation management is heavily impacted by how they assess their technical environment. This thorough assessment entails assessing the organization's current technology setup, pinpointing areas needing development, and coordinating the results with its strategic objectives. Using this evaluation, the CIO can learn about new technology, possible hazards, and innovative opportunities in various geographic regions. The CIO can adopt a dynamic approach to innovation management that promotes collaboration, adjusts to regional differences, and strategically incorporates cutting-edge technologies by having a thorough awareness of the global IT landscape. This guarantees that the company maintains flexibility, adapts to market fluctuations, and is well-positioned for long-term success in the rapidly changing digital environment. By regularly assessing the state of technology, the CIO can identify emerging trends and disruptive innovations. With this awareness, CIOs can evaluate potential impacts on the organization and make informed decisions.

Cultivating a Culture of Innovation: CIOs are essential in leading enterprises toward success in global IT management by fostering an innovative culture. A multimodal strategy considering organizational culture modifications and technology improvements is necessary to manage innovation in a global IT context. CIOs need to encourage an innovative, risk-taking, and collaborative environment amongst diverse teams. This entails cultivating a culture that fosters experimentation, prioritizes lifelong learning, and reacts quickly to technology disruptions. . CIOs can enable their global IT teams to interact with emerging trends proactively, keep ahead of market obstacles, and create sustainable growth in a constantly changing digital ecosystem by fusing technological strategy with a dedication to promoting innovation. Encouraging an innovative culture in the IT department and the corporation at large is a significant responsibility of the CIO. This entails promoting risk-taking, innovation, and failure-based learning. New ideas and solutions can be sparked by putting initiatives like hackathons, innovation laboratories, and cross-functional cooperation into practice.

Investment and Resource Allocation: A global IT operations CIO faces a challenging environment in innovation management, where strategic investment and resource allocation are vital. When pursuing technological innovation, the CIO must carefully combine short-term objectives with long-term vision, considering the opportunities and difficulties presented by diverse global marketplaces. In addition to keeping up with new technological developments, the CIO's approach to innovation management entails encouraging an environment of ongoing learning and flexibility within the IT staff. In order to distribute resources efficiently, it is necessary to understand legal frameworks, regional differences, and the dynamic needs of a global user base. In addition, the CIO must make strategic investments in state-of-the-art technologies that complement the organization's overall objectives to guarantee that technology facilitates rather than impedes global business operations. How well a CIO strategically blends investment and resource allocation will determine their success in navigating the rapidly evolving world of global IT innovation. The CIO assigns financial and human resources to assist innovative projects. This entails determining which technologies have the potential to provide substantial value for the company and making investments in them. For long-term success, short-term objectives and long-term innovation investments must be balanced.

Collaboration and Partnerships: A CIO plays a crucial role in fostering innovation through strategic alliances and collaboration in the dynamic sector of global IT operations. Understanding that innovation is frequently a team effort, CIOs actively interact with industry peers, technology providers, and external stakeholders to keep up with new developments, best practices, and innovative solutions. These collaborations provide valuable information about potentially game-changing technologies and help CIOs better understand the rapidly evolving IT landscape. A forward-thinking CIO can harness a variety of viewpoints and experiences by building a network of relationships, enabling a comprehensive approach to innovation management. The CIO can proactively guide the organization into the future of technology with a collaborative culture, which will transcend the traditional borders of the business and create an ecosystem where shared knowledge and resources drive constant innovation. The CIO can access outside expertise and stay updated with industry developments by interacting with startups, industry ecosystems, and external partners. Joint ventures and strategic partnerships are examples of collaborative endeavors that can give access to resources and complementing abilities.

Agile and Adaptive Frameworks: The CIO who is in charge of global IT operations navigates a dynamic environment where innovation is critical to organizational success. The CIO utilizes Agile and Adaptive Frameworks to manage innovation efficiently because they understand that adaptability and responsiveness are essential in the rapidly changing technology landscape. Using these frameworks, the CIO may inspire their team to embrace collaboration, iterative development, and continuous improvement, creating an environment where flexibility is valued highly. Agile techniques enable the CIO to respond swiftly to technological and market developments and expedite the delivery of innovative solutions. In addition, an adaptive framework guarantees that the IT strategy stays aligned with the overarching business objectives, enabling the CIO to take proactive measures to tackle new issues and seize opportunities. The CIO is positioned as a strategic partner in leading the company toward global digital excellence with this integrated approach to innovation management. The IT department may react swiftly to evolving market dynamics and requirements by using agile approaches and adaptable frameworks. To quicken innovation cycles, the CIO might advocate using cloud computing, DevOps techniques, and other agile approaches.

Data-Driven Decision Making: Adopting Data-Driven Decision Making (DDDM) is essential to a CIO's overall approach to innovation management in global IT management. Making intelligent and well-informed decisions requires utilizing data-driven insights, which are becoming increasingly critical as technology advances at an unparalleled rate. Using extensive information from many sources, the CIO can obtain valuable insights, recognize patterns, and anticipate possible obstacles, ultimately facilitating the better direction of innovation endeavors. DDDM empowers the CIO to make decisions based on facts, allocate resources as efficiently as possible, and coordinate innovation activities with the changing demands of the global IT ecosystem. This strategy puts the CIO at the forefront of innovation in the digital age and improves the organization's capacity to adjust to changing market conditions. It also cultivates an agile and continuous improvement culture inside the IT infrastructure. The CIO can make data-driven decisions to locate opportunities, optimize workflows, and pinpoint areas for improvement by employing business intelligence and data analytics solutions. Implementing a robust data governance framework guarantees the quality and security of data used in innovation projects.

Digital Transformation: The growing alignment of the CIO's position with digital transformation in global IT management has established a new paradigm for innovation management. Digital transformation helps companies keep up with the quickly changing technological landscape by utilizing cutting-edge technology to transform and streamline business processes. A practical approach to innovation management in the context of digital transformation requires a CIO in charge of global IT to pay close attention to how new technologies align with broader business objectives. This entails keeping up with developing technologies that can advance the company, promoting cooperation between geographically separated teams, and cultivating a culture of constant learning and adaptation within the IT ecosystem. The CIO may foster innovation, optimize operational effectiveness, and guarantee that the global IT framework stays flexible and sturdy when confronted with ever-changing business obstacles by methodically incorporating digital solutions. Leading the charge in digital transformation initiatives, the

CIO uses technology to improve customer experiences, streamline business operations, and generate new revenue sources. This could entail embracing digital platforms, using cutting-edge technology like artificial intelligence and the Internet of Things, and updating legacy systems.

Continuous Learning and Adaptation: A CIO in charge of global IT operations must constantly learn and adapt as part of an efficient innovation management strategy. In today's IT landscape, staying abreast of new developments, market trends, and changing user requirements is critical. A CIO should cultivate an environment where team members constantly learn new skills and stay abreast of technical developments inside the IT department. Furthermore, quickly integrating novel ideas and techniques depends on a flexible and adaptable attitude.

Effective innovation management requires the capacity to adjust to changing conditions quickly, learn from both triumphs and failures, and use those lessons to improve strategy. A CIO who supports continuous learning and adaptation ensures that the global IT team is adaptable, responsive, and well-positioned to spur innovation. Because technology changes quickly, the CIO must encourage an ongoing learning and adaptability culture inside the IT department. Upskilling the group and keeping abreast of market developments fall under this category.

To sum up, the CIO employs various strategies for managing innovation, including resource allocation, cultural development, data-driven decision-making, adaptive frameworks, digital transformation, strategic alignment, technology assessment, and a dedication to ongoing learning. The CIO may put the company in a position to succeed in a constantly changing business environment by adopting these ideas.

10.6 BALANCING INNOVATION WITH OPERATIONAL STABILITY

Organizations looking to succeed in the long-term business climate have a crucial challenge of finding a balance between innovation and operational stability. Long-term growth requires stability and creativity, yet these qualities frequently call for different approaches, resources, and ways of thinking. Finding the ideal balance between the two is essential for encouraging innovation, adjusting to change, and guaranteeing dependable daily operations.

Finding the proper equilibrium between innovation and operational stability requires a strategic approach. Below are some key considerations:

Strategic Alignment: Reaching the ideal balance between innovation and operational stability necessitates a sophisticated strategy based on strong strategic alignment. Companies must create a dynamic atmosphere supporting creativity while preserving operational stability. This entails matching creative endeavors with strategic aims to ensure that the search for novel concepts enhances the current framework of operations. To unite these seemingly disparate components, departments must effectively communicate and collaborate. Identifying changes for innovation to increase operational effectiveness and customer value is more accessible when strategic alignment exists. Businesses can successfully traverse the problematic balance between stimulating creativity and upholding a solid operational foundation by developing a strategic mentality that integrates innovation into the organization's objectives. This will ultimately lead to sustainable success in a continuously dynamic landscape. A CIO should ensure that innovation initiatives support the organization's long-term strategy by coordinating them with overarching business objectives.

Resource Allocation: The correct balance between innovation and operational stability can only be reached by carefully applying efficient resource allocation techniques. Organizations must carefully manage resource allocation to promote an innovative culture while preserving the stability of ongoing operations. Strategic allocation of financial, human, and technological resources enables organizations to support R&D activities, foster experimentation, and cultivate a creative atmosphere. In addition, some resources should be allocated to guarantee the stability and effectiveness of ongoing activities, protecting against any disturbances. This dynamic approach to resource allocation allows businesses to embrace innovation without compromising the stability required for long-term success, creating a harmonious balance that propels them ahead in the business landscape. A CIO should use resources wisely and balance the requirement for reliable operations and expenditures in innovation. A CIO should also consider establishing departments or teams committed to innovation while keeping core operational resources.

Risk Management: Reaching the ideal equilibrium between innovation and operational stability depends on implementing a robust risk management system. However, this goal should be moderated by a sharp understanding of the hazards and disruptions that could arise. An efficient risk management plan serves as the cornerstone, enabling businesses to anticipate, evaluate, and address possible risks to operational stability while also promoting creative initiatives. By integrating risk management into decision-making procedures, enterprises can effectively traverse uncertain situations, guaranteeing that innovation occurs in a regulated setting with minimal adverse effects. Finding the right balance allows businesses to take advantage of growth and transformational opportunities while retaining the resilience required to face unforeseen obstacles. Recognize and control the risks connected to both operational stability and innovation. Determine how new initiatives affect current procedures and find strategies to reduce risks.

Feedback Loops: Finding the correct balance between innovation and operational stability is challenging but essential for businesses. A key component of creating a harmonious equilibrium is having efficient feedback loops. The feedback loops are an ongoing, iterative method of collecting input from stakeholders, such as partners, employees, and customers. Organizations can accelerate innovation by quickly adapting to shifting market demands and technical improvements by cultivating a culture that values and integrates feedback. Furthermore, feedback loops promote operational stability by providing instantaneous insights into the efficiency of present systems and procedures, enabling timely adjustments and improvements. Robust feedback loops enable the synergy between innovation and operational stability, ensuring enterprises stay ahead of the curve in a fast-changing world while maintaining the efficiency and dependability necessary for long-term success. A CIO can create feedback loops so that an organization can gain knowledge from operational difficulties and successful ideas. A CIO can utilize this feedback to improve procedures and strategies iteratively.

In summary, maintaining the delicate balance between innovation and operational stability requires ongoing work and necessitates adaptability, strategic planning, and a thorough comprehension of the company's goals. Businesses that can effectively strike this balance will be well-positioned to prosper in the quickly changing business environment.

CHAPTER 11
CASE STUDIES

INTRODUCTION

The role of the CIO has changed significantly in the intricate structure of modern businesses to meet the diverse demands of a rapidly evolving technological landscape. This chapter delves into some interesting case studies that shed light on CIOs' complex struggles and victories in various corporate settings. We start by examining Case Study 1, which examines how a CIO function has changed inside the boundaries of a traditional corporation.

Case Study 2, which explores digital entrepreneurship in greater detail, puts us in the fast-moving, technologically advanced startup environment where CIO leadership is essential. We examine the strategies CIOs employ to navigate the intricate landscape of innovation, growth, and competitiveness in the face of disruptive technologies and agile frameworks. As our journey continues, Case Study 3 allows us to delve deeper into global workforce management by thoroughly examining strategic excellence in outsourcing within an MNC. Due to the intricate interplay between local and global elements, CIOs face numerous challenges in assisting a cohesive, geographically distributed workforce.

Case studies 4-6 take us into global IT operations, supply chain management, technology adoption, and legal compliance, each revealing a different aspect of the CIO's strategic role. Our investigation is set against an MNC aiming for global excellence, from changing global supply chains through strategic IT operations (Case Study 4) to navigating the ship of legal and compliance in international IT operations (Case Study 6). The common thread that runs through these disparate stories is that a CIO's strategic expertise is not limited to technology; it is a dynamic force reshaping modern business strategy globally.

CASE STUDY 1
THE EVOLUTION OF A CIO ROLE IN A TRADITIONAL ORGANIZATION

One of the well-established manufacturing companies needs an updated IT infrastructure to be more efficient. The leadership is aware that leading a digital transformation requires a CIO. The CIO has to deal with inefficient decision-making procedures, outdated technology that limits adaptability, and a growing need for data-driven insights. A mismatch between the organization's goals and technology strategy has resulted from the absence of a CIO. Outdated systems and manual processes have caused inefficiencies in the organization. A significant area for improvement was the company's need for a centralized IT strategy and administration, in addition to its inadequate cybersecurity measures and weak data analytics capabilities.

In this case study the same problem statement was categorized according to past, present, and future CIO positions to demonstrate the change in the CIO roles from Past, Present and future. For this problem statement, the CIO's responsibilities up until now included assessing technology, identifying problem areas, and laying the groundwork for future developments. Typical responsibilities of a CIO included overseeing IT infrastructure, managing vendor relationships, and handling pressing technical problems. The CIO used to deploy cutting-edge ERP systems to streamline operations, create a progressive digital transformation plan, fund employee training initiatives to promote technology adoption and conduct exhaustive IT audits to find vulnerabilities. The CIO conducted an analysis and found that this would result in enhanced cybersecurity measures to reduce the risk of data breaches, a 30% reduction in manual processes, a 30% increase in operational efficiency, better decision-making through data analytics capabilities, and enhanced departmental collaboration through integrated systems.

On the other hand, modern CIOs will leverage cutting-edge technology like artificial intelligence, machine learning, and the Internet of Things when they observe the same issue. The duties of modern CIOs are expanded to include driving innovation, creating digital strategies, and overseeing data. Among various actions, the CIO will launch initiatives to integrate IoT devices for real-time monitoring, establish a data governance framework, employ advanced analytics to forecast market trends and cultivate an innovative culture through hackathons and idea incubators to enhance data quality. The current strategy would primarily increase revenue through data-driven decision-making and customized digital experiences. Modern CIOs will position the company as an industry leader in technology adoption, innovative culture development, employee engagement, etc.

When future CIOs' handling strategies for the same problem statements are expected to be entirely focused on directing the organization's digital destiny, A proactive cybersecurity strategy against evolving threats is one of the responsibilities expected of future CIOs. Other responsibilities include addressing ethical concerns in AI and data usage, implementing AI-driven automation to improve efficiency further, and leading initiatives for a sustainable and environmentally conscious IT infrastructure. More cybersecurity resistance to emerging threats, ethical and sustainable technological practices, enhanced employee and customer experiences via cutting-edge technologies, and more are the expected results.

CASE STUDY 2

CIO LEADERSHIP IN A STARTUP

A rapidly growing IT company that is one of the startup wants assistance building its infrastructure. IT leadership needs to be more organized, which has led to inefficiencies and a mismatch between business goals and technological aspirations. The problem statement of this organization is that it is growing, yet it requires assistance from outside sources to stay up with its IT infrastructure. Disjointed technology projects, limited scalability, and security vulnerabilities have resulted from the absence of a CIO. The organization identified several areas for improvement, such as the lack of a centralized IT strategy and governance, the limited scalability and flexibility of the current IT architecture, inefficient and compartmentalized technological solutions, and security issues stemming from a targeted cybersecurity approach.

Modern CIOs can give strategic direction for technical projects compared to former CIOs who used to handle just the challenges. The CIO's top priorities are assessing scalability issues, understanding the state of technology today, and setting the stage for future expansion. The CIO's predecessors would implement collaborative technologies to increase productivity and communication, adopt a cloud-first strategy to improve scalability and conduct a full technology review to identify bottlenecks and scalability difficulties. They would also assess cybersecurity, implement critical security controls, encourage collaboration and communication, reduce present cybersecurity threats by taking preventative action, use cloud computing to boost flexibility and scalability and create the framework for future technological initiatives.

As the company grows, the CIO's responsibilities evolve, focusing increasingly on data-driven decision-making, strategic technology leadership, and fostering an innovative culture. Consequently, the current CIO is inclined to leverage advanced analytics for data-driven decision-making and oversee the development of a comprehensive IT strategy aligned with company objectives. Particular emphasis will be placed on recruiting and retaining qualified IT personnel, launching innovative initiatives to unleash the creativity of staff members, and achieving outcomes such as enhanced business agility through data-driven decision-making. These technological endeavors align with business objectives, facilitate the recruitment of top IT talent, establish a high-performing IT team, promote an innovative culture, and accelerate continuous improvement.

It is expected that the CIO will play a significant role in deciding how the company will lead in technology. The duties of a CIO include keeping up with technological developments, leading the digital transformation, and ensuring long-term security and scalability. It is anticipated that future CIOs will take the following actions: proactively addressing cybersecurity challenges with state-of-the-art measures, spearheading a comprehensive strategy for digital transformation, continuously observing and embracing emerging technologies for innovation, and guaranteeing the IT architecture's scalability and flexibility. Anticipated outcomes include establishing the company as a market leader in adopting new technology, ensuring a competitive edge in the marketplace, seamless scalability to facilitate future growth, advanced cybersecurity measures to protect against evolving threats, and more.

CASE STUDY 3

STRATEGIC EXCELLENCE IN GLOBAL TALENT MANAGEMENT: A CIO CASE STUDY ON OFFSHORING IN AN MNC

The CIOs are crucial in creating strategies that support global expansion and personnel management. This case study focuses on offshore and international people management by analyzing the strategic choices and actions of a CIO overseeing a multinational company. An MNC aimed to reduce costs and boost operational effectiveness by embracing outsourcing. However, this project brought significant challenges in managing a dispersed global workforce, including differences in time zones, cultural nuances, and skill sets.

In order to solve the problem statement, the CIO has taken the following approaches:

- ❖ A talent mapping that included the CIO and IT department carried out a comprehensive talent mapping study to determine the skill sets needed for tasks that are offshored, worked in tandem with HR departments to match recruiting tactics to the recognized skill gaps on a national and global scale.

- ❖ The outcomes of the talent mapping process determined the establishment of offshore centers in critical places. To promote cooperation between onshore and offshore teams, these centers had strong communication lines and committed leadership.

- ❖ All team members underwent cultural sensitivity training programs to improve teamwork and overcome cultural gaps. The CIO promoted virtual team-building exercises and cross-cultural exchange initiatives to promote togetherness and a common goal.

- ❖ The CIO has invested in cutting-edge communication systems and collaboration tools to enable real-time interactions across time zones. Organized frequent video conferences to facilitate transparent and open communication among the team members, no matter where they are.

❖ The CIO and IT standardized performance measures, and KPIs were implemented to monitor the efficiency and productivity of offshore and onshore staff, and routine performance evaluations were used to pinpoint areas needing development and acknowledgment.

The above strategy of the CIO has resulted in the following outcomes:

❖ Offshoring helped the organization achieve significant cost reductions while preserving and sometimes increasing operational efficiency. This approach improved flexibility and scalability in project execution, enabling the company to react quickly to shifting market demands.

❖ The organization was able to utilize the varied skill sets in various geographic places to guarantee that the organization has access to a global talent pool. The strategy also resolved the requirement for specific knowledge by utilizing regional sources of knowledge.

❖ The strategy helped the organization to promote an environment of cooperation at work that cut across borders and improved team morale and satisfaction. Effectively brought together various teams, establishing a unified corporate culture with shared values and objectives.

❖ The CIO strategy has established an agile organizational structure that allows for rapid adaptation to market changes and continuously refines talent management strategies based on feedback, ensuring an adaptive and resilient approach to offshoring.

In conclusion, the case study shows how an MNC may overcome obstacles and build a robust and resilient framework for its global IT operations by taking a strategic approach to offshore and global talent management led by an innovative CIO. The organization established a harmonious combination of operational excellence, cost efficiency, and a globally empowered staff by emphasizing talent mapping, cultural integration, agile communication, and performance measurements.

CASE STUDY 4
TRANSFORMING GLOBAL SUPPLY CHAIN MANAGEMENT THROUGH STRATEGIC IT OPERATIONS

This case study looks at a CIO's strategic role in an MNC that wants to improve its supply chain management (SCM) by leveraging global IT operations. The MNC operates in multiple nations and needs help optimizing its supply chain procedures, guaranteeing effectiveness, and adjusting to constantly changing market circumstances. The CIO spearheads the effort to incorporate technological solutions into the global supply chain, with the responsibility of coordinating IT strategy with business goals. This MNC encountered obstacles in its supply chain, such as inefficiencies, delays, and issues adjusting to various regulatory contexts. Due to the company's rapid development and international expansion, a robust IT strategy is essential to maintaining a competitive edge and optimizing supply chain processes. The main goal was to leverage technology to improve global operations' collaboration, inventory management, and supply chain visibility. The CIO sought to tackle these issues by implementing an all-encompassing IT plan to guarantee flexibility, scalability, and adherence to local laws.

The CIO has taken the following strategy:

❖ A decision was made for global ERP integration, in which the company unified its ERP system to optimize operations in many geographical areas. Additionally, the company made real-time data sharing possible, improving communication and decision-making amongst supply chain partners.

❖ The organization used data analytics and predictive modeling in which the CIO leveraged advanced analytics and predictive modeling to forecast demand, optimize inventory levels, and reduce lead times. The organization also applied machine learning algorithms to identify patterns and trends, enabling proactive decision-making in supply chain management.

❖ In order to increase traceability and transparency throughout the supply chain, the company considered transparency and implemented blockchain technology. The company enhanced its cooperation with distributors, suppliers, and logistical partners by offering a safe, unchangeable ledger for information exchanged.

❖ The idea of switching to a cloud-based supply chain platform was planned in order to improve accessibility, scalability, and flexibility for global operations. Additionally, the company enabled information sharing and real-time cooperation between international teams and outside partners.

❖ Robust cybersecurity implementations were planned to safeguard confidential supply chain data, and adherence to local data protection laws and industry-specific requirements was considered.

The above strategy has the helped the organization to achieve the following results and outcomes:

❖ The CIO strategy has enhanced productivity and cost savings were attained through optimized supply chain procedures, decreased overhead and increased overall effectiveness, and reduced lead times and inventory holding expenses via improved demand projections and inventory management.

❖ Additionally, the technique improved supply chain visibility, which made proactive problem-solving possible. Improved collaboration with overseas partners results in smoother operations with fewer disruptions.

❖ The strategy helped the organization adapt to market dynamics and has evolved due to the strategy's enhanced responsiveness to market shifts, enabling the multinational corporation to promptly adjust to changing customer needs and supply chain interruptions.

❖ The strategy also mitigated legal and regulatory risks by ensuring compliance with various regional legislation. This approach also increased resistance to supply chain interruptions and geopolitical unpredictability.

In conclusion, by implementing important IT projects, the CIO successfully changed the MNC's global supply chain operations. The incorporation of cutting-edge technologies enhanced cooperation, flexibility, and compliance in addition to streamlining procedures. This case study demonstrates a CIO's critical role in spearheading digital transformation and utilizing IT strategically to enable global supply chain management within an international organization.

CASE STUDY 5

DRIVING GLOBAL EXCELLENCE: A CIO STRATEGY CASE STUDY ON TECHNOLOGY ADOPTION IN MANAGING GLOBAL IT OPERATIONS IN AN MNC

MNCs rely significantly on effectively utilizing technology in the quickly changing global business environment. This case study examines the strategic steps a top MNC took, led by its CIO, to improve and expedite its global IT operations by embracing cutting-edge technologies. This broad, multi national company operates in multiple sectors, such as manufacturing, finance, and technology solutions. The organization has a global presence; thus, it must effectively manage various IT activities in different nations.

The organization faced the following challenges:

Diversity in IT Infrastructure: Due to the company's disparate global IT architecture, there were operational inefficiencies and higher maintenance expenses.

Communication Barriers: Inability of International teams to collaborate and communicate easily with one another hampered the timely completion of IT projects and reduced output overall.

Security Concerns: One major challenge was managing compliance and data security across many jurisdictions.

The CIO of the MNC came up with a thorough plan to deal with these issues and set up the business for success in the future. The following fundamental pillars served as the strategy's focal points:

Standardization of IT Infrastructure: Established a global standardization procedure of IT infrastructure, guaranteeing uniformity in networking, software, and hardware solutions throughout all overseas offices, and embraced virtualization technology to lessen reliance on hardware and increase scalability.

Unified Communication and Collaboration: By deploying a single platform for communication and collaboration the global teams were able to collaborate on projects and communicate in real-time. They incorporated instant messaging, document sharing, and video conferencing capabilities to eliminate communication obstacles.

Cybersecurity and Compliance: Established a robust cybersecurity architecture to guarantee data security and adherence to global laws and conducted frequent security audits and training courses to raise staff members' cybersecurity awareness.

Cloud Adoption: Adopted cloud computing to increase IT operations' cost-effectiveness, scalability, and flexibility, moved essential data and apps to cloud platforms, facilitating simpler management and network accessibility globally.

The above strategies adopted by the CIO have helped the organization to achieve the following results:

Operational Efficiency: Significant cost savings and increased operational effectiveness were made possible by standardizing IT infrastructure, allowing quicker IT service launch and decreased downtime.

Enhanced Collaboration: Due to the unified communication and collaboration platform, international teams could exchange expertise and innovation and interact more successfully across borders.

Enhanced Security: Strong cybersecurity safeguards reduced security threats and guaranteed adherence to data protection regulations, improving the business's standing and winning over new clients.

Agile and Scalable Operations: Adopting the cloud gave the organization the scale and agility required to react swiftly to shifting market conditions and foster corporate expansion.

In conclusion, by deliberately implementing cutting-edge technologies, this MNC's CIO was able to effectively manage the challenges of overseeing global IT operations. In addition to resolving issues, the company's dedication to standardization, cooperation, cybersecurity, and cloud adoption established it as a technology-driven leader in the international market. This case study is an invaluable resource for other MNCs seeking to maximize their IT strategy for global success.

CASE STUDY 6
STRATEGIC MANAGEMENT OF LEGAL AND COMPLIANCE IN INTERNATIONAL IT OPERATIONS

This case study considered another MNC offering a wide range of products and services. This company needed to enhance its legal and compliance practices and manage global IT operations. The CIO faced the challenge of coordinating the organization's IT goals with various legal and regulatory requirements spanning multiple jurisdictions. This MNC operates in several countries, each with its own regulatory and compliance landscape. As part of its global IT operations, the corporation has its development teams, support services, and data centers spread across multiple continents. The complexity of global operations made it challenging to maintain data privacy, control legal risks associated with IT activities, and ensure compliance with multiple regulations.

The organization is facing the following challenges:

Diverse Legal Landscapes: The organization operates in multiple jurisdictions and has to align with different regulatory frameworks in different nations, like the CCPA in the US, the GDPR in Europe, and the need for data localization in several Asian nations.

Data Privacy Concerns: The organization faces challenges in protecting customer and employee data in compliance with evolving privacy regulations and preventing data breaches.

Contractual Compliance: The organization faces challenges in aligning IT contracts and agreements with local legal requirements, intellectual property laws, and vendor management regulations.

Cybersecurity Regulations: The organization faces challenges in adapting to different cybersecurity regulations and standards in each country of operation to mitigate cyber threats effectively.

In order to mitigate the above problems, the CIO has come up with the following strategic initiatives:

Global Legal and Compliance Team: The CIO created a thorough plan that calls for enlisting local government teams with knowledgeable legal and compliance teams to help them navigate the intricacies of local laws and ordinances. Regular training sessions were implemented as a proactive measure to guarantee that IT staff members know industry best practices and legal duties.

Comprehensive Risk Assessment: A comprehensive risk assessment strategy was also implemented to find possible legal and compliance issues related to global IT operations. Plans were created for risk reduction and implementation into the overall IT strategy.

Standardized Policies and Procedures: The CIO has implemented a strategy for consistent IT policies and procedures that comply with the most stringent legal and regulatory standards across the board. Regulations were updated regularly to consider law and industry best practices changes.

Data Governance and Privacy Measures: The CIO has implemented robust data governance mechanisms to guarantee adherence to privacy regulations and protect sensitive data by utilizing data anonymization, access limits, and encryption.

Vendor Management and Contractual Compliance: The CIO implemented a centralized vendor management system strategy to track contractual obligations and compliance and also implemented strategies for reviewing and updating vendor agreements to ensure they abide by local regulations.

Incident Response and Cybersecurity Framework: The CIO created an incident response strategy by adhering to international cybersecurity standards, working with law enforcement authorities as needed, and responding to cybersecurity issues quickly and legally.

The above strategies adopted by the CIO have helped the organization to achieve the following results:

Enhanced Legal Compliance: The organization achieved higher compliance with international and local legal frameworks, reducing the risk of legal actions and penalties.

Improved Data Privacy Practices: The company tightened its privacy policies, giving stakeholders and consumers more faith that their information is handled responsibly.

Streamlined Vendor Relationships: The organization established more robust relationships with vendors by ensuring compliance with contractual obligations, leading to improved service delivery.

Reduced Legal Risks: The organization was able to mitigate legal risks associated with IT operations, protecting the company's reputation and fostering a culture of legal and ethical responsibility.

Adaptive Cybersecurity Measures: The organization implemented adaptive cybersecurity measures, reducing the likelihood and impact of cyber threats across the global IT infrastructure.

In conclusion, this MNC successfully negotiated the challenging world of foreign regulations by strategically focusing on legal and compliance considerations when managing multinational IT operations. In the end, the proactive attitude of the CIO supported the company's performance in the global marketplace by ensuring regulatory compliance and fostering a more robust and secure IT environment.

REFERENCES

"15 Characteristics of IT Digital Maturity." CIO, www.cio.com/article/219824/15-characteristics-of-it-digital-maturity.html.

"2018 RSA Winter Conference Special Sessions." RSA Main, www.regionalstudies.org/news/2018-winter-special-sessions/.

"Analysis – Quant AG." Quant.swiss, quant.swiss/en/analyse-english/.

"Answer These 6 Questions before Investing in PEO Services." Stumbleforward.com, stumbleforward.com/2020/01/28/answer-these-6-questions-before-investing-in-peo-services.

"Arabnet | CIOs in the Age of Digital Disruption: Key Trends & Insights at This Year's Arabnet Riyadh." Www.arabnet.me, www.arabnet.me/english/editorials/events/conferences/cio-innovation-forum.

"Azure Global - Sahara Net." Sahara Net, 28 July 2021, sahara.com/cloud/azure-global/.

"Benefits of Business Analyst Workshop in 2023." Blog-Directory.org, blog-directory.org/BlogDetails?bId=79864&catId=46&t=Benefit s%20of%20Business%20An...&v=.

"Best-Android-App-For-Speeding-Up-Phone." Phone-Halo.com, 2024, phone-halo.com/best-android-app-for-speeding-up-phone/.

"CIOs Play a Vital Role in Customer Experience." Gartner, www.gartner.com/smarterwithgartner/cios-play-a-vital-role-in-customer-experience.

"Compensation 101 - Chapter 1 - How to Pay." Aon.com, 2022, rewards.aon.com/en-us/insights/compensation-101/how-to-pay.

"Competition #3 Making Connections." Topical Talk, talk.economistfoundation.org/competitions/festival-2023-competitions/competition-3/.

"Contact Us – the True Test of Leadership Is How Well You Function in a Crisis." Empowermentprojectintl.org, 2024, empowermentprojectintl.org/contact-us/.

"COSO - Committee of Sponsoring Organizations of the Treadway Commission." Optiv, www.optiv.com/cybersecurity-dictionary/coso-committee-of-sponsoring-organizations-of-the-treadway-commission.

"Cx Success Measurement | European Customer Consultancy."
ECC, www.eucustomerconsultancy.com/cxsuccess.

"Digital Migration." Stepping Stone, steppingstone.io/digital-
migration/.

"Digital Strategy Consulting: A Guide for Businesses |
ChangeMASTR." Www.changemastr.com, 16 May 2023,
www.changemastr.com/digital-strategy-consulting-a-guide-
for-businesses/.

"Governance." Atlas Honda, www.atlashonda.com.pk/governance/.

"Grateful Dead Gear: The Band's Instruments, Sound Systems and
Recording Sessions from 1965 to 1995." Rowman.com,
rowman.com/ISBN/9780879308933/Grateful-Dead-Gear-
The-Band%27s-Instruments-Sound-Systems-and-
Recording-Sessions-From-1965-to-1995.

"Home." Peer Learning Institute, peerlearninginstitute.com/pli-
blog-5-redefining-workplace-learning-for-the-21st-century/.

"How to Build a Demand Center." Ledger Bennett,
ledgerbennett.com/resources/how-to-build-a-demand-
center/.

"Industry Leaders Awards 2019: Fund Services Technology Vendor of the Year Nominees - Global Custodian." Www.globalcustodian.com, www.globalcustodian.com/industry-leaders-awards-2019-fund-services-technology-vendor-year-nominees/.

"InfoSec Assessment: Evaluating Your Security Risks." Www.6clicks.com, www.6clicks.com/resources/glossary/information-security-assessment.

"Introduction to Sales and Operations Execution (S&OE)." 3scsolution.com, SS Supply Chain Solutions (3SC), 12 Jan. 2023, 3scsolution.com/insight/sales-and-operations-execution-soe.

"John Marcante | the Enterprisers Project." Enterprisersproject.com, enterprisersproject.com/user/john-marcante.

"Maintenance Lead | Leclerc." Leclercfoods.com, leclercfoods.com/us/careers/posts/4975.

"Matt Murrie." Be You., 19 Apr. 2013, redefineschool.com/matt-murrie/.

"May 2023." Creative Partner, www.creativepartner.ca/2023/05/.

"MY Salary Guide 2022_23_v5.Pdf." Www.slideshare.net, 23 Mar. 2023, es.slideshare.net/SANJANRAVI3/my-salary-guide-202223v5pdf.

"Navigating Challenges and Seizing Opportunities: The Future of Victim Advocacy - an Interview Essay for Legal Professionals." Rongoldmanfoundation.org, rongoldmanfoundation.org/navigating-challenges-and-seizing-opportunities-the-future-of-victim-advocacy-an-interview-essay-for-legal-professionals.

"Oracle HCM Cloud to Manage Complex Workforce Effectively." Gemini Consulting & Services, 24 Nov. 2022, www.gemini-us.com/oracle/oracle-hcm-cloud-to-manage-complex-workforce-effectively/.

"Palafox Associates." Www.palafoxassociates.com, www.palafoxassociates.com/news/leyte-ecological-industrial-zone-master-development-plan-technical-working-group-presentation.

"Partners Guide: Educating Customers on Cloud Security." Www.threatkey.com, www.threatkey.com/partners/how-to-educate-your-customers-on-the-importance-of-cloud-security.

"PCI DSS Archives." CISO Global (Formerly Alpine Security), www.alpinesecurity.com/blog/tag/pci-dss/.

"Pru Life Data Center Archives." Back End News, backendnews.net/tag/pru-life-data-center/.

"Q&A: Strengthening Supply Chains to Create and Protect Value." CohnReznick, www.cohnreznick.com/insights/q-a-strengthening-supply-chains-create-protect-value.

"Quality over Quantity | Rathbones." Www.rathbones.com, www.rathbones.com/blog/quality-over-quantity.

"ServiceNow Developer | Tezza Business Solutions LLC." Tezzasolutions.catsone.com, tezzasolutions.catsone.com/careers/23509-General/jobs/16146380-ServiceNow-Developer/.

"SupplyChainBrain." Www.supplychainbrain.com, www.supplychainbrain.com/articles/20814-top-5-reasons-sop-belongs-in-the-cloud-integrating-cloud-sop-with-erp-vs-customizing-erp-for-so.

"Top 7 Cybersecurity and Compliance Foundations for RIAS." Itsynergy.com, itsynergy.com/7-cybersecurity-and-compliance-foundations-for-rias/.

"Uncovering the Hidden Gems: How to Find and Hire Top IT Executive Talent in the Digital Age." Uncovering the Hidden Gems: How to Find and Hire Top IT Executive Talent in the Digital Age, www.pronixinc.com/blog/uncovering-the-hidden-gems-how-to-find-and-hire-top-it-executive-talent-in-the-digital-age.

"Understanding Moments of Truth and How They Connect to Customer Journeys | Merchants." Business Process Outsourcing Services | Merchants CX SA, 20 Dec. 2017, www.merchantscx.com/news/understanding-moments-of-truth-and-how-they-connect-to-customer-journeys.

"Use Gamification Progress Bars to Drive Customer Engagement." Www.comarch.com, www.comarch.com/trade-and-services/loyalty-marketing/blog/use-gamification-progress-bars-to-drive-customer-engagement/.

"Vooban - Awwwards SOTD." Www.awwwards.com, www.awwwards.com/sites/vooban.

"WHAT IS 5 FORCES STRATEGY?" Meticulous, 26 Dec. 2022, www.meticulousoffices.com/single-post/what-is-5-forces-strategy.

"What Is the Meaning of Planned Change? – Pvillage.org."
Pvillage.org, pvillage.org/archives/18330.

"Who's the Boss? Trends in CIO Reporting Structure." Deloitte
Insights, 2019, www2.deloitte.com/us/en/insights/focus/cio-
insider-business-insights/trends-in-cio-reporting-
structure.html.

"Why Digital Transformation? Explore Our 5 Answers Why."
Digital Adoption, 8 Aug. 2019, www.digital-
adoption.com/why-digital-transformation/.

Abebe, Rediet, et al. "Roles for Computing in Social Change."
Proceedings of the 2020 Conference on Fairness,
Accountability, and Transparency, 22 Jan. 2020,
https://doi.org/10.1145/3351095.3372871.

Admin. "6 Compelling Reasons That Justify the Need to Launch a
Loyalty Program." Sbzbusiness.com, 22 Mar. 2022,
sbzbusiness.com/6-compelling-reasons-that-justify-the-
need-to-launch-a-loyalty-program/.

Annals-XXI, Economic. "Role of Chief Information Officer within
the System of Human Resource Development in Service
Organizations (Tourism)." Economic Annals-XXI, 11 Oct.
2017, ea21journal.world/index.php/ea-v165-20/.

Artemis. "Predictions for 2016: Susan Lane, Co-CEO, Tokio Solution Management Ltd. - Artemis.bm." Artemis.bm - the Catastrophe Bond, Insurance Linked Securities & Investment, Reinsurance Capital, Alternative Risk Transfer and Weather Risk Management Site, 21 Jan. 2016, www.artemis.bm/news/predictions-for-2016-susan-lane-co-ceo-tokio-solution-management-ltd/.

Back to the Office: Learning from the Pandemic | Boostalab. boostalab.com/en/remote-and-hybrid-work/back-to-the-office-challenges-of-reopening/.

Banker, Rajiv D., and Cecilia (Qian) Feng. "The Impact of Information Security Breach Incidents on CIO Turnover." Journal of Information Systems, vol. 33, no. 3, 1 Aug. 2019, pp. 309–329, https://doi.org/10.2308/isys-52532. Accessed 8 Oct. 2020.

Barnes, Stuart, et al. "Empirical Identification of Skills Gaps between Chief Information Officer Supply and Demand: A Resource-Based View Using Machine Learning." Industrial Management & Data Systems, vol. 121, no. 8, 13 May 2021, pp. 1749–1766, https://doi.org/10.1108/imds-01-2021-0015.

Battifarano, Matthew, and Zhen (Sean) Qian. "Predicting Real-Time Surge Pricing of Ride-Sourcing Companies." Transportation Research Part C: Emerging Technologies, vol. 107, Oct. 2019, pp. 444–462, www.sciencedirect.com/science/article/pii/S0968090X1930 1627, https://doi.org/10.1016/j.trc.2019.08.019.

Behera, Mukti Prakash, and Dibyajyoti Mohapatra. "Strategic Imperatives of Training and Development Practices on Sales Performance: A Case Analysis of Insurance Company in Bhubaneswar City, Odisha." Training & Development Journal, vol. 8, no. 2, 2017, p. 103, https://doi.org/10.5958/2231-069x.2017.00013.0. Accessed 15 Mar. 2021.

Bellisario, Andrea, et al. "The Role of Performance Measurement in Aligning Operations with Strategy: Sustaining Cognitive Processes of Internal Alignment." International Journal of Operations & Production Management, vol. ahead-of-print, no. ahead-of-print, 29 Oct. 2021, https://doi.org/10.1108/ijopm-02-2021-0081.

Belyh, Anastasia. "21 Best Zoho Alternatives for CRM and Project Management." FounderJar.com, 7 Dec. 2021, www.founderjar.com/zoho-alternatives/.

Bensla , Aastha. "6 Reasons Why Remote Work Trend Is Not Going Away Any Time Soon - Risely." Www.risely.me, 17 May 2023, www.risely.me/reasons-why-remote-work-trend-is-not-going-away/.

Bernes, Tom. "Enhancing Patient Safety: Technology and Nurse Practitioners in Virginia." The next Hint, 7 Aug. 2023, www.thenexthint.com/enhancing-patient-safety-technology-and-nurse-practitioners-in-virginia/.

Björkdahl, Joakim. "Strategies for Digitalization in Manufacturing Firms." California Management Review, vol. 62, no. 4, 5 May 2020, p. 000812562092034, journals.sagepub.com/doi/abs/10.1177/0008125620920349, https://doi.org/10.1177/0008125620920349.

Blockchain Technology: The Future of Financial Services and Banking - Cessummit. 15 June 2023, cessummit.com/blockchain-technology-the-future-of-financial-services-and-banking/.

Bongiorno, Giorgio, et al. "CIOs and the Digital Transformation: A New Leadership Role." CIOs and the Digital Transformation, 1 Aug. 2017, pp. 1–9, https://doi.org/10.1007/978-3-319-31026-8_1.

Carton, Andrew M., et al. "A (Blurry) Vision of the Future: How Leader Rhetoric about Ultimate Goals Influences Performance." Academy of Management Journal, vol. 57, no. 6, Dec. 2014, pp. 1544–1570, https://doi.org/10.5465/amj.2012.0101.

Chadwick, John. "AWWA Water Science Author Spotlight." Journal - American Water Works Association, vol. 112, no. 4, Apr. 2020, pp. 18–19, https://doi.org/10.1002/awwa.1477. Accessed 14 Dec. 2020.

Chechi, Haris. "What Is Digital Transformation?" Les Roches, 28 Dec. 2022, lesroches.edu/blog/digital-transformation/.

De Tuya, Manuel, et al. "The Leading Role of the Government CIO at the Local Level: Strategic Opportunities and Challenges." Government Information Quarterly, Jan. 2017, p. 101218, https://doi.org/10.1016/j.giq.2017.01.002.

Definition of Success Archives | Holistic Strong. holisticstrong.com/tag/definition-of-success.

Denford, James Stephen, and Kurt Schobel. "Public Sector CFOs and CIOs: Impacts of Work Proximity and Role Perceptions." Journal of Accounting & Organizational Change, vol. ahead-of-print, no. ahead-of-print, 25 Mar.

2021, https://doi.org/10.1108/jaoc-09-2019-0099. Accessed 2 Apr. 2021.

Desk, Lioness News. "XLIVE 2016: Industry Leaders to Share Latest in Festival Music, Food, Culture and "Live Event" Tech." Lioness Magazine, 13 Oct. 2016, lionessmagazine.com/xlive-2016-industry-leaders-share-latest-festival-music-food-culture-live-event-tech/.

Dhlamini, Thabani, and Tendani Mawela. "Critical Success Factors for Information Technology and Operational Technology Convergence within the Energy Sector." Innovations in Bio-Inspired Computing and Applications, 2022, pp. 425–434, https://doi.org/10.1007/978-3-030-96299-9_41.

Drechsler, Katharina, et al. "The Changing Roles of Innovation Actors and Organizational Antecedents in the Digital Age." Wirtschaftsinformatik 2019 Proceedings, 2 Mar. 2019, aisel.aisnet.org/wi2019/track07/papers/3/.

Durán, Orlando. "Computer-Aided Maintenance Management Systems Selection Based on a Fuzzy AHP Approach." Advances in Engineering Software, vol. 42, no. 10, Oct. 2011, pp. 821–829, https://doi.org/10.1016/j.advengsoft.2011.05.023. Accessed 10 Nov. 2020.

FIAU. "Industrial Training Fund (ITF)." FIAU, 11 Mar. 2023, fiau.org/industrial-training-fund-itf/.

Ghazal, Taher M, et al. Internet of Things Connected Wireless Sensor Networks for Smart Cities. 1 Jan. 2023, pp. 1953–1968, https://doi.org/10.1007/978-3-031-12382-5_107.

Guarda, Teresa, et al. "Blockchain and Government Transformation." Advances in Intelligent Systems and Computing, 1 Jan. 2021, pp. 88–95, https://doi.org/10.1007/978-3-030-68285-9_9. Accessed 18 Nov. 2023.

Guerrero, Jose E., and Eric Hansen. "Cross-Sector Collaboration in Oregon's Forest Sector: Insights from Owners and CEOs." International Wood Products Journal, 17 Feb. 2021, pp. 1–9, https://doi.org/10.1080/20426445.2021.1889164. Accessed 9 Mar. 2021.

Guerrini, Aimitis Design-Valentina Frate, Luca. Interoperability of Track and Trace Systems: Key to Public Health Protection | Intuslegerechemia. www.intuslegerechemia.com/2021/11/16/interoperability-of-track-and-trace-systems-key-to-public-health-protection/.

HAYNE, CHRISTIE, and MARSHALL VANCE. "Information Intermediary or de Facto Standard Setter? Field Evidence on the Indirect and Direct Influence of Proxy Advisors." Journal of Accounting Research, vol. 57, no. 4, 17 July 2019, pp. 969–1011, https://doi.org/10.1111/1475-679x.12261. Accessed 23 May 2022.

Heidari, Alireza, et al. "Strategic Analysis of Iran's Energy System." Strategic Planning for Energy and the Environment, vol. 37, no. 1, 30 May 2017, pp. 56–79, https://doi.org/10.1080/10485236.2017.11878952. Accessed 11 June 2020.

Henryjjackson. How to Choose the Right Conversion Rate Optimisation Agency for Your Business? 15 May 2023, idealnewshub.com/how-to-choose-the-right-conversion-rate-optimisation-agency-for-your-business/.

Hilgetag, Claus C., and Alexandros Goulas. ""Hierarchy" in the Organization of Brain Networks." Philosophical Transactions of the Royal Society B: Biological Sciences, vol. 375, no. 1796, 24 Feb. 2020, p. 20190319, https://doi.org/10.1098/rstb.2019.0319.

Hospital UMRA - Tourism Selangor. 7 Jan. 2022, selangor.travel/listing/hospital-umra/.

How AI Is Driving Innovation in the Automotive Industry. rejolut.com/ai/ai-in-automotive-industry/.

How UX Is Shaping the Future of ECommerce. 3 Mar. 2023, www.webguru-india.com/blog/ecommerce-ux-trends/.

Hütter, Alexander, and René Riedl. "Chief Information Officer Role Effectiveness: Literature Review and Implications for Research and Practice." Chief Information Officer Role Effectiveness, 2017, pp. 1–30, https://doi.org/10.1007/978-3-319-54753-4_1.

Impact of Artificial Intelligence on Banking Sector Globally - Special Report News Journal,Stocks News. 11 Aug. 2023, www.srjnews.com/impact-of-artificial-intelligence-on-banking-sector-globally/10613/?utm_source=rss&utm_medium=rss&utm_campaign=impact-of-artificial-intelligence-on-banking-sector-globally.

Innes, E. "Education and Training Programs for the Prevention of Work Injuries: Do They Work?" Work, vol. 9, no. 3, 1997, pp. 221–232, https://doi.org/10.3233/wor-1997-9304. Accessed 22 Feb. 2020.

Johnston, Jay. "App Commerce: A Step beyond Digital." RIS News, risnews.com/app-commerce-step-beyond-digital.

Joia, Luiz Antonio, and José Carlos P. Correia. "CIO Competencies from the IT Professional Perspective." Journal of Global Information Management, vol. 26, no. 2, Apr. 2018, pp. 74–103, https://doi.org/10.4018/jgim.2018040104. Accessed 4 Mar. 2020.

Jones, Mary C., et al. "Pathways to Being CIO: The Role of Background Revisited." Information & Management, vol. 57, no. 5, July 2020, p. 103234, https://doi.org/10.1016/j.im.2019.103234.

Kautz, Manuel. "How Amazon Delivers Your Items so Fast: The Science behind the Speed." AgaPe Press, 30 Jan. 2023, agapepress.org/how-does-amazon-deliver-so-fast/.

Khatoon, Asma. "A Blockchain-Based Smart Contract System for Healthcare Management." Electronics, vol. 9, no. 1, 3 Jan. 2020, p. 94, https://doi.org/10.3390/electronics9010094.

Kitsios, Fotis, and Maria Kamariotou. "The Impact of Information Technology and the Alignment between Business and Service Innovation Strategy on Service Innovation Performance." 2016 International Conference on Industrial

Engineering, Management Science and Application (ICIMSA), May 2016, https://doi.org/10.1109/icimsa.2016.7504042.

Koleva, Viktoria. "Work Together on Your Videos - with the New Comment Mode in Simpleshow Video Maker." Simpleshow, 19 Apr. 2023, simpleshow.com/blog/work-together-new-comment-mode/.

La Paz, Ariel. "How to Become a Strategist CIO." IT Professional, vol. 19, no. 1, Jan. 2017, pp. 48–55, https://doi.org/10.1109/mitp.2017.2. Accessed 20 Feb. 2020.

Li, Yehong, et al. "Identifying Stakeholders and Key Performance Indicators for District and Building Energy Performance Analysis." Energy and Buildings, vol. 155, Nov. 2017, pp. 1–15, https://doi.org/10.1016/j.enbuild.2017.09.003.

Madakam, Somayya, et al. "The Future Digital Work Force: Robotic Process Automation (RPA)." Journal of Information Systems and Technology Management, vol. 16, no. 1, 4 Jan. 2019, www.scielo.br/j/jistm/a/m7cqFWJPsWSk8ZnWRN6fR5m/, https://doi.org/10.4301/s1807-1775201916001.

Mangulabnan, Gingerlin. "Ways to Simplify and Improve Your Business Workflow." Nuve, 18 May 2023, www.gonuve.co/post/ways-to-simplify-and-improve-your-business-workflow.

Mattice, Catherine. "3 Questions to Reflect on Your Employer Brand." Civilitypartners.com, 9 Dec. 2020, civilitypartners.com/3-questions-to-reflect-on-your-employer-brand/.

Media, Sublime Designs. "Harness the Power of Change." Sublime Designs Media, 27 Mar. 2018, www.sublimedesignsmedia.com/resources/harnessing-the-power-of-change/.

Midgley, Gerald, and Raghav Rajagopalan. "Critical Systems Thinking, Systemic Intervention and Beyond." Hull-Repository.worktribe.com, 20 Aug. 2021, hull-repository.worktribe.com/output/1220089/critical-systems-thinking-systemic-intervention-and-beyond, https://doi.org/10.1007/978-981-15-0720-5.

Mike. "Benefits of IT in Business." Daily Business, 17 Aug. 2021, dailybusinessguide.com/benefits-of-it-in-business/.

Nambisan, Satish, et al. "Digital Innovation Management: Reinventing Innovation Management Research in a Digital World." MIS Quarterly, vol. 41, no. 1, 1 Jan. 2017, pp. 223–238, https://doi.org/10.25300/misq/2017/41:1.03.

Neves, Julia. "Productivity vs Efficiency: A Deep Dive into Their Differences and Pathways to Improvement." Day.io, 14 May 2023, day.io/blog/productivity-vs-efficiency/.

Nwankpa, Joseph K., et al. "Process Innovation in the Digital Age of Business: The Role of Digital Business Intensity and Knowledge Management." Journal of Knowledge Management, vol. ahead-of-print, no. ahead-of-print, 16 Aug. 2021, https://doi.org/10.1108/jkm-04-2021-0277.

Object, object. "Organisational Change Experienced by HR Professionals : Case Nordea." Core.ac.uk, core.ac.uk/download/198011060.pdf.

Online, Liquor Store, and Liquorstore-online.com. "Cockburns 20 Year Old Tawny Port 750ml Rated 94WS." Liquorstore-Online.com, www.liquorstore-online.com/53513/cockburns-20-year-old-tawny-port-500ml-rated-94ws.

Patel, Ankit R. "What Is SaaS ERP? Best ERP SaaS in 2024 | Ximple Solution." Ximple Solutions, 14 Dec. 2022, www.ximplesolution.com/saas-erp/.

PCI DSS SAQ Types: Which Type Is Right for Your Business? | AWA. 16 Aug. 2022, www.ispartnersllc.com/blog/pci-dss-3-2-self-assessment-questionnaire-preparation/.

Picco, Gian Pietro, et al. "Software Engineering for Mobility: Reflecting on the Past, Peering into the Future." Future of Software Engineering Proceedings, 31 May 2014, https://doi.org/10.1145/2593882.2593884.

Pinho, Cláudia, and Mário Franco. "The Role of the CIO in Strategy for Innovative Information Technology in Higher Education Institutions." Higher Education Policy, vol. 30, no. 3, 5 Jan. 2017, pp. 361–380, https://doi.org/10.1057/s41307-016-0028-2. Accessed 6 July 2020.

Point, Crypto News. "India Hosted 2nd Edition of Singapore-India International Hackathon." Crypto News Point, 9 Oct. 2019, www.cryptonewspoint.com/post/india-hosted-2nd-edition-of-singapore-india-international-hackathon.

Porter, Katherine R., and Todd Woerner. "On the Way to the Virtual Laboratory." Science & Technology Libraries, vol. 16, no. 3-4, 15 Jan. 1998, pp. 99–114, https://doi.org/10.1300/j122v16n03_07. Accessed 4 Aug. 2022.

Prasad, K.V, and Venkatesan Vasugi. Readiness Factors for Sustainable Lean Transformation of Construction Organizations. Vol. 15, no. 8, 10 Apr. 2023, pp. 6433–6433, https://doi.org/10.3390/su15086433. Accessed 20 July 2023.

PrimoStats. "8 Project Management Tips for Small Businesses." Www.primostats.com, 23 May 2023, primostats.com/blog/project-management-tips-for-small-businesses/.

Puspita, Henny, and Heeju Chae. "An Explorative Study and Comparison between Companies' and Customers' Perspectives in the Sustainable Fashion Industry." Journal of Global Fashion Marketing, vol. 12, no. 2, 5 Feb. 2021, pp. 133–145, www.tandfonline.com/doi/full/10.1080/20932685.2020.1853584, https://doi.org/10.1080/20932685.2020.1853584.

Quote – TranStream®. transtreamglobal.com/quote/.

Ramadan, Ahmed. "Breaking down Silos: How Building Information Modelling Is Transforming Facility Management." PlanRadar, 10 Apr. 2023, www.planradar.com/ae-en/building-information-modelling-transforming-facility-management/.

Rasenberg, Marlou, et al. "Alignment in Multimodal Interaction: An Integrative Framework." Cognitive Science, vol. 44, no. 11, 29 Oct. 2020, https://doi.org/10.1111/cogs.12911.

Research,https://www.vantagemarketresearch.com, Vantage Market. "Artificial Intelligence in Genomics Market Share Worth $ 5.5 Billion by 2030 | CAGR 43.2%." Vantage Market Research, www.vantagemarketresearch.com/press-release/global-artificial-intelligence-in-genomics-market-93764.

Revolutionize Healthcare with Artificial Intelligence. www.etc-expo.com/revolutionize-healthcare-with-artificial-intelligence/.

Sadjiarto, Arja, et al. "Analysis of the Effect of Business Strategy and Financial Distress on Tax Avoidance." Papers.ssrn.com, 17 Feb. 2020, papers.ssrn.com/sol3/papers.cfm?abstract_id=3539036.

Serhii. The Synergy of Bitcoin and Artificial Intelligence: Shaping the Future of Finance – Home | AIIN. www.aii-network.org/bitcoin-and-artificial-intelligence/.

Sesay, Amin kef. Orange SL Accelerates Digital Business Transformation - the Calabash Newspaper. 24 Mar. 2023, thecalabashnewspaper.com/orange-sl-accelerates-digital-business-transformation/.

Share, Info Tech. "Traits of Cell Phone Repair Store Technicians in Burlington." Info Tech Share, 27 Apr. 2023, infotechshare.com/traits-of-cell-phone-repair-store-technicians-in-burlington/.

Sieber, Marcel R., et al. "Conceptualizing Organizational Culture and Business-IT Alignment: A Systematic Literature Review." SN Business & Economics, vol. 2, no. 9, 8 Aug. 2022, https://doi.org/10.1007/s43546-022-00282-7.

Sjödin, David, et al. "An Agile Co-Creation Process for Digital Servitization: A Micro-Service Innovation Approach." Journal of Business Research, vol. 112, no. 1, May 2020, pp. 478–491, www.sciencedirect.com/science/article/pii/S0148296320300175, https://doi.org/10.1016/j.jbusres.2020.01.009.

Skills for Web Developers – Big Foot Web Marketing. 15 Feb. 2023, bigfootwebmarketing.com/web/skills-for-web-developers/.

Skope. "Making Use of Commercial Real Estate IT Consultants and IT Consulting for Business Success." Skope Entertainment Inc, 13 Aug. 2023, skopemag.com/2023/08/13/making-use-of-commercial-real-estate-it-consultants-and-it-consulting-for-business-success.

Snoeck, Monique, and Yves Wautelet. "Agile MERODE: A Model-Driven Software Engineering Method for User-Centric and Value-Based Development." Software and Systems Modeling, 16 June 2022, https://doi.org/10.1007/s10270-022-01015-y.

Spike, and Spike Team. "Integrated Teams: Critical Success Factors for Business Growth." Spike, 14 May 2023, www.spikenow.com/blog/team-collaboration/integrated-teams-the-key-to-business-growth/.

Team, HRHQ Editorial. "Leading a Remote Team Presents Unique Challenges - HRHQ Ireland's No1 Choice for HR News & Resources." Www.hrheadquarters.ie, 8 Mar. 2023, www.hrheadquarters.ie/featured/47203/.

The Importance of Fashion - Caribbeanpoultry. 28 Apr. 2023, caribbean-poultry.org/the-importance-of-fashion/.

Tursunbayeva, Aizhan, et al. "People Analytics—a Scoping Review of Conceptual Boundaries and Value Propositions." International Journal of Information Management, vol. 43, Dec. 2018, pp. 224–247, www.sciencedirect.com/science/article/pii/S0268401218301750, https://doi.org/10.1016/j.ijinfomgt.2018.08.002.

Urbach, Nils, et al. "The Impact of Digitalization on the IT Department." Business & Information Systems Engineering, vol. 61, no. 1, 10 Dec. 2018, pp. 123–131, https://doi.org/10.1007/s12599-018-0570-0.

User. "Top 3 Best Free Cannabis Reports API 2022 - Micro-SaaS." Micro-SaaS, 20 Nov. 2022, ec2-52-90-15-253.compute-1.amazonaws.com/top-3-best-free-cannabis-reports-api-2022/.

Van Toorn, Christine, et al. "CC's for the CIO (Core Competencies for the Chief Information Officer)." ICIS 2019 Proceedings, 6 Nov. 2019, aisel.aisnet.org/icis2019/practice_is_research/practice_is_research/4/.

Wasmer, Noah. "Announcing Our Acquisition of Mindville." Work Life by Atlassian, 30 July 2020, www.atlassian.com/blog/announcements/atlassian-acquires-mindville.

Williams, Amanda, et al. "Backstage Interorganizational Collaboration: Corporate Endorsement of the Sustainable Development Goals." Academy of Management Discoveries, vol. 5, no. 4, Dec. 2019, pp. 367–395, https://doi.org/10.5465/amd.2018.0154.

Wim Van Grembergen, and Steven De Haes. Introduction to IT Governance and Its Mechanisms Minitrack. 1 Jan. 2017, https://doi.org/10.24251/hicss.2017.626. Accessed 31 May 2023.

Workforce Identity Management vs. Access Management: Understanding the Differences | Bridgesoft. 14 Mar. 2023, bridgesoft.com/workforce-identity-management-vs-access-management-understanding-the-differences/.